2 TIMOTHY

Readings: A New Biblical Commentary
General Editor
John Jarick

2 TIMOTHY

Craig A. Smith

SHEFFIELD PHOENIX PRESS
2016

Copyright © 2016 Sheffield Phoenix Press

Published by Sheffield Phoenix Press
Department of Biblical Studies, University of Sheffield
Sheffield S3 7QB

www.sheffieldphoenix.com

All rights reserved.
No part of this publication may be reproduced or transmitted in any form or by any means, electronic or mechanical, including photocopying, recording or any information storage or retrieval system, without the publisher's permission in writing.

A CIP catalogue record for this book
is available from the British Library

Typeset by CA Typesetting Ltd
Printed on acid-free paper by Lightning Source

ISBN-13 978-1-910928-04-2 (hardback)
978-1-910928-05-9 (paperback)

I dedicate this book to Ron and Shirley Baxter, my in-laws, of whose sincere faith I am reminded daily and with whose love I am blessed unequivocally.

Contents

Figures	ix
Foreword	xi
Preface	xiii
Abbreviations	xv
Introduction	1
2 Timothy 1.1-2: Opening	18
Introductory Comment	18
Author (1.1)	18
Recipient (1.2a)	20
Greeting (1.2b)	20
Changes in the Opening of 1 Timothy and 2 Timothy	22
2 Timothy 1.3-5: Thanksgiving	24
The Thanksgiving as a Distinct Literary Form	24
Paul's Attitude toward Ministry (1.3a)	25
Frequency of Paul's Prayers for Timothy (1.3b)	26
Paul's Desire to See Timothy (1.4-5)	27
2 Timothy 1.6-18: Paul's First Request for Timothy: Suffer Shamelessly for the Gospel with Paul	29
Overview	29
Relationship between the Request and the Thanksgiving	30
Fan into Flame the Gift of God (1.6)	30
Paul's Reason for Engaging the Struggle of Ministry: Character of the Spirit (1.7)	32
Timothy Is Not to Be Ashamed (1.8a)	33
Timothy Is to Be a Fellow Sufferer for the Gospel (1.8b)	34
First Basis for Paul's Request to Suffer: God's Grace and Sovereignty (1.9-10)	35
Second Basis for Paul's Request to Suffer: Paul's Testimony (1.11-12)	38
Paul's Appeal for Timothy (1.13-14)	43
Paul's Two Examples of Servants for Timothy to Consider (1.15-18)	47

viii *Contents*

2 Timothy 2.1-7: Paul's Second Request: Suffer for the Ministry with Him (2.1-7)	52
Threefold Exhortation (2.1-3)	53
Three Metaphors (2.4-7)	60
2 Timothy 2.8-13: Paul's Basis for Suffering for the Gospel	69
Overview	69
Call to Imitate Jesus the Paragon of Suffering (2.8)	70
Timothy's Invitation to Imitate Paul in Suffering (2.9-10)	71
Faithful Saying: Support for Paul's Thesis to Suffer (2.11-13)	75
2 Timothy 2.14–3.17: Paul's Concern with the False Teachers	85
Paul's Charge to Timothy against False Teachers (2.14-26)	86
Denunciation of the False Teachers (3.1-9)	108
Paul's Appeal to Timothy for his Commitment to Him and the Gospel (3.10-17)	123
2 Timothy 4.1-8: Paul's Final Charge to Timothy	141
The 'Charge' as a Distinct Literary Form	141
Paul's Charge to Timothy before God (4.1)	143
Content of the Charge (4.2)	144
Reason for the Charge: It is a Time of Intolerance of Truth (4.3-4)	147
Content of the Charge Continued (4.5)	149
Paul's Autobiographical Comments (4.6-7)	151
Implications of the Charge (4.8)	160
2 Timothy 4.9-22: Closing	162
Final Remarks (4.9-18)	163
Final Greetings (4.19-22)	173
Bibliography	178
Scripture Index	187

Figures

Figure 1	Typical Structure of a Graeco-Roman Letter	17
Figure 2	Typical Structure of a Pauline Letter	17
Figure 3	Thanksgiving Form	24
Figure 4	Chiastic Structure of 2 Tim. 2.1-6	60
Figure 5	Structure of a Faithful Saying	76
Figure 6	Structure of Paul's Argument in 2 Tim. 2.14-26	86
Figure 7	Vice List in 2 Tim. 3.3-5	112
Figure 8	Contrast between the False Teachers and Timothy	130
Figure 9	The Structure of the Charge Form	142
Figure 10	Comparison of a Charge and an Exorcism	142
Figure 11	Chiastic Structure of 2 Tim. 4.1-8	143
Figure 12	*Inclusio* in 2 Tim. 4.1-8	144
Figure 13	Comparison of Ps. 21 (LXX) and 2 Tim. 4.9-18	163
Figure 14	Structure of 2 Tim. 4.9-22	164
Figure 15	Greetings Form in 2 Tim. 4.19-22	174

Foreword

The best commentaries are those that take into account the full context of the text. This means a careful examination of grammar, literary form, purpose for writing, argument, and social, cultural, and historical settings. For early Christian writings this entails a great deal of hard work. The Pastoral Letters are especially difficult, for it is not obvious exactly how they fit within the historical and chronological framework provided by the book of Acts. Moreover, the style of writing, content, and tenor of these letters noticeably differ from what we observe in the other letters attributed to Paul. For these reasons and others interpretation of the Pastoral Letters has been especially challenging.

It is not surprisingly, therefore, that many modern critics have concluded that Paul was not in fact the author of these letters. It is usually argued that the Pastorals were composed long after Paul's death, perhaps as late as the middle of the second century. The letters are seen as efforts to counter second-century heresies, promote firmer eecclesiastical structures and control, and perhaps to lionize Paul himself. In short, the Pastorals, we are to believe, offer us little or nothing of the apostle's teaching or of the challenges faced by the first-century Church, while their many personal details are nothing more than fictions. But not all scholars agree with this widely held view.

Showing how weak theories of pseudonymity really are Craig Smith offers a strong defense of Pauline authorship of the Pastorals in general and of 2 Timothy in particular. He believes, quite plausibly, that Luke assisted Paul in writing the letter during the apostle's incarceration in Rome, perhaps in the Mamertine prison, sometime in the early 60s. The letter, contends Smith, is not a Last Testament or Farewell Speech, as commonly thought, but a paranaetic letter including something called a Charge Form, in which the apostle summons Timothy to prepare for further ministry (2 Tim. 4.1-8). The apostle does not expect to die soon; rather, he expects to be released from prison. Accordingly, he summons Timothy and Mark to join him in Rome, so that he, along with Luke, can engage in further evangelism and teaching.

It is against this background that Smith writes his commentary on 2 Timothy. He provides readers with a plausible account of Paul's travels and activities. He surmises that Tychicus delivered the letter to Timothy and that

Timothy was to try to reach Paul in Rome, hopefully before winter. Timothy is instructed to bring with him a cloak, books, and 'especially the parchments', things Paul had left behind at Troas with one Carpus (2 Tim. 4.13). Smith rightly underscores the importance of these details, for these kinds of details do not appear in pseudonymous letters. One immediately thinks of the Cynic Letters, most of which are probably fictive. In these letters we find affirmations of the Cynic lifestyle but none of the details one should expect to find in authentic letters or, for that matter, the details that are present in the Pastorals. There are simply too many personal names and specific details for the Pastorals to be no more than second-century forgeries.

Having made a strong case for Pauline authorship Smith then interprets 2 Timothy in this light. He offers a compelling description of the false teachers and false teaching in Ephesus, a description that is coherent and plausible because the details reflect real people and their teaching, not a fictional scenario of a later age. In my view, Smith offers readers a far better account of the Pastorals than the ones offered by scholars who assume the letters are pseudonymous.

Of special interest is Smith's interpretation of 2 Tim. 4.6, where the apostle speaks of being 'poured out' and his 'time of departure'. Smith concludes that Paul is not expressing his expectation of death but of release from prison and further evangelism and missionary work. Unfortunately Paul's expectation of release was not realized, for the apostle suffered martyrdom (in my view shortly after the fire that destroyed a great part of Rome in AD 64).

Readers will find Professor Smith's commentary very stimulating and a refreshing change in direction. Above all, it exemplifies the way commentary writing ought to be done and so serves well as a model.

Craig A. Evans
Payzant Distinguished Professor of New Testament
Acadia Divinity College, Acadia University

Preface

I have had the desire to write a commentary on 2 Timothy since the time I was completing my ThM several years ago. This desire only grew as I wrote my PhD dissertation on 2 Timothy at Trinity College through the University of Bristol, England. So when Sheffield Phoenix Press offered me the opportunity to write such a commentary, I was delighted.

The first book I published with Sheffield Phoenix, *Timothy's Task, Paul's Prospect*, looked at the issue whether 2 Timothy was indeed Paul's Last Will and Testament or Farewell Speech, looking particularly at 2 Tim. 4.1-8 from which most scholars derive their position. Looking at the issue from a form-critical approach based foremost on structure it was clear that this text was neither a Last Will and Testament nor a Farewell Speech but a unique literary form called a 'Charge Form', the strongest command in Greek. Therefore this commentary distinguishes itself from other commentaries since it is not based on the idea that Paul is writing his farewell to Timothy and passing the baton of leadership to him as he about to die. On the contrary Paul expects to be released from prison, based on his difficult though effective first trial, and is calling Timothy to come to his side with Mark and join him and Luke in further ministry. Unfortunately his hope is not realized since he is martyred in Rome. This perspective will be worked out throughout this commentary.

It is easy to get bogged down in the issue of authorship and many commentators do so to the detriment of the commentary on the text. I have not avoided this issue but have put it in perspective since so much can and has already been written on this topic. A section of the introduction is dedicated to this issue and is dealt with in the commentary on specific texts when this issue comes to the forefront. I take the position of authenticity though Paul uses Luke as his amanuensis and will assume this perspective throughout the commentary. It is with this understanding that I use the name of 'Paul' throughout this commentary.

This commentary is not written for Greek NT readers though the reader can be assured that my work is based on a careful consideration of the Greek text. Greek words will be transliterated and translated (my own) when the word's meaning and usage is significant. Hopefully this will lead to a deeper understanding of the text and a deeper appreciation of the Greek text (and possibly provoke one to learn *Koinē* Greek).

A work like this is not without struggles. This one is no exception. A move from Sterling College in Sterling, Kansas to Carey Theological College in Vancouver, extended the time taken to complete this book. I am thankful for the support of my colleagues at Carey Theological College, Colin Godwin, Barbara Mutch, Jonathan Wilson, Axel Schoeber, Joyce Chan and Paddy Ducklow. Too often it goes without saying that I am thankful for Anne, an extraordinary wife, mother and pastor, and my two great children Johanna and Adam with whom life is richer and this book is made possible.

Abbreviations

AB	Anchor Bible
AnBib	Analecta biblica
ANRW	Hildegard Temporini and Wolfgang Haase (eds.), *Aufstieg und Niedergang der römischen Welt: Geschichte und Kultur Roms im Spiegel der neueren Forschung* (Berlin: W. de Gruyter, 1972).
AsSeign	Assemblées du Seigneur
Bib	Biblica
BiTod	Bible Today
BZNW	Beihefte zur ZNW
CBQ	Catholic Biblical Quarterly
Exp	The Expositor
ExpTim	Expository Times
GBS	Guides to Biblical Scholarship
HBT	Horizons in Biblical Theology
HE	Historia ecclesiastica
HNTC	Harper's New Testament Commentaries
HTR	Harvard Theological Review
IBS	Irish Biblical Studies
ICC	International Critical Commentary
JBL	Journal of Biblical Literature
JQR	Jewish Quarterly Review
JR	Journal of Religion
JSJ	Journal for the Study of Judaism
JSNTSup	*Journal for the Study of the New Testament,* Supplement Series
JTS	Journal of Theological Studies
LCL	Loeb Classical Library
LSJ	H.G. Liddell, Robert Scott and H. Stuart Jones, *Greek–English Lexicon* (Oxford: Clarendon Press, 9th edn, 1968).
NBD	J.D. Douglas (ed.), *New Bible Dictionary* (Leicester: Inter-Varsity Press, 1982).
NCB	New Century Bible
Neot	Neotestamentica
NIBC	New International Biblical Commentary
NICNT	New International Commentary on the New Testament
NIDNTT	Colin Brown (ed.), *The New International Dictionary of New Testament Theology* (3 vols.; Exeter: Paternoster Press, 1975).
NovT	Novum Testamentum
NovTSup	Novum Testamentum Supplements
NTL	New Testament Library
NTS	New Testament Studies
PBTM	Paternoster Biblical and Theological Monographs

RSPT	Revue des sciences philosophiques et théologiques
RSR	Recherches de science religieuse
SBL	Society of Biblical Literature
SBLDS	Society of Biblical Literature Dissertation Series
SBLSP	Society of Biblical Literature Seminar Papers
SR	Studies in Religion/Sciences religieuses
TDNT	Gerhard Kittel and Gerhard Friedrich (eds.), *Theological Dictionary of the New Testament* (trans. Geoffrey Bromiley; 10 vols.; Grand Rapids: Eerdmans, 1964–).
THAT	Ernst Jenni and Claus Westermann (eds.), *Theologisches Handwörterbuch zum Alten Testament* (Munich: Chr. Kaiser, 1971–76).
TNTC	Tyndale New Testament Commentaries
TynBul	Tyndale Bulletin
VT	Vetus Testamentum
WBC	Word Biblical Commentary
ZNW	*Zeitschrift für die neutestamentliche Wissenschaft*

Pseudepigrapha

2 En.	*2 (Slavonic) Enoch*
3 Macc.	3 Maccabees
4 Macc.	4 Maccabees
Apoc. Elij.	Apocalypse of Elijah
Ep. Arist.	*Letter of Aristeas*
Jos. Asen.	Joseph and Asenath
Odes	Odes of Solomon
Ps.-Phoc.	*Pseudo-Phocylides*
Sib. Or.	*Sibylline Oracles*
T. Jud.	Testament of Judah
T. Levi	Testament of Levi
T. Reub.	Testament of Reuben
T. Sol.	Testament of Solomon

Qumran

CD	Damascus Document

Targums

Pal. Tgs.	Palestinian Targums
Tg. Ps.-J.	Targum Pseudo-Jonathan

Mishnah

m. Naz.	*Nazir*
P. Ab.	*Pirke Aboth*

Philo

Aet. mundi	De aeternitate mundi
Agr.	De agricultura
Conf. ling.	De confusione linguarum

Dec.	De decalogo
Ebr.	De ebrietate
Flacc.	In Flaccum
Fug.	De fuge et inventione
Leg. all.	Legum allegoriae
Leg. gai.	Legato ad Gaium
Migr. Abr.	De migratione Abrahami
Plant.	De plantatione
Quaest. in Gen.	Quaestiones in Genesin
Rer. div. her.	Quis rerum divinarum heres sit
Spec. leg.	De specialibus legibus
Vit. Mos.	De vita Mosis

Josephus
Ant.	*Antiquities of the Jews*
Apion	Against Apion
Life	Life of Josephus
War	*The Jewish War*

Ancient Christian authors
1–2 Clem.	*1–2 Clement*
Acts Paul	*Acts of Paul*
Acts Paul and Thecla	*Acts of Paul and Thecla*
Acts Pet.	*Acts of Peter*
Ad Mart.	Tertullian, *Ad Martyras*
Adv. haer.	Irenaeus, *Against All Heresies*
Apost. Const.	Apostolic Constitutions
Barn.	Barnabas
Ep. apost.	Epistula apostolorum
Ep. Diog.	Epistle to Diognetus
Fr. Pap.	Fragments of Papias
HE	Eusebius of Caesarea, *Historia cclesiastica*
Hom.	Chrysostom, *Homilies*
Homil.	Pseudo-Clement of Rome, *Homiliae*
Lib. pont.	Liber pontificalis
Man.	Hermas, *Mandate*
Mart. Pol.	Martyrdom of Polycarp
Or.	Dio Chrysostom, *Orations*
Phil.	Polycarp, *Philippians*
Pol.	Ignatius, *Letter to Polycarp*
Praesc.	Tertullian, *On the Proscribing of Heretics*
Sim.	Hermas, *Similitudes*
Strom.	Clement of Alexandria, *Stromata*
Vis.	Hermas, *Vision*

Other ancient authors
Aen.	Virgil, *Aeneid*
Alex.	Lucian, *Alexander*

xviii   *Abbreviations*

Ann.	Tacitus, *Annals*
Ant. rom.	Dionysius of Halicarnassus, *Antiquitates romanae*
Ars rhet	Julius Victor, *Ars rhetorica*
Chrono. 354	Valentinius, *Chronography of 354*
Cyr.	Xenophon, *Cyropaedia* De mat. med. Galen, *De materia medica*
Diod. Sic.	Diodorus Siculus
Dionysius Hal., *Ant. rom.*	Dionysius of Halicarnassus, *Antiquitates romanae*
Disp. Man.	Archelaus, *Disputation with Manes*
Diss.	Epictetus, *Dissertationes*
Elec.	Sophocles, *Electra*
Epodes	Horace, *Epodes*
Ep. Socr.	Epistle of Socrates
Graec. descr.	Pausanias, *Description of Greece*
Hdt. *Hist.*	Herodotus, *Histories*
Hist.	Polybius, *Histories*
Hist. Pelop.	Thucydides, *History of the Peloponnesian War*
Hist. Alex. Mag.	Quintus Curtius Rufus, *Historiae Alexandri Magni*
Hist. mir.	Antigonus of Carystus, *Historiae mirabiles*
Mor.	Plutarch, *Moralia*
Nat. hist.	Pliny the Elder, *Naturalis historia*
Od.	Homer, *Odyssey*
De plac. phil.	Plutarch, *Doctrine of the Philosophers*
Pisc.	Lucian, *Piscator*
Rhet.	Aristotle, Rhetoric
Sat.	Juvenal, *Satires*
Sent.	Ps.-Phocylides, *Sentences*
Senten.	Secundus of Athens, *Sententiae*
Sublime	Longinus, *On the Sublime*
Symp.	Methodius, *Symposium*
Var. hist.	Aelian, *Varia historia*
Zen.	Demosthenes, *Zenothemis*

Introduction

Authorship

Identifying the author is important for understanding any letter. For almost 1,800 years 2 Timothy was considered to be written by Paul. This changed when Friedrich Schleiermacher (1768–1834) questioned the authenticity of 1 Timothy. Later Johann Eichhorn (1752–1827) expanded this by rejecting Pauline authorship of 1 and 2 Timothy and Titus. His work led to the presumption that 1 and 2 Timothy and Titus were one body of writing, called the 'Pastorals', that were inauthentic. Subsequent scholars until today have largely assumed this position as they have interpreted these Epistles.

It is certainly beyond the scope of this commentary to examine all the aspects of Pauline authorship as it pertains to all Pastoral Epistles so I will try to limit my scope to 2 Timothy though there is some interrelatedness. Today, apart from Pauline authorship, there are generally four other positions.

Four Popular Positions of Authorship

a. *Pseudonymous*

Pseudonymous authorship is the prevailing hypothesis among scholars today. These scholars believe that an unknown author drawing upon the authority of Paul's name wrote 2 Timothy. Postulations about the identity of the author are tied with the time of writing. The speculations range from an acquaintance or close associate of Paul writing not too long after Paul's death to a contemporary of Marcion (AD 140) or even later though the most common position among these scholars is that the pseudepigrapher is believed to be writing well after the death of Paul around the time of Ignatius (AD 100–35). It is generally agreed among these proponents that the pseudonymous author's reason and motive for writing in this manner is altruistic. This author, who had great respect for Paul and a desire to preserve the Pauline tradition, writes to a new situation (i.e. one Paul has not addressed before) but in a manner that would be consistent with Paul's thinking in an attempt to make the audience believe it was Paul's authoritative apostolic writing. Of course he was not successful since these readers today are convinced the letter is not authentic.

b. *Fragment Theory*

Some scholars believe they can identify authentic elements of Paul within the letter though they still hold to the pseudonymity of 2 Timothy. This has led to the development of the Fragment Theory. These adherents propose that genuine fragments of Paul's writings were in circulation long after his death, which an editor(s) wove together with his own material so that he might address his own particular situation. Most of these fragments are usually detected in the 'historical sections' of 2 Timothy (e.g. 4.9-12, 16-18) and even on these there is sadly no clear consensus on their authenticity, which should caution the present reader to its validity. Advocates of the Fragment Theory look to letters like 2 Corinthians and particularly Philippians as examples of support for their position.

c. *Allonymous*

This hypothesis is really a nuanced form of pseudonymity though these aficionados are very quick to stress that the allonymous authors had no intent to deceive the audience; their motives were pure and they sought only to bring new expression of Paul's teaching in order to deal with challenging problems in the church, in particular false teaching and the need for church order. 2 Timothy was therefore written soon after Paul's death probably drawing upon an authentic work of Paul. The production of this letter and the subsequent Pastoral Epistles was a group effort, possibly including Timothy and Titus. These letters are not like later pseudonymous letters that sought to use the names of important past figures in order to legitimize their spurious teaching. Rather 2 Timothy (and so too 1 Timothy and Titus) is written more like the *Didache*, which has no stated author but rather a disclaimer that it is written according to and consistent with the witness and teaching of the apostles. Because of the orthodox nature of the teachings, the early church accepted 2 Timothy as Pauline, as subsequent generations forgot how it came into being.

d. *Amanuensis*

The use of amanuenses was common in the Graeco-Roman world and Paul himself certainly made use of this benefit (Rom. 16.22). There are three variables with respect to this position: when did this person write the letter, how much freedom did he/she have when writing and how familiar was this person with Paul?

The time of writing is difficult to pinpoint but certainly it was written when Paul was in prison, after his first trial and possibly not too long before his death. Opinions differ on how much freedom the secretary had in the composition of the letter though generally these proponents believe the amanuensis exercised enough freedom to account for the differences between this letter and Paul's undisputed letters. Most of these scholars agree 2 Timothy was written by someone who was a close associate of Paul (e.g. Luke, Tychicus) and possessed a sophisticated theological understanding of the faith and the needs of the Church.

Evidence to Be Considered
In this section I will examine this evidence as it pertains to the respective positions in order to determine the identity of the most likely author.

a. *Style*
I use the term broadly, as the ancient rhetoricians did, to include language and manner of writing (e.g. syntax, method of argumentation). Antagonists of the authenticity position are quick to point to the difference of style between the undisputed letters of Paul and the Pastorals. Initially the issue was the large number of hapax legomena found in the Pastorals and subsequently the number of words included in them but not found in the undisputed letters. The introduction of computers led to more statistical analysis on which far-reaching claims of certainty of authorship were made. Unfortunately there are problems methodologically.

First, it is assumed that there is a distinct unequivocal Pauline style to which every other letter can be compared. Clearly this is not the case. Ancient writers, Paul included, would have been trained to write according to the purpose and intention of the letter needed in that given situation and therefore style was not viewed as a form of self-expression as it is today. Rhetorical handbooks are filled with examples on how to write appropriately for the task at hand. Paul would have been taught to adapt the style to the situation and, given his educational background, he was probably influenced as a writer by both Greek and Jewish writers.

Second, related to the first point is the certainty with which some scholars today reject the authenticity of 2 Timothy because they know what constitutes truly Pauline style. I find this quite amazing, even presumptuous. There are no writers of the early church who rejected 2 Timothy on the basis of style, although Hebrews came under this scrutiny. It is worth considering that these ancient historians and theologians, who were near contemporaries of Paul and who were immersed in the understanding and practice of style, might possibly be better judges of style than we are today with our limited understanding.

Third, not enough consideration has been taken of how vocabulary is directly related to the subject matter being addressed. Advocates of pseudonymity are quick to point out how the vocabulary of the 'Pastorals' is not found in the undisputed letters. Their first error is to consider the 'Pastorals' as a group instead of individually as I mentioned above. The vocabulary of 2 Timothy should be examined by itself. In Paul's letters, when the subject matter is the same there is a similarity of vocabulary; so for example,

Romans and Galatians have a shared vocabulary (e.g. 'flesh', 'law'). But if you compare the vocabulary of Romans with 1 Thessalonians you will see differences (e.g. 'righteousness' is found 12 times in Romans but never in 1 Thessalonians). Does this mean 1 Thessalonians is not Pauline? Comparison of vocabulary has no significance unless the subject matter is taken into consideration. Even a cursory reading of the Pauline corpus in comparison with 2 Timothy and the other two Pastorals demonstrates that the unique vocabulary is found in those sections in which the subject matter differs from that found in the undisputed letters.

Some scholars try to make an argument against Pauline authorship based on syntax (e.g. sentence length, use of particles). It is true that the type of writing has a large bearing on the syntax used. For example, an exhortatory letter will be characterized by shorter sentences and more imperatives. Philippians, a friendship letter, has one imperative for every 65 words whereas 2 Timothy, a paranaetic letter, has one imperative for every 37 words. Most of the studies on this topic have tended to be inconclusive since they do not take into account the letter type.

Most scholars do take enough note of the use of rhetoric and the similarity of the vocabulary of 2 Timothy and Luke/Acts. These should be borne in mind when considering authorship and will be discussed later in this chapter.

b. *Historical Setting*
Proponents of 'pure' pseudonymity propose that the historical details in the letter are fictional and proof of their pseudepigraphic nature. Those in the 'fragments theory' camp suppose that these historical details, which have come from authentic Pauline correspondences, are inserted into 2 Timothy. The purpose in both cases is to make the letter sound more credible and historical, and to make the audience believe (deceive them into believing?) it has the authority of Paul's hand.

A few scholars have tried to fit 2 Timothy into the lifeline depicted in Acts suggesting that 2 Timothy fills in details not found in Luke's account. Most of these scholars do so with the intention to show Pauline authenticity. Every attempt to reconcile 2 Timothy with Acts fails since there are too many inconsistencies (e.g. Trophimus being left sick in Miletus but suddenly showing up with Paul in Jerusalem; Acts 21.29).

In spite of the limited amount of information, the best and most likely scenario is that Paul is imprisoned a second time in Rome from where he writes 2 Timothy. Paul was released from his first Roman imprisonment, referred to in Acts 28, around AD 62, after which he carried on his missionary activity to Spain and later to Asia Minor. He left Titus in Crete and Timothy in Ephesus, wrote Titus and 1 Timothy and was subsequently arrested and taken to Rome. For fuller explanation of this timeline see 'Historical Situation'.

Resolving the historical setting does not solve the problem of authorship though it does strongly suggest that 2 Timothy depicts a real situation faced by Paul and Timothy and this letter is a response written to this situation during their lifetimes in the mid-sixties AD.

c. *Church Order*

Many scholars in favour of the pseudonymous position believe that the organization of the church found in the Pastorals depicts a situation much later, around AD 100 or later, rather than the decade of AD 60–70. Of course there is no mention of church order whatsoever in 2 Timothy but because of their assumption that 2 Timothy belongs to the 'Pastoral letter group' it is considered to be written later too for an audience promoting egalitarianism for women or for a church needing more formal structure since it no longer was expecting an immediate parousia or was no longer being led charismatically.

There are many arguments against considering the Pastorals to represent a later situation. First, the categories of leadership found in 1 Timothy are also found in Phil. 1.1 and Rom. 16.1, both undisputed letters. Second, it is naïve to think that no formalized structure existed before AD 100. Acts 6 shows clearly that the church began, early on, to organize itself based on the needs of the community. The formation of structure for these communities probably drew on the background (e.g. Jewish synagogue, Guilds) most familiar to the audience and emissaries sent to help these churches. Third, it seems that the names associated with leadership (e.g. elder, deacon, overseer) are known by the audience and are not created in response to a problem of leadership structure within Ephesus. In fact Paul predicts several years earlier that their leaders will become corrupt which assumes there were leaders in place in Ephesus already (Acts 20.28-30). The goal of 1 and 2 Timothy is not to establish structure but rather to replace the problematic leaders within the existing church structure.

The topic of church order does not support a later date for 2 Timothy; in fact it does quite the opposite. Church order in the Pastorals is consistent with the undisputed Pauline letters and Acts and supports a situation sometime during the later years of Paul's life.

d. *Identification of Recipient*

Each of the Pastorals is addressed to individuals and therefore differs from the undisputed letters of Paul, which are addressed to churches with the exception of Philemon (although even this letter, like 2 Timothy, is also addressed to others: Apphia, Archippus and the church; Philemon 2). Having a single recipient, of course, is not a basis for rejecting authenticity.

Pseudonymists propose that the letters are not written to the historical Timothy but to leaders of later generations who are functioning in the same capacity as Timothy and Titus had done. Part of their logic is that since Timothy and Titus had been coworkers with Paul for many years, it seems odd to think they would need this elementary teaching on church order and the life of the servant of the Lord.

The main problem with the pseudonymists's logic is that while 1 and 2 Timothy are written to Timothy they also include a plural greeting at the end of each letter. 1 Timothy clearly includes teaching on church order but it is done with the understanding of instructing leaders not to teach false teaching. The theme of church order fades into the background in 2 Timothy but the concern about the character of church leaders remains the same: servants of the Lord must be characterized by holy godly lives, sustained by the orthodox teaching of Scripture, and be people who are willing to suffer for the gospel and reprove those who deviate from it. Paul sends these two letters to Timothy in part as a reminder of his teaching on this matter but also that Timothy might have an authoritative word from him in writing to present before the erring leaders and straying congregants. Having this letter in hand would be particularly important if the church was not willing to accept Timothy's authority.

e. The Image of Paul

Some have tried to discount the authenticity of 2 Timothy on the basis that the image of Paul portrayed in this letter and the other Pastorals does not coincide with that in the undisputed letters. These scholars propose that in the Pastorals Paul is portrayed as the all-authoritative apostle whose teaching is the sole norm to which the church must conform. Paul's word is final and there is no discussion of contentious issues, as there were for example in 1 Corinthians. For these scholars, Paul is also the final authority for Timothy's ministry, without any sense of collegiality or independent authority. Similarly these proponents believe that Paul is presented as *the* paradigm of conversion and *the* unequivocal representative of what it means to be a believer. Finally, they point out that Paul's self-references in the Pastorals seem unusual. For example, Paul refers to himself as 'persecutor, blasphemer and a violent man' (1 Tim. 1.13), which they believe is hard to reconcile with his self-description in Phil. 3.4-6. Other examples include 2 Tim. 1.11. For them these portrayals are not representative of the thoughts and heart of Paul and therefore represent an image of Paul created after the death of Paul in honour of him.

In general these scholars have overstated their case and have tried to force the evidence in an unnatural way. Paul's use of his apostolic authority in 2 Timothy and the Pastorals in general is not inconsistent with how Paul uses his apostolic authority in the undisputed letters. In Galatians Paul holds up his authority before the Galatians to justify his condemnation of their 'false gospel'. Similarly in 1 and 2 Corinthians, Paul presents his apostolic power and rights to confront the Corinthians's misunderstandings of apostleship and their misuse of Christian freedom for licentiousness (1 Cor. 2.6–5.13; 9; 2 Corinthians 2–4; 10–12).

In the undisputed letters, Paul unabashedly sets himself up as a model of the Christian life to follow just as he follows Christ (1 Cor. 11.1). Similarly in 2 Timothy, he is honest about his former life and the extraordinary grace he experienced as an example for others to note on how Christ and his gospel can change lives. In Gal. 1.13-17 he refers to his former life of pride, his misguided zeal and his attempts to destroy the church. Thus, to refer to himself as a 'persecutor, blasphemer and a violent man' is probably not out of character since I am sure he saw his actions with respect to the persecution of the Church, and Stephen in particular, before his Damascus Road experience within this framework.

f. *Theology*
Probably the theology of the Pastorals in comparison with the undisputed letters provides the possible strongest case to be made for pseudonymity, though in my mind it is still weak. Most of the argument about theology is developed around the material found in 1 Timothy and Titus and less so in 2 Timothy. The challenge is determining whether the differences represent changes due to different authorship or whether they represent authentic Pauline thought which has developed over the course of time and/or presented in a unique way due to new circumstances or simply expressions of his creativity.

Two areas of theology which cause some scholars to doubt 2 Timothy's authenticity are eschatology and the seeming disparity of the teaching in 2 Timothy.

(i) *Eschatology*. Paul, in his undisputed letters, held firmly to an eschatological viewpoint with respect to salvation and the Christian life. Christ's life, death and resurrection marked the watershed moment in history by which salvation and redemption have come in the present but are to be fully realized when Christ returns. Believers live according to the Word and Spirit as they wait in eager expectation for the return of Christ. Scholars espousing pseudonymity believe the eschatology of the Pastorals is different since Paul expects to die before the Parousia and they presume that these letters have been written to prepare, equip and establish the church due to the delay of Christ's return.

When one examines 2 Timothy, it is clear that the theological framework is eschatological and Pauline. Christ has come and destroyed death (2 Tim. 1.10) but he will return again at which time there will be a judgment and reward (4.8). Based on this perspective Paul exhorts Timothy to embrace suffering, as he has (2.12), in order to receive the future reward.

The character and actions of the false teachers are viewed as expressions of the end times (3.1) and the inevitability of God's eschatological judgment (4.1). Clearly Paul's perspective in 2 Timothy (in particular) is no different than in the undisputed letters; he is eagerly awaiting the return of Christ but in the meantime he is eagerly seeking the maturity in Christ of every believer and every Church.

Some point out how *epiphaneia* is used in 2 Timothy coupled with the fact this word is used in Hellenistic religions and therefore suppose that this might support pseudonymity. The word *epiphaneia* means 'appearance, appearing' and can have the connotation of 'suddenness' or 'something hidden now visible' (2 Macc. 2.21; 3.24; 5.4). *Epiphaneia* is used to refer to the Second Advent of Christ in 2 Thess. 2.8 and has the same meaning as *parousia* (1 Thess. 5.23). It is used in the same way in 2 Tim. 4.1, 8; 1 Tim. 6.14; Tit. 2.13. The different usage that concerns some scholars is the way it is used in 2 Tim. 1.10 where it refers to the First Advent of Christ. It is possible that this usage suggests a different author though more likely it is a creative development in Paul's thought using the same term to refer to both events when Christ comes to earth and staying true to the meaning of *epiphaneia*.

(ii) *Teaching*. Pseudonymists are quick to point out that there are several examples in 2 Timothy where the teaching seems to differ from the undisputed letters or is missing entirely. Most of these claims are either overstated or can be explained.

'Righteousness', *dikaiosunē*, is found in the undisputed letters primarily as the saving activity of God (Rom. 3.21) and justification of God (Rom. 1.17) but this meaning is not found at all in 2 Timothy. Probably the main reason for their omission in 2 Timothy is because it is not the problem in Ephesus as it was in Galatia and Rome. The issue in Ephesus is not about the relationship between the Law, works and justification before God. The third, though less common, use of 'righteousness' in the undisputed letters, the justice of God (Rom. 3.25), is found in 2 Tim. 2.22.

Pseudonymists point out that in the undisputed letters Paul refers to a 'weak' or 'strong' conscience whereas in the Pastorals one has either a 'good/pure' (2 Tim. 1.3) or 'bad/seared' conscience (1 Tim. 4.2). What they do not point out is that in the undisputed letters Paul refers to the conscience as a moral compass (Rom. 9.1), which discerns good and evil or can remain neutral (1 Cor. 10.27). Paul sought to keep his conscience 'good' and 'blameless' (Acts 23.1; 24.16) which suggests that his conscience could be 'bad' and 'with fault'. The reference to conscience in 1 Corinthians is influenced by the issue at hand: believers attending pagan feasts without a firm faith are being taken to these feasts by other believers, which could harm their faith. The situation in Ephesus is much different. There are false teachers who have had their 'moral compasses' (i.e. consciences) harmed by choosing to accept a false gospel and they are attempting to spread this teaching to others. Therefore the concept of conscience is the same in the Pastorals as it is in the undisputed letters but it is nuanced for the situation of their respective audiences.

Another example put forward by pseudonymists is the term *pistis*, 'faith'. In the undisputed letters, they believe that 'faith' refers to the response of obedience to God (Rom. 4.5), whereas in the Pastorals 'faith' is an objective reality equivalent to doctrine (i.e. content of belief) on which they cite several examples, mostly from 1 Timothy (1.19; 2.7; 3.9), but also in 2 Timothy (1.5; 2.22; 3.8; 4.7). There are a couple of problems with their postulation. First, several of the texts they cite, as examples of 'doctrine', are better understood in a subjective manner as in the undisputed letters (2 Tim. 1.5, 13; 3.15; 4.7) or as a 'double entendre' holding both meanings in tension (2 Tim. 2.22; 3.8, 10). But even if faith is taken in the objective sense of referring to doctrine then this is not inconsistent with Paul in the undisputed letters since he uses 'faith' in this sense too (Rom. 1.5; Gal. 1.23; Phil. 1.25, 27).

Pseudonymists see the use of 'godliness', *eusebeia*, a word associated with Hellenistic philosophy and religion, as another piece of evidence against authenticity since it is never used in the undisputed letters. The most likely reason is that 'eusebeia' was the term the false teachers used to describe their 'gospel'. Paul uses their term but fills it with his meaning (much as he does with 'wisdom' in 1 Corinthians). There are two sides to godliness: the objective side, which includes teaching that coincides with the life and teaching of Christ (1 Tim. 3.16; 6.3), and the subjective side, which includes the manner in which one lives (1 Tim. 2.2; 4.7-8; 6.6, 11). The false teachers lack both, godliness (1 Tim. 6.5) and doctrine (2 Tim. 3.5) in their lives.

In spite of the insistence of pseudonymists, even the theology of 2 Timothy is not supportive of inauthenticity. Most of the issues against authenticity can be shown to be non-existent or explained as Paul's creative expression or a development of Paul's thought which is consistent with his earlier writings but presented in a new way due to the changed circumstances under which he is writing 2 Timothy.

g. Canon and External Evidence
Ascertaining the usage of 2 Timothy in the Apostolic Fathers is just as difficult as in the undisputed Pauline Epistles since one must rely on allusions to the texts. It is very likely that Polycarp (AD 66–155) was familiar with 2 Timothy because of the clear allusions to this letter (2 Tim. 2.12; 3.5, 6; 4.10 found respectively in Polycarp, *Phil.* 5.2; 6.3; 9.2). It is possible that 2 Timothy had been in the hands of Ignatius of Antioch (AD 35–110) since

there is a possible allusion to 2 Tim. 3.16 in *1 Clem.* 45.2 (but see also 16.1-2). The unknown author of *2 Clement* (*circa* AD 98–100) makes use of 2 Tim. 2.5 and 4.8 in *2 Clem.* 7.4 and 7.1-3, 20.1-4 respectively.

Writings from the latter half of the second century demonstrate familiarity with 2 Timothy too. Clement of Alexandria (AD 150–215) certainly made use of 2 Timothy (e.g. he quotes 2 Tim. 1.7-8 in *Strom.* 4.7). Tertullian (AD 160–220) also quotes from 2 Timothy (2 Tim. 1.14 in *Adv. Haer* 25). Irenaeus (AD 130–202) also quoted 2 Timothy (e.g. 2 Tim. 2.12 in *Praesc.* 3.18.5; see also 2.14.7 where Paul is associated with the quotation; 3.3.3).

It is clear that 2 Timothy was known in the early church. It is also true that 2 Timothy was accepted into most canon lists by the end of the second century (*Muratonian Canon* 59–63). One exception is Marcion. It is not clear if he omitted 2 Timothy intentionally or was unaware of its existence. Tertullian is certain that Marcion rejected it (*Praesc.* 5.21). Given Polycarp's proclamation when he met Marcion, 'I recognize you as the firstborn of Satan' (Irenaeus, *Adv. Haer*, 3.4), and given that 2 Timothy speaks out against false teachers, then his trustworthiness in issues of the canonicity of 2 Timothy is suspect.

2 Timothy is omitted from the ancient manuscript, P^{46}, which includes all the letters of Paul (and the Epistle to the Hebrews) except 2 Thessalonians, Philemon and the Pastoral Epistles. There are seven leaves missing at the end of the codex, which has led to different conjectures. Some suggest that there was enough room for all of the missing books to be included especially since the words per page are increasing in the subsequent pages (similar to P^{75}) suggesting that the scribe was aware of the limited space remaining. If there was not enough space then additional pages could have been added. Others propose that P^{46} comprises a list of Paul's letters to churches and therefore Philemon and the Pastoral Epistles are omitted because they were addressed to individuals; 2 Thessalonians is missing due to deterioration. This form of categorizing Paul's letters would be consistent with the *Muratorian Canon* (40–41, 59–60). In conclusion there is a reasonable explanation for the omission of 2 Timothy from this codex.

The formation of the canon was surely a complex prolonged process but certainly one that was taken seriously by the early church and given due diligence. So all the issues mentioned above would have been evaluated and scrutinized. On the basis of this, the early church accepted 2 Timothy into the canon as authentic. Even the most contentious issue, theology, was no barrier for its inclusion. This suggests that who wrote it and the letter's authenticity were fundamentally important which in turn means the early church would have been concerned about inauthentic letters and the use of deception. Too often the debate about authorship overlooks the concern the early church had with respect to deception and pseudonymous writing. The fact is, throughout this process, the early church was alert for deceptive writings and it was looking for real words addressed to a real situation from a real author under the inspiration of the Holy Spirit and not some nebulous 'tradition of Paul'. In conclusion, both the historical canonical process and external evidence support authenticity.

Conclusion

Determining the authorship of any NT letter is a complicated endeavour. Even the undisputed letters of Paul are problematic. Almost without exception scholars accept that Paul wrote Romans, yet he clearly used an amanuensis (Rom. 16.22). What degree of freedom did Tertius have in writing this letter? Most would say 'very little'. Similarly most everyone would agree that Paul wrote 1 Corinthians, yet Sosthenes' name is placed alongside Paul's as the sender of this letter. To what degree was this letter a joint project? Only Paul's name is given in the opening of 2 Timothy, so does this mean that he was the sole author? Could anyone else be involved in the writing process?

As was shown in this section, there is little merit in the pseudonymous, fragment theory or allonymous hypotheses. These solutions create more problems than they solve. This leaves two options: either Paul wrote it himself or he used an amanuensis. There are two factors that must be considered. First, there is a significant amount of overlap in the vocabulary of Luke–Acts and 2 Timothy (e.g. 'traitors' in Lk. 6.16; Acts 7.52; 2 Tim. 3.4; 'madness' in Lk. 6.11; 2 Tim. 3.9). This could account for some of the difference in language. Second, Paul's circumstances have changed from his first imprisonment. He is incarcerated, likely in the Mamertine prison, and therefore his movements would have been quite restricted. The text says only Luke is with Paul. Luke is Paul's long-time companion, who is well acquainted with Paul's teaching and thinking and therefore would make a good amanuensis. The most likely scenario is that Paul explained to Luke what he wanted to say and gave a basic structure for the letter. There was probably some give and take in the process of composition which is reflected in the thought and language. When agreed, the letter was sent via Tychicus. From the perspective of Paul and Luke this letter came from Paul and was endued with his authority. This is the perspective taken in this commentary.

Date

The date of writing for this epistle is integrally connected with one's position on authorship. There is a wide range of dating for those taking a pseudonymous authorship position, from shortly after the death of Paul to sometime in the second century. In this commentary, 2 Timothy is taken as having been written during Paul's lifetime. The events leading up to the date of writing include Paul likely having already travelled to Spain and having been arrested and sent to Rome while travelling through Asia. Paul was probably incarcerated after the Great Fire of Rome (AD 64) and during the ensuing persecution of the church, which lasted until Nero's death in AD 67/68. Paul almost certainly wrote this letter sometime between AD 65 and AD 67 before he was martyred.

Provenance

Since pseudonymists consider the details in 2 Timothy to be the author's creation then they are left with little to determine the provenance of letter. Nevertheless the most common unsubstantiated claim is Rome.

When one does take the internal evidence seriously then a fairly clear picture of the provenance of 2 Timothy appears. Paul makes it clear that he is suffering in his present conditions (2 Tim. 1.12) and that he is in prison in Rome (1.16-17). Exactly where Paul was being held is a mystery. If he is under house arrest with an assigned guard as he was in his first Roman imprisonment in AD 60–62 (Phil. 1.13) then he could possibly be in the NE area of Rome, *Campus Martius*, where the camp of the Praetorium Guard was located. From the tone and content of the letter it seems that his circumstances are substantially different since now he is fettered (2.9) and has undergone one lonely difficult trial and is awaiting the outcome (4.16-17). If he were being held in a prison like the Mamertine Prison, as tradition suggests, then the conditions would have been very poor. In this particular prison, the inmates were lowered down into the cell, where they were shackled either individually or to each other or the wall. The sanitary conditions would have been grim and he would have had little freedom for writing.

Having Luke with him is significant (2 Tim. 4.11) since Paul would have been dependent on him for his needs. Visiting Paul would have been dangerous for Luke since 'helpers' were subject to bribes, mistreatment and arrest for associating with a criminal. Prison guards would interrogate visitors to gain information about others associated with the 'Way'. It was during these visits that Paul and Luke collaborated to create 2 Timothy.

Historical Situation

Circumstances

It is most likely that Paul was released from imprisonment around AD 62 after spending two years of incarceration in Caesarea and two more years in Rome. Several sources suggest this. Both Festus and Agrippa agreed that Paul had done nothing wrong and would be released if he had not appealed to Caesar. Paul also expected to be released from prison when he wrote to the Philippians late in his Roman imprisonment (Phil. 2.24). The church historian Eusebius states that Paul was released from Roman imprisonment in order to preach again but only to find himself subsequently in prison in Rome under Nero where he was martyred (Eusebius, *HE* 2.22.2, 3). During this time Eusebius states that Paul wrote 2 Timothy and that 2 Tim. 4.16-18 is a reference to this imprisonment.

Upon release from prison, around AD 62, Paul desired to renew his preaching ministry. His original intention four years earlier was to go to Spain via Rome. It is possible that he carried through on this intention and got to Spain. The author of *1 Clem.* 5.6-7 states that Paul taught righteousness to the whole world and went to the western limit. If the author writes from the perspective of Corinth then by 'western limit' he may mean 'Rome'. But, if the author is writing from the perspective of Rome then by 'western limit' he may mean 'Spain'. There is also a reference in the Muratorian Canon (*Mur.* 34–39; AD 180) referring to Paul departing from Rome and proceeding to Spain (*Acts Pet.* 1–3).

Paul heads towards Crete. Two options are possible. First, he arrives there after being released from prison in Rome *circa* AD 62. It is not clear how much time it took for him to arrive in Crete, whether he stayed in Rome for a while or set off for Colossae (Philemon 22). Second, he arrives in Crete after spending time in Spain in the company of Timothy, fellow prisoner Aristarchus (Acts 27.2; Col. 4.10) and Titus, and possibly Demas, Mark and Luke (Philemon 23). After they evangelize throughout Crete, Titus stays there with the task of creating the necessary infrastructure to maintain a viable church (Tit. 1.5).

The goal of the group was to pass through Asia Minor and get to their destination of Macedonia but when they arrive in Ephesus they discover the church is being adversely affected by false teachers and their teaching. This problem predicted earlier (Acts 20.29-30) is pervasive and requires immediate corrective measures. Paul excommunicates Hymenaeus and Alexander, who were possibly former church leaders or infiltrators and were likely the main 'instigators' responsible for corrupting the church. Timothy remains in Ephesus as Paul's apostolic delegate to correct the existing situation while Paul heads off to Macedonia (1 Tim. 1.3).

Paul, probably with Luke (since he is with him later in Rome; 2 Tim. 4.17), follows the typical shipping route along the coast of Asia Minor heading towards Macedonia, following the *Via Egnatia* and then on to his final destination of Nicopolis where he spends the winter (Tit. 3.12). Some time during this period of travelling from Ephesus to Nicopolis, Paul almost certainly writes Titus and then 1 Timothy (since there is no mention of his arrest in these letters). Paul may have stopped in Troas on his way to Macedonia and left his books and parchments there (2 Tim. 4.13). More likely he pressed on to Macedonia since he seems to be eager to get there (1 Tim.

1.3). It is not clear how long or where he stayed in Macedonia but eventually he arrives in Nicopolis, 'victory city'. Although there are nine cities in the Roman Empire with this name, it is quite certain Paul landed at this strategic metropolis along the Adriatic Sea, founded by Octavian in 31 BC after his victory over Mark Antony in nearby Actium. Paul's hope is that Titus will join him here (Tit. 3.12) after Artemas arrives in Crete to relieve Titus of his duties.

Meanwhile in Ephesus, Hymenaeus and Philetus have joined ranks and are continuing to cause trouble with their false teaching (2 Tim. 2.17).

In the spring Paul leaves for Corinth for an undetermined period of time and Titus, after spending a little time with Paul in Nicopolis, heads off to Dalmatia, which lies just to the north (2 Tim. 4.11). Paul arrives in Corinth, possibly in an attempt to recruit Erastus, though he chooses to remain in Corinth (4.20). It is likely that Trophimus, the Ephesian (Acts 21.29), has joined company with Paul on his return to Ephesus. At this point there are two likely scenarios largely due to the difficulty of fitting Paul's visits to Corinth and Troas into his journey. Under the first scenario, these two men stay in Troas, at Carpus's house where Paul is arrested leaving behind his books and outer garment. Paul is taken by boat to Rome under Roman guard via Miletus. Trophimus, who has accompanied Paul, falls sick and is left in Miletus (2 Tim. 4.20) and Paul travels the remainder of the trip to Rome without him. Under the second scenario, Paul has left his books and garments in Troas on his way to Nicopolis. On his return to Ephesus from Corinth, he takes an indirect route to Troas, to pick up his books and cloak, via Miletus (where he drops off Trophimus who has fallen sick [maybe on the boat ride across the sea]; 2 Tim. 4.20) and presses on to Troas to pick up his belongings but is soon arrested. Regardless of which scenario is the case (though the former is more likely), Alexander the metal worker, who after his excommunication by Paul (1 Tim. 1.19-20) had left Ephesus for Troas, creates trouble for Paul upon Paul's arrival in Troas, resulting in Paul's arrest and immediate departure to Rome (2 Tim. 4.14).

Paul is imprisoned in Rome where he has had one trial. Some of his close associates have left him for good reasons (Titus to Dalmatia; Crescens to Galatia; 4.10b) but Demas has abandoned suffering with Paul and the gospel for love of the world (4.10a). Only Luke is with him (4.11), though previously he received much help from Onesiphorus (1.16-18). Paul stood alone when he gave his first defence (2 Tim. 4.16), yet he felt the Lord's presence as he was strengthened to share the gospel with his accusers (4.17a) which he compares to being poured out like a drink offering (4.6) and a difficult fight (4.7a). Though this was a painful ordeal, he kept the faith (4.7c) and feels certain that he has escaped death (4.17b) and that his release could be soon (4.6b). For this reason he asks Timothy to leave Ephesus when Tychicus arrives (4.12) and to join him before winter in Rome, bringing along

Mark (4.11). Paul warns Timothy to be careful on his journey to Rome since he may run into Alexander who has caused Paul so much grief (4.14-15).

Paul is eager for Timothy and Mark to join him in Rome so that they, plus Luke, might continue to minister together (2 Tim. 4.11) when he is released from prison. Unfortunately Paul does not get out of prison and he is executed sometime before Nero's death in AD 67/68 though at the time of writing he is quite confident he has been 'delivered from the Lion's mouth' (4.17).

Problem of False Teachers and False Teaching in Ephesus

In a farewell speech to the Ephesian elders Paul predicts that false teachers, likened to 'savage wolves', will infiltrate their church and other false teachers arising from their own leadership will distort the truth (e.g. denying the resurrection; 2 Tim. 2.18) and lead congregants away (Acts 20.29-31). The fulfillment of this word came when Paul and company returned to Ephesus on their way to Macedonia. This false teaching was derived from a misuse and misinterpretation of the Law. They promoted asceticism in terms of abstinence from certain foods (1 Tim. 4.3b) and prohibition of marriage (4.3a). These men either used contemporary Jewish myths in circulation or created strange interpretations of OT stories that resembled Jewish myths more than the truth. Similarly they had an eccentric preoccupation with genealogies to promote their cause. In this sense these false teachers looked and functioned more like the charlatans Jannes and Jambres, who were magicians in the Pharaoh's court (2 Tim. 3.8), than Christ-centered leaders building on the 'truths of the faith and good teaching' (1 Tim. 4.6).

Paul's concern throughout 1 and 2 Timothy is that Timothy differentiates himself from the false teachers in his conduct and teaching. There are two particularly insidious characteristics of the false teachers that Paul addresses. First, he asks Timothy to treat people with honour and respect, particularly women. The false teachers were able to snare some weak-willed women and may have been relating to them in an inappropriate manner (thus the injunction to treat 'old women as mothers and young women as sisters with absolute purity'; 1 Tim. 5.2) and using them to disseminate their false teaching (1 Tim. 5.13). Second, Timothy is to flee greed, not use ministry for a pretence for gaining wealth and to be content with the essentials. This attitude will expose the false teachers, who are using their ministry as a means to get wealthy because of their inordinate attachment to money and teaching others to put their trust in money instead of God.

In Paul's first letter to Timothy, he left him with the mandate to remove and replace the false teachers with reliable leaders (1 Tim. 1.3). By the time of writing 2 Timothy, this problem still has not been resolved, possibly because Timothy is having a hard time removing poor leaders and finding good replacements (2 Tim. 2.2). He is being careful, realizing the long-term effect leaders have on a community.

Purpose

The purpose for writing 2 Timothy is threefold. First, Paul wants to exhort Timothy to be faithful to his calling (1.14), to Paul himself as Timothy's mentor and example (2.1-13) and to the gospel (3.10–4.5) in terms of both his behaviour (2.15) and service (2.24; 4.2, 5).

Second, in light of the presence of the false teachers he wants Timothy to continue in the endeavour of appointing reliable men to be leaders (2.2) so that the gospel may continue to be preached regardless of the cost of suffering. Paul assures Timothy of his confidence that God is doing more to ensure that the gospel and ministry will not be thwarted by these false teachers since 'the gospel cannot be chained' (2.9), 'God will remain faithful' (2.13), 'God's solid foundation stands firm' (2.19) and 'the crown of righteousness awaits' the believers (4.8).

Third, Paul writes to request Timothy to come to Rome help him (4.9) in his future ministry. The tone of this letter is much more personal than 1 Timothy and in it Paul expresses his affection for Timothy as a colleague and a son.

There are many instructions in this letter for Timothy but they may be just as much for Tychicus's sake. Tychicus is likely the carrier of this letter to Timothy and the replacement for Timothy in Ephesus. So these instructions on how to deal with the false teachers are given for Timothy to help train Tychicus and prepare him to take over the situation in Ephesus with the goal that Timothy might get to Paul before winter.

Structure

Paul was a creative letter-writer but also a very practical one. He used letters because they provided him the quickest means of communication available by which he could correspond with people. Though he preferred personal contact to quill and parchment, he accepted letters as an excellent substitute (1 Cor. 5.3; 2 Cor. 2.11). Frequently, Paul is responding to issues and problems in a specific church. For example, in 1 Corinthians, Paul rejoins to a letter (1 Cor. 7.1) and a report (1 Cor. 1.11) he has received. In other instances, he writes simply to reiterate what he has said before (2 Thess. 2.5) or to disclose new information or teaching on a subject (1 Thess. 4.13) using the *disclosure formula* ('I don't want you to be ignorant'). 2 Timothy is slightly different from other letters in the Pauline corpus. It does not include a lot of teaching or new information though Paul does remind Timothy of earlier events and teaching he has passed on. In general, 2 Timothy is a *paraenetic* letter. Most of the material included by Paul is used to exhort Timothy through persuasion and dissuasion to take a particular course until the end of the letter when he sums up his thinking by giving Timothy a strong command through the use of a *charge* form (2 Tim. 4.1-8).

2 Timothy is one of the shorter of Paul's letters (around 1,338 words). Nevertheless it follows the structure characteristic of other Pauline letters based on a slightly altered form of the typical structure of the contemporary Graeco-Roman letter.

Opening/Prescript
    Apollinarios to his mother, Taesis   author to addressee greeting:
    greeting,   some form of *charein* ('to greet')
    I pray that you are well,   health wish (optional)
    and make obeisance on your behalf   prayer (optional)
    to the gods

Body
    I want you to know mother   disclosure formula ('I want you to know...')
    that I arrived safely in Rome...
    I request that you attend to yourself...
    Do not worry about me...
    Please send me a letter about your
    welfare and that of my brothers and
    of all your people.
    And if I ever find someone (to carry my
    letter), I will write to you.

Closing
    I greet my brothers much and Apollinarios   final greeting
    and his children. I greet all your friends,   (or wish for health)
    each by name.
    I pray that you are well.   sentence prayer

Figure 1. *Typical Structure of a Graeco-Roman Letter*

Opening
    author (usually an extended description)
    addressee (extended description)
    greeting:
        grace and peace

Thanksgiving Form
Body
Closing
    final greeting
    sentence prayer

Figure 2. *Typical Structure of a Pauline Letter*

2 Timothy 1.1-2
Opening

Introductory Comment

A great deal can be learned about a letter through examining the opening. 2 Timothy is no exception. An observant reader will immediately notice the expanded appellations attached to the names of 'Paul', the author, and 'Timothy', the addressee. This is consistent with the practice of Graeco-Roman letter-writers. Julius Victor writes in *Ars rhet.* 27 that 'the openings and closings should conform with the degree of friendship (one shares with the recipient) or with his rank, and should be written according to customary practice'. This phenomenon is clearly demonstrated in the Egyptian Official Petitions of the first century BC. The descriptions (e.g. King, procurator, pontifex maximus, imperator etc.) attached to the names in the opening depict the status of the two parties and thereby set out the relationship between them. By means of the opening, Paul does three things. First, he establishes the type of relationship between him and Timothy and thereby how this letter is to be received by Timothy. Second, he sets the tenor of the letter. Third, he introduces some ideas that will be woven into the fabric of the entire letter.

Author (1.1)

Paul begins by calling himself 'an apostle of Christ Jesus'. The term 'apostle' can mean 'messenger', as it does in reference to Epaphroditus (Phil. 2.25), or it can refer to 'the twelve who were with Jesus'. But the usage here conforms to the more specific meaning of those who are specially gifted by God and play a significant, even unique, role in the development of the church (cf. Eph. 4.11; 1 Cor. 12.28). The technical sense of the word as referring to an eyewitness of Christ (1 Cor. 9.1) and one who performs signs, wonders and miracles (2 Cor. 12.12) may also not be too far from his mind.

Paul roots his apostleship in the person of Jesus Christ though he reverses the order as 'Christ Jesus' (note the opposite order in Tit. 1.1; 1 Pet. 1.1; 2 Pet. 1.1). This order is not unusual in Paul's letters since he uses each roughly the same number of times (i.e. 'Christ Jesus' > 85 times and 'Jesus Christ' > 80 times). What is surprising, is the number of times this phrase is found in 2 Timothy: eleven times in 2 Timothy, and the same number in 1 Timothy (note that the phrase 'Jesus Christ' is only found once in 2 Timothy). The expression 'Christ Jesus' is used in two ways. First, it is used to draw attention to the ramifications of having Christ as Messiah. Typically this usage is tied together with the preposition 'in', thus 'in Christ Jesus' referring to the new sphere of existence and benefits for the one who believes in Jesus Christ. Several examples of this usage are found in 2 Timothy (1.1b; 1.9, 13; 2.1, 10; 3.12), which will be discussed later. Second, it is used in order to draw attention to the word 'messiah' (which means 'anointed one') as the one who is God's anointed King, Priest and Prophet. This is the usage found in 1.1 but it is also found elsewhere in the epistle (1.2, 10; 2.3; 4.1). For Timothy's sake, Paul is drawing attention to the person of Jesus who is known as 'the Messiah' or 'the Christ' and is responsible for his apostleship and the one to whom he belongs and to whom he is accountable. It is this same Jesus, the Messiah, who is the basis of Timothy's call to the ministry.

The term 'apostle' is further modified by two phrases, 'through the will of God' and 'according to the promise of life which is in Christ Jesus'. The former phrase is used in the exact form elsewhere in the Pauline corpus (1 Cor. 1.1; 2 Cor. 1.1; Eph. 1.1; Col. 1.1) and in a slightly modified form in Gal. 1.4. In settings where there is tension between Paul and the recipients (1 Cor. 1.1; 2 Cor. 1.1; Gal. 1.4), the phrase is used to make it clear for Paul's opposition that the source of his calling to the apostleship is found in God and not himself. Where there is no tension, as in 2 Timothy (i.e. certainly Timothy is his ally), Paul is simply reminding Timothy that it was God's will for Paul to be an apostle and to live the lifestyle of one. The idea of the 'will of God' reverberates throughout 2 Timothy. Paul makes it clear that it is God's will that he is suffering as an apostle and for the gospel (2 Tim. 1.11-12). Similarly, it was God's will to choose Timothy for the ministry (1.6). Elsewhere in his Epistles, Paul presents himself as a model for believers to follow (1 Cor. 4.16; 2 Thess. 3.9) in the same way that Jesus set himself up as an example to emulate (Jn 13.15). Paul asks this of believers because he believes that he is imitating Christ (1 Cor. 11.1). He asks this of Timothy now (2 Tim. 1.13; 3.10). Paul is convinced that it is God's will for Timothy to suffer as a minister of God and exhorts him to follow his example (2 Tim. 1.8; 2.3).

The latter phrase lets Timothy know that Paul's apostleship is in accordance with the 'promise of life' and that this life comes through Jesus Christ. By means of this phrase, Paul connects together ministry and life. Paul has become convinced through experience that quintessential life was manifest in Jesus Christ (1.10) and that he is both the paradigm of how to live life well in its truest sense and also the source and sustaining power of life. For this reason Paul can conclude in 1 Tim. 4.8 that Jesus holds the promise of life in the present and future. Here, in this opening, Paul introduces the idea of 'life' for Timothy. Paul will develop this idea in the letter almost as a reminder that they both have embraced this life and that they have received the ministry of making this life known to others in spite of suffering (2 Tim. 1.11-12). Their perspectives differ slightly. Paul writes as one farther along on the journey. His advice, purified on the anvil of experience, is that if one is faithful in the ministry God ordains then one can expect to experience life in the present (1.9) and in the future, eternal life (1.10, 12; 4.8, 18). Paul is a realist so he knows that life comes with sufferings but these do not suggest God's displeasure or personal failure, rather they are signs of an authentic life and ministry (2 Tim. 3.12; cf. 2 Cor. 6.4-10; 11.23-33).

Recipient (1.2a)

The nature of Paul's relationship with Timothy is summed up with the words '[my] beloved child'. Paul does not refer to himself as 'father' in the opening but what is implied here is made specific in Phil. 2.22: 'as a child with his father, Timothy has served with me for [the work of] the gospel'. He considers Timothy like his adopted son. The affection Paul has for Timothy is interwoven into the letter (1.4; 4.9, 21). The word 'beloved' is used frequently in the Gospels to refer to God's beloved son, Jesus (Mk 1.11; 12.6). In Paul's writing it is used generally for those to whom Paul addresses his letters (Rom. 1.7) or more narrowly to certain fellow workers for the gospel (Eph. 6.21). The words which follow in the letter are chosen carefully by a father concerned for the welfare of his child and the gospel they both love.

The language of father and son is also the language taken up by moral philosophers to portray the relationship of teacher and student. The pedagogical posture between them is the *paradigmatic apostle* and the *collegial student*. Timothy is to follow Paul's example (1.13; 3.10-14) so that he may continue to be an example for others in Ephesus regardless of his age or experience (1 Tim. 4.12) just as he has been in other assignments Paul has given him (in Corinth, 1 Cor. 4.17 and Philippi, Phil. 2.19-24). Because Timothy accepts Paul's authority and pedagogical role in his life there is no superfluous expansion of his authority as there is in Galatians and 1 Corinthians. From this perspective, strong words follow in this letter, like the charge in 4.1-8, which Paul expects Timothy to obey. Paul is confident Timothy will be obedient but not so much on the basis of his authority but on the basis of their intimate relationship.

Greeting (1.2b)

The opening ends with the greeting, 'grace, mercy and peace from God [our] father and Christ Jesus our Lord'. Traditionally scholars have understood

Paul's inclusion of 'grace and peace' as an attempt to be inclusive through using both the Greek and the Hebrew greeting respectively. A few have seen it as a customary greeting used at the beginning of worship. But most likely the inclusion of these two important terms is a condensed expression of Paul's theology. Grace is the cornerstone of his theology. Objectively, it refers to the salvation of life and freedom that Jesus procured through his substitutionary death on the Cross. Subjectively, it refers to the ongoing graciousness poured out, leading people to accept and continue in this salvation. Peace has two aspects. First, it refers to the reconciliation that Christ has founded, namely the vertical reconciliation between God and humankind (Rom. 5.2) that should result in horizontal reconciliation between people (e.g. race, Eph. 2.11-14; 4.3) within humankind and creation. Second, it refers to the *shalom* or wholeness found in belonging to God. All this is from God the father and Christ Jesus the Lord. These truths sustain Paul. Now he passes these on to Timothy in the form of a blessing to sustain him as he ministers in a difficult context.

It is important to note that this greeting is unique from all other greetings in Paul's letters, except 1 Timothy, because it includes the word 'mercy'. Why then does Paul sandwich 'mercy' between 'grace' and 'peace'? Some might suggest that the difference in wording may suggest a different author than Paul. Though possible, there is a more plausible explanation. For emphasis, Paul brackets 'mercy' with 'grace' and 'peace'. This new emphasis on mercy may indicate something about the circumstances that Paul and Timothy are facing. God's mercy is close to Paul's heart since it was God's mercy that saved him, the 'worst of sinners' (1 Tim. 1.13, 15). It was this experience of God's mercy that motivated his ministry of mercy to others (1 Tim. 1.16; cf. Lk. 10.37; Rom. 9.23; 11.31). Paul is older now and ministry has taken its toll on him (2 Cor. 6.3-10). He is well aware of the need to keep his experience of God's mercy shown to him in the forefront of his mind in order for him to be merciful to others. This has been his perspective in the past when faced with a tough situation (2 Cor. 1.8-10) and more recently in the present while facing an equally difficult situation, his imprisonment and trial (2 Tim. 4.9-18). The words of Christ, 'blessed are the merciful, for they will be shown mercy', are familiar, tried and true for Paul. Though the exact number of his days on earth is unknown, he is aware that difficulties will always be near (2 Tim. 3.10). Therefore just as grace is needed to live a godly life of ministry, so is mercy, because he knows that without mercy he will come into judgment and his ministry will be discounted. Final mercy will be experienced when he arrives in heaven just as Onesiphorus will soon receive (1.18). It is from this perspective as a weathered saint that Paul wants Timothy to embrace the mercy of God in the present so that he might live a godly life amidst suffering and express mercy to others. If he does then he will receive the fullness of mercy from God on the day of the Lord (cf. 4.8).

Changes in the Opening of 1 Timothy and 2 Timothy

There are a couple of changes in the Opening of 2 Timothy from the Opening of 1 Timothy which give some insight into the situation of 2 Timothy and how it is to be understood.

In 1 Tim. 1.1 Paul states that he is Christ's apostle 'by the command of God our saviour and Christ Jesus our hope' but in 2 Tim. 1.1 he expresses that he is 'an apostle of Christ Jesus by the will of God'. There are two notable changes in 2 Timothy: 'command' versus 'will' and the replacement of the appellations 'God our saviour and Christ Jesus our hope' with 'according to the promise of life'. The situation with the false teachers in 1 Timothy is serious, so much so that Paul depicts his apostleship in terms of a military metaphor. Paul's purpose for doing so is to let Timothy know that he is an apostle, a soldier of Christ, under the authority of God. Similarly, Timothy is a man *under* authority (God and Paul) and must therefore fulfill the commands and heed the advice Paul gives in his letter. But Timothy is also a man *with* authority because he is Paul's apostolic delegate, a soldier of Christ, and therefore he must confront the false teachers and bring them under the authority of God and Paul's 'sound teaching' (1 Tim. 1.10; 6.3). To continue this emphasis on confronting the false teachers, Paul states that the command he is giving Timothy is from 'God our saviour and Christ Jesus our hope'. Paul does this to point Timothy's attention to God since he is the one who can ultimately save and give hope to the false teachers just as he did for Paul (1 Tim. 1.13-16).

In 2 Timothy, Paul's concern has shifted. Whereas in 1 Timothy he spoke of his apostleship in terms of God's authority, now he thinks of it—as he frequently does (1 Cor. 1.1; 2 Cor. 1.1; Eph. 1.1; Col. 1.1)—as a calling predicated on the will of God like his OT predecessors. He also wants Timothy to see his life as a minister of the gospel as God's will which includes living in accordance with God's purposes (contra the false teachers who are doing Satan's will; 2.26) but specifically as suffering for the gospel because it holds the promise of life (1.8; 3.12). In 1 Timothy Paul had his focus on the problem of the false teachers but in 2 Timothy Paul has turned his attention more towards the future and further away from the false teachers and the situation in Ephesus. Paul's concern is for Timothy to remain a faithful minister because he has his sights set on the time when Timothy arrives in Rome (4.9, 13, 21) and Paul is released from prison (4.6) so that they will minister together again.

Another change between 1 and 2 Timothy is found in the way Paul addresses Timothy. In 1 Timothy he refers to Timothy as 'my true child' but in 2 Timothy he refers to Timothy as 'my beloved child'. This difference reflects the change in the tenor of the letter. In the first epistle Paul affirms Timothy as a genuine or true child in the sense that Timothy is a genuine reflection of Paul's beliefs and thus he is fully qualified to confront the false teachers who are the opposite. But in the second epistle, Paul is much more vulnerable and personal in his address to Timothy largely due to his circumstances in Rome which have been difficult. He feels deserted and longs for Timothy's company again (2 Tim. 4.9, 10).

2 Timothy 1.3-5
Thanksgiving

The Thanksgiving as a Distinct Literary Form

The thanksgiving form is a distinct literary form found in the Pauline letters. Some scholars look to the Hellenistic letters as the background for this form and others see behind this form the Jewish custom of bringing a thanksgiving before preaching. More likely it is a creation of Paul, who has expanded the *wish for health* section in secular letters. As a literary form it is characterized by a clear structure and in this sense the thanksgiving in 2 Tim. 1.3-5 is like those found in other letters of Paul.

A	Verb of Thanksgiving and Person Thanked	'I give thanks to God…
B	Manner in which Paul gives Thanks	'as unceasingly…
C	Reason for the Thanksgiving	'because I have received a reminder of your sincere faith…
D	Explanatory Clause for the Reason for the Thanksgiving Clause	'which first dwelt in your mother…and I am persuaded now dwells in you
E	Content of the Prayer for his Addressee(s)	'since I long to see you so that I might be filled with joy.'

Figure 3. *Thanksgiving Form*

The thanksgiving form in Paul's letters served different purposes. It could express genuine thankfulness for the recipient(s) (Phil. 1.3-5), even when that for which he was thankful was minimal (1 Cor. 1.4-9). If the thanksgiving form was missing the reason was obvious (Galatians): he was not thankful. In this situation Paul is genuinely thankful for Timothy, the person and colleague.

Some think it is used to provide a model for prayer in corporate worship or to state his concerns for his readers (1 Thess. 1.2-16). This seems less likely in this case. More importantly the thanksgiving can be used to introduce issues or themes that will be developed in the letter. This usage is evident in 2 Timothy where two themes are introduced which weave their way through the letter. First, it expresses Paul's desire to have Timothy abate his loneliness and to have him at his side as they do further ministry together (4.9, 21). Second, it presents Timothy's loyalty to the gospel and

Paul, thereby setting the foundation for the many exhortations for Timothy to continue to remain faithful and loyal in the face of a difficult situation where false teachers are continuing to succeed (2.14–3.9) and where so many have deserted the gospel (4.10, 14, 16).

Some understand the thanksgiving in quite the opposite manner. These ones believe that Timothy's fidelity as a believer and evangelist is at stake. Thus the thanksgiving and 2 Timothy do not affirm Timothy's faithfulness and loyalty to the gospel but rather expose his deviation from his heritage of faith. The following directives in the epistle serve to get Timothy back on track since he has started to resemble the false teachers more than a faithful minister of the gospel. Several textual clues militate against this position and prove it to be a misinformed interpretation. First, Paul has received yet a new reminder of Timothy's sincere unalloyed faith (1.5a). Second, Timothy's spiritual heritage is presented to show that he has been consistent with and has grown firmly into the orthodox Christian faith passed down to him (1.5b). Third, in 1.5c Paul states unequivocally that he is convinced of Timothy's sincere faith. Fourth, though it is possible for someone to fall away from the gospel (Demas in 4.10; Alexander in 1 Tim. 1.20), Timothy has had a proven track record of faithfulness to the gospel. By the time of the writing of 2 Timothy, Timothy and Paul have had around 15–16 years of joint service (3.10-14) since the time Timothy joined Paul on his second missionary journey (c. 50 AD). Timothy is even mentioned as the co-writer of six letters. Fifth, if Timothy had indeed deviated from the faith and was a compromised minister, it is very unlikely that Paul would ask him to join in doing further ministry together (4.9, 11).

Paul's Attitude toward Ministry (1.3a)

In terms of content 1.3 is similar to Rom. 1.9 in which Paul stresses his service is to God and remembers his recipients. The word *latreuō* can more narrowly mean 'to worship' (Heb. 9.9) but Paul uses the broader meaning of the word 'to serve' (cf. Phil. 3.3; Rom. 1.9, 25) which can include ministering in the context of worship (cf. Phil. 3.3; Heb. 8.5) or preaching (Rom. 15.16). Paul serves with a clean conscience. In his earlier letter he states that he expects to minister in love which is only possible if one has 'a pure heart and good conscience' (1 Tim. 1.5). This purity of thought brings Paul and true ministers in direct contrast to the false teachers who have a 'seared conscience' (1 Tim. 4.2). Paul is wise enough to realize that a clean conscience does not mean that he is innocent since sin and Satan can corrupt the conscience (1 Cor. 4.4) so he leaves judgment of this to God. Elsewhere Paul has boasted of having lived with a clean conscience before God and people. In Acts 23.1 he makes this proclamation before the Sanhedrin for which Ananias immediately judges him and orders that Paul be struck and in doing so proves that he (Ananias) is the real lawbreaker (Lev. 19.15; Deut. 25.1, 2). Later Paul makes the same claim before Felix but this time without any pugilistic repercussions (Acts 24.16). The importance of a clean conscience may be in part the reason he makes it a requirement of deacons (1 Tim. 3.9) though in this text Paul is indirectly reminding Timothy to continue to make it a priority in his own life.

Some translate 1.3a as 'whom I serve as my forefathers did'. These scholars understand Paul to be saying that his service to God stands in direct succession to his OT forefathers. If so, then Paul is stressing the continuity between the message of the OT and the message of the gospel. The OT prophets and forefathers through many ways (e.g. psalms, oracles) gave only parts of the message but it is Christ who has given the complete revelation that Paul is proclaiming (Heb. 1.1-3). This is Paul's heritage to which Timothy is connected. The emphasis on the correct use of the Law (1 Tim. 1.8-11; 2 Tim. 2.8, 19; 3.8, 14-17) in contrast to the false teachers may be further support for this position. Though this is possible, there is a more likely interpretation.

The word translated 'forefather' literally means 'those born before'. This can refer more narrowly to 'relatives' as it does in 1 Tim. 5.4 in which children and offspring are exhorted to repay their parents and grandparents for the care they previously received from them. Thus this word may refer to those born before Paul but not necessarily refer back to the characters of the OT. It is more likely Paul has in mind believers, 'relatives in the faith', who were born before him. Paul has relatives in the faith (Rom. 16.7, 11, 21) but here, as he prays reflecting on his ministry, he remembers those believers who preceded him and may now be dead. As he thinks about this Christian heritage he wants Timothy to remember that this is his Christian heritage too and in fact he even has believers in his immediate family (i.e. his grandmother Lois and his mother Eunice).

Frequency of Paul's Prayers for Timothy (1.3b)

Paul discloses that he prays for Timothy 'night and day'. This may reflect the prayer life Paul developed formerly as a Law-abiding Pharisee, who would pray habitually at set times throughout the day and evening (Ps. 55.17; Dan. 6.10). Textually it is possible to take the phrase 'night and day' with 'long to see' (cf. RSV). In 1 Thess. 2.9 and 2 Thess. 3.8 Paul does use the phrase 'night and day' with 'work' in order to stress how long and hard he worked. But in the three other Pauline references he uses this phrase with 'prayer' (1 Thess. 3.10; 1 Tim. 5.5; 2 Tim. 1.3; cf. Lk. 2.37). 'Night and day', which are qualified by 'unceasingly', suggests that Paul has developed a regular pattern of remembering Timothy in his prayers. This is also consistent with what he expects of the Thessalonians (1 Thess. 5.17).

Paul's Desire to See Timothy (1.4-5)

Paul's remembrance of Timothy in prayer reminds him of their last emotional farewell, when Paul left Timothy in tears. Paul is clearly longing for that same intimacy now in order to quell his loneliness during these days between his first and second judicial hearings in Rome (4.16). The word 'to long for', *epipotheō*, is a typically Pauline word (note that seven of the nine usages are found in the Pauline corpus) which points to his deepest desire for something very significant to happen. It could be to share a spiritual gift (Rom. 1.11) or to receive the resurrection body (2 Cor. 5.2) or to see someone (Phil. 1.8; 1 Thess. 3.6). This word captures the immediacy Paul feels of having Timothy arrive. Only then will Paul's joy be filled. It is for this reason he has sent Tychicus to Ephesus to relieve Timothy of his duties so that he can get to Rome quickly, or at least before winter (4.9, 21). The statement of Paul's desire to see Timothy, found at the beginning and end of the letter, functions similar to bookends stressing the need Paul has for Timothy to return to his side.

Translators differ whether the text should read 'because I remember your sincere faith' or 'because I have received a reminder of your sincere faith'. The former translation suggests that Timothy's sincere faith simply comes to mind as Paul prays. The latter translation implies that a specific incident has occurred or Paul has received a report which he turns into a thanksgiving. Some scholars do not accept this position because there is no specific incident mentioned in the text. In spite of this opposition there is a lot in favour of the latter position since it is more true to the Greek text. First, the meaning of *hupomnēsin* is typically 'reminder' (cf. 2 Pet. 1.13; 3.1; Hermas *Vis.* 16.9). Second, *labōn* is best translated 'I received'. Though the reader is left to surmise in what form the reminder came, clearly Paul has received some news about Timothy that demonstrates his loyalty to the gospel, Christ and Paul.

Though Paul is constantly in prayer for Timothy, the specific reminder that influenced his prayers at that moment had to do with Timothy's sincere faith. The word for 'sincere' (*anupokritos*) carries the idea of doing something with genuine motives so that one does not appear hypocritical to an outsider. Interestingly this word is used three other times in Paul's letters (Rom. 12.9; 2 Cor. 6.6; 1 Tim. 1.5) and in each instance the context has to do with love. True love is easily recognized (Rom. 12.9) particularly when it is costly (2 Cor. 6.6). A sincere faith is necessary to express genuine love (1 Tim. 1.5). Through this thanksgiving Paul is indirectly exhorting Timothy to keep his faith genuine amidst sufferings and temptations. Demas, Paul's long-time friend, exchanged a genuine love and faith for love of this world (4.10) just as the false teachers had (1 Tim. 1.5).

Paul is not surprised by Timothy's sincere faith since he has a good spiritual heritage. The reminder of Timothy's sincere faith in turn reminds Paul of the sincere faith of Lois, Timothy's grandmother, and Eunice, Timothy's mother. Paul is exhorting Timothy to remember his roots, his spiritual heritage just as Paul remembered his. Timothy's father is not mentioned. Acts 16.1 tells us that Timothy's mother was a Jewess and a believer but his father was Greek. It may be that his father was omitted because he was not a believer or that he was deceased or possibly because Paul wants to emphasize the continuity of Timothy's faith and gospel with his Jewish heritage.

2 Timothy 1.6-18
Paul's First Request for Timothy: Suffer Shamelessly for the Gospel with Paul

Overview

This portion of text is part of a larger section (1.6–2.13) in which Paul is encouraging Timothy to continue to join with Paul in suffering for the gospel and to do so willingly and without shame. There are two requests in this section (1.6-14 and 2.1-7) coupled with an example or examples (1.13-18 and 2.8-10) exemplifying these requests. The section ends with a 'saying' which sums up what a minister for Christ can expect (2.11-13). The following is an outline of this section.

> Paul's First Request: Suffer Shamelessly for the Gospel with Paul (1.6-14)
>   Negative Examples: Phygelus and Hermogenes (1.15)
>   Positive Example: Onesiphorus (1.16-18)
> Paul's Second Request: Suffer for the Ministry with Paul (2.1-7)
>   Positive Example: Jesus (2.8-10)
> Trustworthy Saying on Ministry (2.11-13)

The willingness to suffer for Christ and the gospel is the thread that runs through the two requests. There is a slight difference in the content of the two requests. In the first request Paul emphasizes not being ashamed of suffering for the *message* of the gospel whereas in the second request there is more of an emphasis of being willing to suffer as a *minister* of the gospel. Paul is well aware that the gospel can appear like foolishness (cf. 1 Cor. 1.18-25) to some and therefore it can be tempting not to proclaim it and to shrink away from one's calling as a minister for Christ. For this reason he presents a few examples to show the consequences. Phygelus and Hermogenes represent two people who were ashamed of Christ and Paul and unwilling to suffer for the gospel. Onesiphorus, on the other hand, represents a person who was not ashamed of Christ or Paul's suffering. Rather, he was quite the opposite, gladly and energetically joining in suffering for the gospel with Paul. The final example is Jesus who stands as the paragon of suffering and provides the perfect example of a true minister for God.

Relationship between the Request and the Thanksgiving

Structurally this passage of Scripture is one unit. It begins (1.6-7) and ends (1.14) with the need for the power of the Holy Spirit in order to be faithful and loyal to God and the gospel and to be willing to suffer for it. The text is connected with the preceding thanksgiving through the use of an unusual phrase that is often translated 'for this reason'. This phrase is found four times outside 2 Timothy (Lk. 8.47; Acts 22.24; Tit. 1.13; Heb. 2.11) and in each case it is used for emphasis. The same phrase is found in 2 Tim. 1.12 where Paul wants to make a strong connection between his calling (as herald, apostle and teacher; 1.11) and suffering (1.12) in order to show that the two are inextricably related. Similarly here, Paul builds on the truth he asserted in the thanksgiving (1.3-5): Timothy is a tested and proven minister with a sincere faith. Because this is true Paul reminds Timothy to continue to build on this foundation and to continue to suffer yet more for the gospel (1.6) by fanning into flame the gift of God. For Paul the ministry is all about moving forward, not shrinking back (Phil. 3.12-14), because the prize is found at the end of the race (2 Tim. 4.8).

Fan into Flame the Gift of God (1.6)

The key issue in this text is establishing to what event is Paul referring. Is it the same event he mentions in 1 Tim. 1.18 and 4.14 or is it a different event?

Traditionally scholars point to 1 Tim. 4.14 (and 1.18) as the time when Timothy was ordained for the ministry by a body of elders. He received this ministry (*charisma*) when the elders laid hands on him and shared prophecies with him as confirmation from God for this task. These scholars propose that Paul is referring to this event in 2 Tim. 1.6 since the word *charisma* is found in both passages, both texts mention 'laying on of hands' and because they find a parallel in the language of 'do not neglect' and 'fan into flame'. Under this interpretation some believe that Timothy may be flagging and growing timid in the ministry. For this reason Paul has to encourage Timothy to 'keep 'er lit' (to quote an Irish expression), namely to rekindle his passion for the ministry, in spite of the difficult circumstances, by living a life characterized by power, love and self-discipline.

Though this position is attractive and I concur that the meaning of 'the gift in you' in 1 Tim. 4.14 does refer to Timothy's gift of ministry, I suggest that Paul is referring to a different event. He is looking back to a moment when Paul laid hands on Timothy, whereby he was empowered by the Holy Spirit. In the following section I will present several reasons that suggest Paul may be referring not to public ordination but to a specific moment when Paul laid his hands on Timothy.

First, the meaning of 'gift' (*charisma*) in the Pauline corpus largely gains its meaning from the surrounding context. For example the exact phrase 'gift of God' is found in Rom. 6.23. But there it refers to 'eternal life' which is in direct contrast to the 'wages of sin'. A similar wording, 'gift from God', is found in 1 Cor. 7.7 yet the context suggests that this gift from God is the gift of being married or unmarried. In several contexts the word can refer generally to the gifts of the Holy Spirit (Rom. 12.6; 1 Cor. 12.4) or specifically to particular gifts of the Holy Spirit (1 Cor. 12.28, 'gifts of healing'). In 1 Tim. 4.14 the meaning of 'ministry' for 'gift' is confirmed by the surrounding context. Paul encourages Timothy to devote himself to the public aspects of ministry, namely teaching and preaching (1 Tim. 4.13), not neglecting this gift (1.14), being diligent as a minister (1.15a, 16b), watching his doctrine (1.16a) so that people might watch his lifestyle (1.15b) and be saved by his ministry (1.16b). The phrase 'gift of God' in 2 Tim. 1.6 similarly is affected by its context. There are three important contextual factors that confirm that Paul is referring to the Holy Spirit as the gift of God. The first factor is located in 2 Tim. 1.7. Here Paul elaborates on the experience of the 'gift of God' as the Spirit which does not lead to cowardice but to power, love and a sound mind. The second factor is found in 1.6a where Paul asks Timothy to fan into flame this gift. The close connection between the Holy Spirit and fire is an image Paul uses elsewhere (1 Thess. 5.19). Whereas in 1 Thess. 5.19 Paul warns against 'extinguishing' the fire of the Spirit, here in 2 Tim. 1.6 Paul encourages Timothy to 'fan this gift' into flame. The third factor is that this entire section 1.6-14 is held together by an emphasis on the power of the Holy Spirit to enable Timothy to fulfill his calling.

Second, the means by which the 'gift' is received differs between the two texts; in 1 Tim. 4.14 the gift is received through the *elders'* laying on of hands but in 2 Tim. 1.6 the gift is received through *Paul's* laying on of hands. The use of the laying on of hands for setting apart and commissioning individuals for ministry is well established in the NT (Stephen and others in Acts 6.6; Paul and Barnabas in 13.2-3). Using almost identical wording, the use of the laying on of hands for receiving the Holy Spirit is also well established in the NT. Peter and John place their hands on the apostles of Samaria to receive the Spirit but refuse to do so for Simon the Sorcerer (Acts 8.17-19). Paul experienced first healing and then the reception of the Spirit after his Damascus road experience through the laying on of Ananias's hands in Damascus (Acts 9.12, 17). Sometime later Paul shares what he previously experienced by laying his hands on some disciples of John (Acts 19.6). Thus the laying on of hands can equally refer to either commissioning or reception of the Holy Spirit. The difference is that one is done with Paul alone but the other with the body of elders.

The language used to convey the means by which the gift is transferred is also inconclusive since in both passages it is said that the 'gift is given' to

Timothy (1 Tim. 4.14; 2 Tim. 1.7). But there is a particular emphasis in the NT on the Spirit being given to the individual which is not so emphasized with respect to commissioning. In three other Pauline texts it is emphasized that the Spirit is 'given' to a person in order for him to reside 'in' him or her (1 Cor. 6.19; 2 Cor. 1.22; 1 Thess. 4.8). Of particular importance too is the fact that it is God who is singled out as the one who gave Timothy and Paul this gift (1.7), which is a stress found in those other passages too.

In conclusion, given the emphasis on the Holy Spirit in the immediate and greater context, the strong linguistic connections between Spirit and gift, the stress on Paul's hands being laid on Timothy, coupled with the direct action of God in the process makes it likely that Paul has a different situation in mind than the one described in 1 Tim. 4.14.

Paul's Reason for Engaging the Struggle of Ministry: Character of the Spirit (1.7)

In this verse Paul contrasts the *pneuma* of cowardice and the [*pneuma*] of power, love and sound mind. Scholars have debated whether *pneuma* ('spirit') refers to the Holy Spirit or the human spirit and whether the same referent is used in both places. One possible idea is that Paul is saying, 'God did not give us [believers in general, not just Paul and Timothy] a *spirit* [i.e. an attitude or disposition] but rather the *Holy Spirit*, characterized by power, love and sound mind'. It is probably more plausible that Paul could be paraphrased as saying 'when we [Paul is speaking of his personal experience and Timothy's in 1.6] received the *Holy Spirit*, it was not the "*Holy Spirit*-which-makes-us-cowardly Holy Spirit" but rather it was the Holy Spirit of God, the gift from God (1.6), who works inwardly to give us power in weakness, love amidst struggle and a sound mind amidst compromised thinking'. The latter view is certainly consistent with Paul's usage in Rom. 8.15, 'you did not receive the Spirit which enslaves us to fear but the Spirit which embraces us as sons and daughters', and in 1 Cor. 2.12 where Paul shows the Corinthians that they did not receive the Spirit characterized by worldliness but the Spirit who is God and thus characterized by holiness.

The main point Paul is driving home is the need for Timothy to stay connected to the source (i.e. the Holy Spirit) if he is to continue to have a vital ministry. Ministry is not for the faint of heart. It requires courage. Cowardice (a better translation than 'timidity'; cf. Lev. 26.36), which is rooted in fear, is not compatible with the Christian faith (Rev. 21.8), which is rooted in love and trust (Heb. 10.38, 39). Yet, even the disciples were susceptible to it (Mt. 8.26) and examples of cowardly ministers come to mind quickly for Paul (Demas, 2 Tim. 4.9; some Asians including Hermogenes and Phygelus, 1.15). The opposite of cowardice is power, love and sound-mindedness all in abundance through the Spirit and all necessary for effective ministry. The *power* from the Spirit sets people apart (Rom. 1.4), leads people into hope (Rom. 15.13), enables an extraordinary ministry of preaching (1 Cor. 2.4) and healing (Rom. 15.19) and strengthens one's inner being (Eph. 3.16; Phil. 3.10). It is the same power that raised Christ from the dead (Eph. 1.19-20) but only needs a humble vessel to indwell in order to be effective (2 Cor. 12.9). *Love*, the essence of God, brings Timothy in direct contrast with the false teachers (2 Tim. 2.22) and it is needed as he instructs those who oppose him (2.25). In doing this Timothy will be following the pattern set by Christ and Paul (1.13). The last term, *sound-mindedness*, is the aspect of the Holy Spirit, which affects the mental capacities. Sound-mindedness is the state of mind that one enjoys from having knowledge, wisdom, insight and revelation (cf. Eph. 1.18; Phil. 1.9) resulting in discernment and godly living. It enables one to live humbly and to consider oneself with sober judgment (Rom. 12.3). For this reason it is required of overseers who are placed in the church as examples for others (1 Tim. 3.2). This is particularly important for Timothy who is faced with unrestrained false teachers (6.8) and women adversely affecting the community (2.15) both of which exhibit little sound-mindedness.

Timothy is Not to Be Ashamed (1.8a)

The first request in this letter is comprised of three imperatives: 'fan into flame the gift of God', 'don't be ashamed' and 'join in suffering with me'. The first appeal points Timothy toward the Spirit and the need for him in ministry. The latter two appeals direct his attention to the Lord and Paul respectively, and the need to be faithful to both regardless of the pain and shame of ministry. The emphasis is loyalty to Christ and his kingdom at all costs.

In v. 8, Paul draws a conclusion from vv. 6 and 7. Because of the Spirit's empowerment Timothy can serve in a difficult ministry situation with a shameless commitment to Christ, the Gospel, and Christ's suffering servants. Paul knows that ministering for Christ can lead to a feeling of shame much like captured prisoners marching in a procession (2 Cor. 2.14). Paul is insistent that Timothy rejects this shame.

Some commentators's examination of the Greek leads them to suggest that Paul has omitted a verb of teaching or preaching, thereby proposing the text be read as 'do not be ashamed [to teach/preach] the testimony about Christ and me'. This reading should be rejected on the grounds of its awkwardness (i.e. requesting Timothy not to be ashamed to teach or preach about Paul) and because typically the verb for 'to be ashamed' is immediately followed by a noun (Mk 8.38; Lk. 9.26; Rom. 1.16), not an infinitive.

It is not clear in the phrase 'testimony (*marturion*) of our Lord' whether Paul is referring to the 'testimony which Jesus left on earth' or to the 'testimony of others about Jesus'. Both uses are valid and Paul may be intentionally unspecific. The word for 'testimony' carries the idea of 'proof', that is specific actions which serve to substantiate or prove something. What is this testimony that Christ gave? In particular it refers to the sacrificial death of atonement Christ made at God's appointed time (1 Tim. 2.6), his teaching (2 Thess. 1.10) and his actions, like but not exclusively the testimony he gave before he died his sacrificial death (1 Tim. 6.13). The potential shame for Timothy would be aligning himself with a person who died a gruesome death as a criminal of the state which would offend Jews and Gentiles (1 Cor. 1.23), both cultures with which he was familiar (cf. Acts 16.1). The temptation for Timothy would be to water down the gospel in order to make it more palatable (cf. 2 Tim. 4.3) and acceptable or in today's terms more marketable. Timothy is to keep his hope in Christ and his message and in this way he will never be put to shame as he witnesses for the Lord because he knows that his vindication will come (cf. Ps. 25.1-3).

Timothy is equally not to be ashamed of 'Paul, the Lord's prisoner'. The reference to Paul here picks up the nuance that Timothy is not to be ashamed of Paul and 'his testimony about Jesus'. From Paul's perspective being a prisoner of the Lord is not a source of shame for him, nor should it be a source of shame for Timothy. On the contrary, it is a source of humble pride (Eph. 3.1) since he knows that he is not a prisoner of Caesar but of Christ, who makes him free to serve in any context, incarcerated or not (Phil. 1.12-13). Paul wants Timothy to embrace Paul's incarceration as an expression of his testimony about Jesus. From Paul's perspective he is following the very path of his Lord, who also was a prisoner of the state. Later Paul reminds Timothy about Onesiphorus who is an example of someone who was not ashamed of his chains.

Timothy is to Be a Fellow Sufferer for the Gospel (1.8b)

To 'suffer' (*kakopatheō*, a rarely used word inside and outside the NT: three times in the NT, once in the LXX and once in the Apostolic Fathers) is an expected part of life though one needs strength to endure it (Js 5.13). Clement goes so far as to say that suffering in the world is a sign of God's blessing and approval (2 Clem. 19.3). But in this instance and later in 4.5, Paul is focusing on a particular aspect of suffering which only believers can understand. This is the suffering which one experiences for the gospel. The paradigm of suffering for believers is Jesus, who made it clear that he would suffer many things (*patheō*, Mk 8.31) and that his followers would experience suffering in the same way (8.34). For Paul, suffering and fellowship are tightly fused. The person who embraces Christ, thereby becomes part of the body of Christ and, as a member of this body, he or she seeks to share in Christ's sufferings (Phil. 3.8) even though he is absent (Col. 1.24).

These sufferings are not redemptive in nature but an inevitable consequence of the missional endeavour of proclaiming the gospel. Paul later acknowledges that these sufferings can include imprisonment (2 Tim. 2.9) which some have mistakenly taken as a sign of God's displeasure (Phil. 1.15-18). But from Paul's perspective these sufferings are signs of the heartfelt dedication of a good soldier of Christ (cf. 2 Tim. 2.3; the same word *kakopatheō* is used here) to his 'commanding officer'.

The word that Paul uses in 1.8b, 'suffer together', *sugkakopatheō*, is very rare, found only twice in the NT and not at all in the LXX or Apostolic Fathers. The meaning is clear that Paul wants Timothy 'to suffer together with him for the sake of the gospel'. The imperative does not convey the idea that Timothy needs to start joining in suffering as though he were not presently doing so. Rather it is a reminder of the need of suffering on behalf of the local church for their benefit at a personal cost (cf. 2 Cor. 1.3-7 for an example of this vicarious suffering). If Timothy is not ashamed of the message or Paul's ministry then he will be more likely to continue to suffer for it. Paul asks this of him now.

To suffer for something requires strength. It will require the power of God. Paul speaks from experience (2 Tim. 3.11), knowing that only in these instances will the power of God suffice. So Paul assures Timothy that God's power will be there in direct proportion to his need. In the Pauline corpus, there are several instances where the Holy Spirit is related and sometimes even inextricably related to power (Rom. 1.4; 15.13, 15.19; 1 Cor. 2.4; Eph. 3.20). Thus Paul probably uses 'power of God' as a reference to the Holy Spirit in order to emphasize the strength the Spirit gives in suffering and to make a connection with the previous verse, 'God gave us the Spirit of power...' (1.7).

Paul's point is that he wants Timothy to continue in the humiliation of being associated with Christ, his message and his servants. He must be loyal to these. At this point in the letter, Paul does not reveal the outcome of suffering together for the gospel. This comes later when he connects this idea of receiving a crown of righteousness (4.8) with a faithful ministry. There is glory attached to suffering, though it comes at the end of the race (Jn 13.31; 12.27-28).

First Basis for Paul's Request to Suffer: God's Grace and Sovereignty (1.9-10)

The request to suffer shamelessly for the gospel is founded on two bases. The first basis is God's grace and sovereignty demonstrated through the salvific work of Jesus and the calling of sinners as his ministers (1.9-10). The second basis is Paul's testimony, which is an expression of God's grace, sovereignty, salvation and calling (1.11-12).

Verses 9 and 10 are creedal in style and comprise a compact explanation of the gospel. The style of the material has led some scholars to believe that it is formed from an earlier creed and therefore not Pauline. But their conclusion may be ill founded since Paul frequently includes creedal-like material in his undisputed letters (Gal. 4.4-7; Rom. 8.15-16; 1 Thess. 1.9-10; 5.9-10). In typical Pauline fashion, he roots the exhortation of 1.6-8 in the person and work of the Father and Son (cf. Rom. 14.15, 20; 15.7). The point Paul wants Timothy to see is that just as he and Timothy trusted God's sovereign action to give them salvation and their callings, likewise they can trust God to see them through their sufferings. So Paul adapts this material to the needs of Timothy as a reminder of the gospel he embraced and of which he is part. This highly christological material also serves a second purpose. Because the letter is written for the sake of the Ephesians too, this orthodox theological matter may serve as a gentle reminder for them about the importance of rooting themselves and their teaching on the person and work of Christ and rejecting false teaching.

Paul states that the gospel of salvation was founded in Christ Jesus in eternity past (*pro chronon aionion*, lit. 'before eternal time'; cf. Tit. 1.2). Here we have a reference to the pre-existence of Christ. The idea of the saving purpose of God expressed in the gospel predates time, as we know it. The expression of this saving action came after 'eternal time' (cf. Rom. 16.25; the same phrase is used) through the appearance of Christ Jesus. The word used for 'appearance' (*epiphaneia*) is used four times in the two Epistles to Timothy (1 Tim. 6.14; 2 Tim. 1.10; 4.1, 8). Of the four usages, three of them refer to the appearance of Christ at his second coming (1 Tim. 6.14; 2 Tim. 4.1, 8). But in this instance it clearly refers to the first appearance of Jesus, his incarnation. This event marks the beginning of the saving action of God that culminates in his death and resurrection.

The appearance of Jesus the saviour, as expressed in the gospel, has two implications: it nullifies death and brings to light life. Death, the result of sin (Rom. 5.12), has reigned since Adam's fall (5.14) and was overcome at the cross (6.9). The spiritual sense of death is found in 1 Tim. 5.6 with respect to the widows who live for pleasure. It is the last enemy of God to be destroyed (1 Cor. 15.26; note that the same verb is used). For the believer death is still a reality but its sting has been removed (1 Cor. 15.55) and therefore it is not to be feared. This is particularly important in light of the fact Paul could face death and the same may be required of Timothy in the future.

The other side of the gospel coin is that it brings to light life and imperishability. Paul uses this verb 'bring to light' elsewhere with respect to exposing sin (1 Cor. 4.5) and to revealing God's mysteries (Eph. 3.9). It is the latter sense that is found in 2 Tim. 1.10 whereby the gospel reveals to a person what life and imperishability are, thereby providing the opportunity to experience them. The term 'life' is used thirty-seven times in the Pauline corpus primarily to describe the experience of the person who is in Christ. A person without Christ is considered dead (Eph. 2.1) and alienated from life (4.8) but through Christ one is transferred from death to life resulting in a qualitatively different lifestyle (Rom. 6.4). Generally speaking 'life' in the Pauline corpus refers to the believer's present life, which is *true life* because of a person's salvific relationship with Christ. Occasionally this term includes life beyond death (1 Cor. 15.19; Col. 3.4). When Paul refers to life after death he typically uses the phrase 'eternal life' (Rom. 2.7). The phrase 'eternal life' is more commonly found in the Gospels (twenty-four times) with the Gospel of John having the majority of occurrences (sixteen times). Surprisingly this phrase is found eight times in the Pauline corpus, half of these in Romans (2.7; 5.21; 6.22, 23; cf. Gal. 6.8) and three occurrences in the Pastorals (1 Tim. 1.16; Tit. 1.2; 3.7).

The same usages of 'life' and 'eternal life' are found in the Pastorals but there are some nuanced differences too. Paul understands life as the renewed experience in Christ now and in the afterlife (1 Tim. 4.8). Whereas in most of the Pauline corpus there is a fairly strong distinction between the usages of 'life' and 'eternal life', in the Pastorals their meanings are much more blurred. The meaning of the phrase 'eternal life' in the Pastorals resembles its usage in the Gospel of John in which eternal life refers to the qualitative and quantitative aspects of life. Paul's life is an example of this (1 Tim. 1.16) and one which he wants Timothy and others to follow (6.12). So in 2 Tim. 1.10 Paul is referring to the true life he has experienced (1 Tim. 6.19) and will continue to experience into eternity when he lives in glory (2 Tim. 4.8). It is this promise of life now and in the future which serves as the basis for his calling and purpose (1.1) even when it means suffering.

The gospel also brings to light a future 'incorruptibility' or 'immortality'. Being in Christ promises life now and an immortal existence in the future and therefore Paul assures Timothy that it is worth fighting for. The word for 'immortality' (*aphtharsia*) is only found in Paul's letters (Rom. 2.7; 1 Cor. 15.42, 50, 53, 54; Eph. 6.24). In 1 Corinthians 15 this word is used to describe the incorruptible nature of the resurrection body in contrast to the perishable bodies on earth. Without an incorruptible body a person cannot be in heaven or in the presence of God. It is possible that Paul has been influenced with respect to this concept by Hellenistic Jewish writings. Interestingly in Wis. 2.23 the author suggests that people are made for immortality since they are made in the image of God but unfortunately this plan was foiled by the devil. Later this author states that immortality is needed to be near God (6.19). Possibly more significant to the usage in 2 Tim. 1.10 is the reference in *4 Macc.* 9.22 and 17.12 where immortality is the reward for seven Maccabean youths and their mother who suffer intensely for obeying the law and refusing to bow to Antiochus IV's demands for comprising their faith (cf. Wis. 6.18). Paul has taken this Hellenistic Jewish word and adapted it to his context, stressing that through the gospel immortality is revealed and by suffering for it Timothy can expect the promised reward of immortality.

In v. 9, Paul points Timothy's attention to two aspects of God's grace that he has experienced (i.e. salvation and calling) which should help him to suffer for the gospel. In both areas, Paul emphasizes the role of God acting or conceptualizing on Timothy's behalf. Timothy's salvation, as in all believers' salvation, is not 'by works' but according to the grace and purpose of the Father. This statement runs parallel to the thought in Eph. 2.8-9 which states that salvation was in the mind of God before the creation of the world (i.e. conceptualization) and expressed in grace through the death and resurrection of Jesus Christ (i.e. action). Paul is emphasizing the stability of their salvation demonstrated in how God foresaw the need and provided the solution. Therefore Timothy can have confidence in God's grace and purpose in the midst of trials.

Similarly their callings are also an expression of God's own purpose and grace. The Greek in 1.9a is slightly ambiguous. It could mean 'they were called by means of a holy calling', thus stressing God as the one who called them. But it could also mean 'they were called for the purpose of living a holy life', thereby underscoring the quality of life consistent with this calling. Highlighting God's gracious action makes the former attractive. Though this idea is never far from Paul's mind it is more likely the second reading fits better since in 1.11-12 Paul will elaborate on his calling. Timothy's and Paul's calling is holy in the sense of them being set apart by God, for God, and as such they are to reflect his character regardless of their circumstances. Thus Paul's reflection on their salvation and calling serves to assure Timothy that God will bring Timothy to the desired goal, for his life and ministry, even if there are obstacles.

Second Basis for Paul's Request to Suffer: Paul's Testimony (1.11-12)

In the previous section Paul presented God's grace and sovereignty as the first basis for his request for Timothy to continue suffering for the gospel. Within that section he emphasized the nature and power of the gospel to transform and call people. Now, in 1.11-12, Paul presents the proof of these former statements in 1.9-10 with the example of his own life.

Behind his appointment Paul sees the hand of God placing him into this position. The word for 'appoint' typically means 'to place' (Rom. 14.13; 1 Cor. 3.10, 11; 9.18; 15.25; 16.2; 2 Cor. 3.13) but of the sixteen usages in the Pauline corpus, in the majority of cases, he uses the technical meaning of 'appoint'. So just as God appointed Abraham (Rom. 4.17), Jesus (9.33), different members in the Body of Christ (1 Cor. 12.18, 28) and people for salvation (1 Thess. 5.9), likewise he appointed Paul for the ministry (1 Tim. 1.12; 2.7), thus emphasizing the concepts of grace and sovereignty.

The text of 2 Tim. 1.11 is really a condensed form of the same statement made in 1 Tim. 2.7 which says 'to which I was appointed herald and apostle (*I speak the truth, I do not lie*), teacher *of the Gentiles in faith and truth*'. The elements in italics are omitted in the 2 Timothy pericope. Though there is some good textual support for including 'teacher of the Gentiles' (e.g. corrected version of Codex Sinaiticus) in 2 Tim. 1.11, it is likely 'Gentiles' was intentionally added later in order to make it consistent with 1 Tim. 2.7. Whereas in 1 Tim. 2.7 Paul includes the solemn oath and the 'Gentiles' because he is stressing his authority and calling to the Gentiles, in 2 Tim. 1.11 he omits these since he is highlighting the different roles to which he has been called as signs of God's grace and sovereignty.

Paul has received a holy calling which points back to his earlier statement in 1.9. The first term Paul uses to describe his calling is 'herald'. This word is not common in Jewish and Christian circles; it is not found in the LXX, it is used only three times in the NT (1 Tim. 2.7; 2 Pet. 2.5) and only four times in the Apostolic Fathers (1 Clem. 5.6; MPoly. 2.4; 12.1, 2). It is more commonly found in secular contexts for a person who summons an assembly or carries messages between enemies. This shows that the word never took on the Christian meaning of 'preacher' although the cognate verb (*kērussō*, 'to preach') is used twenty times in Paul's letters generally to describe the act of preaching the gospel. Paul probably uses this word because it conveys the idea of 'someone who conveys a message on behalf of someone else'. This same meaning is found in MPoly. 12.1, in which the herald pronounces on behalf of Polycarp to the entire stadium that he is a Christian. Similarly Noah is referred to as the 'herald of righteousness' (2 Pet. 2.5) because he speaks out to the ungodly on behalf of God about the incipient flood. Paul is a herald for the gospel on behalf of Christ. It is possible that Paul uses this term since it is also used to refer to the cultic heralds of the Ephesian cult of Artemis. In doing this, Paul would be taking an Ephesian term but filling it with his meaning (cf. 'wisdom' in 1 Cor. 1.18-25 for the same method of argumentation).

The second term Paul uses to describe himself is 'apostle'. Typically this word is found in the openings of Paul's letters usually in order to underscore his authority. It serves the same function here.

The third term of Paul's self-description is 'teacher'. He has already described himself as a teacher of the Gentiles with respect to issues of faith and truth (1 Tim. 2.7). For this reason Paul is a model for Timothy of what a true teacher should be and he encourages Timothy to follow the same pattern (2 Tim. 1.13; 4.3). Keep in mind that it is the false teachers's lack of understanding in these two areas that has caused such trouble in Ephesus.

Paul is so convinced of the uniqueness and the transforming power of the gospel, and the sheer grace of having this holy calling, that he is willing to suffer for them. He is not specific in his reference to his sufferings when he says, 'indeed I am suffering *these things*' though he is probably referring to his imprisonment (2 Tim. 1.8; 4.16) which seems harsher than his first Roman imprisonment (Acts 28.30-31). According to Paul, believers are to expect sufferings since they have been graciously given the gift both to believe in Christ and also to suffer on behalf of Christ (Phil. 1.29). God does not send sufferings to punish people and to force learning, rather he uses whatever situation that presents itself for their good, namely to transform people into his son's image (Rom. 8.28-29). Sufferings cause people to depend less on themselves and more on God's Spirit. Through this refining process, believers develop character, perseverance, hope and trust in God (Rom. 5.3-4) in order to help them through their trial. Paul's ideas on sufferings are an extrapolation of Jesus' teaching that 'those who humble themselves will be exalted' (Lk. 14.11). Expressing love and faith amidst suffering is proof of belonging to the kingdom (2 Thess. 1.5) and necessary for living a godly life (2 Tim. 3.12). Paul also sees in his claim to suffer a willingness to suffer vicariously on behalf of others (1 Cor. 12.26; 2 Cor. 1.6a) though ultimately he sees this as a participation in Christ's sufferings (Col. 1.24). This is something of which Paul has a lot of experience and is clearly presented in his lists of sundry hardships (2 Cor. 6.3-13; 11.23-33). Timothy was familiar with Paul's hardships too. On the second missionary journey Timothy would have had the chance to remember with Paul the sufferings he endured as they traveled through the towns of Lystra (Timothy's hometown; Acts 16.1-4), Iconium and Pisidian Antioch. These are the towns Paul refers to later in the letter (2 Tim. 3.11) as examples of great hardship. But of the examples of extreme adversity that Paul faced none was as difficult as his time in Asia (2 Cor. 1.8-9). For this reason Paul is sympathetic as Timothy ministers in this same geographical area. The lesson Timothy will have to continue to learn is the same one Paul had to learn: 'this happened that we might not rely on ourselves but on God, who raises the dead' (1.9).

Ephesus, the fourth largest city in the Roman Empire, was an area of great learning and a hotbed for philosophy (cf. Acts 19.9). Given this context it is possible that Paul may be appealing to the Ephesians's understanding of suffering as seen through the lens of the moral philosophers of the time. For them, suffering was a means by which one could attain wisdom and happiness, though for Paul suffering demonstrates his weakness and the surpassing greatness and sufficiency of God's power by which he is able to endure and glorify God (2 Cor. 12.7-10).

Paul is not ashamed of the sufferings he is presently enduring (or has endured in the past). When Paul pens these words, Jesus' teaching may be in the back of his mind: 'whoever wants to be my disciples must deny themselves and take up their cross and follow me' (Mk 8.31) and 'whoever is ashamed of me and my words...the Son of Man will be ashamed of this one when he comes in glory' (Mk 8.38). Suffering and faith in Christ are not mutually exclusive. His suffering is not a cause for shame but boasting for he knows the gospel is not chained (cf. Phil. 1.15-18) since it the power of God regardless of one's circumstances (Rom. 1.16). For this reason he knows that his work is never in vain (1 Cor. 15.58) and neither is Timothy's.

The first reason for Paul's willingness to suffer as a herald, apostle and teacher is founded on a personal relationship with Christ. His Hebrew background probably influences his use of 'know' since it suggests a level of intimacy foreign to the Greek mind (cf. Mt. 1.25, Joseph did not 'know' her until after Jesus was born; Gen. 4.1, Adam 'knew' Eve and she conceived a child). Though the Greek allows the translation 'I know *what* [possibly referring to the gospel] I have believed' it is quite certain that Paul is using the personal pronoun thereby referring to Christ and thus translated, 'I know *whom* I have believed'. Paul knows the character of Christ. Initially he experienced this on the road to Damascus (Acts 9.3-10). He may have had other significant encounters like the heavenly vision (2 Cor. 12.1-10) and the dream in Corinth (Acts 18.9, 10) contributing to this knowledge and trust of Christ but most likely the majority of his trust in Christ came through a steady reliance on him in the midst of daily life, prayer and Scripture.

The second reason for Paul's willingness to suffer for his holy calling is that he knows the power of God. One translation is 'I am convinced that he is able to guard what I have entrusted to him for that day'. There are two difficulties in this passage (1.14b) and they are inextricably related. To what does 'that which was entrusted' (sometimes translated 'deposited') refer? And who is entrusting this deposit to whom?

The rare Greek word used in this text, *parathēkē*, literally means 'that which is entrusted to one's care', sometimes referred to as 'a deposit'. It is found only in 1 and 2 Timothy (1 Tim. 6.20; 2 Tim. 1.12, 14). It is only found twice in the LXX (Lev. 5.21, 23 LXX or Lev. 6.2, 4 in English translations). Both passages depict a situation in which someone has been entrusted with something from a neighbour. A story is told in 2 Macc. 3.15 about money entrusted to the temple which then was stolen and taken to the King's treasury. The people were horrified and recognized this as a violation of the principle of caring for someone else's property. In a touching story about a much more valuable commodity, a mother gives a charge to her son-in-law as she entrusts her daughter to him (Tob. 10.13). Whatever this *parathēkē* is, it is certainly of great value.

Some scholars understand *parathēkē* in 2 Tim. 1.12 to connote 'that which *God* entrusted to Paul', namely the gospel message or possibly the ministry of proclaiming the gospel. They say this understanding fits with the usage in 1 Tim. 6.20 in which Paul encourages Timothy to guard the gospel against the godless chatter of the false teachers. Similarly they point to 2 Tim. 1.14 in which Paul tells Timothy to guard the *parathēkē* (i.e. gospel) with the help of the Holy Spirit. Other scholars suggest that *parathēkē* signifies 'that which *Paul* has entrusted to God', in particular his life or his commitment to Christ and his gospel. This position makes good sense of the surrounding context in which Paul talks about the sufferings he is enduring as an apostle and the importance of Timothy to rely on the Spirit in order to fulfill his ministry. How does one solve this dilemma?

First, it is likely that the meaning of *parathēkē* will be the same in vv. 12 and 14 given their close proximity and in fact the meaning is probably to be expected to be the same in 1 Tim. 6.20 since this word appears to be unique to 1 and 2 Timothy.

Second, whatever this *parathēkē* is, it is something that is required to be guarded by both God and the individual. In 1.12 Paul believes that God has the power to guard it. Just two verses later Paul exhorts Timothy to guard this deposit but with the help of the Holy Spirit. Similarly in 1 Tim. 6.20 Paul expects Timothy to guard this deposit from the aberrations of the false teachers.

Third, who is entrusting what to whom, is to be determined from the context. Some scholars believe that it is significant that in 2 Tim. 1.12 the text states 'my *parathēkē*' thus suggesting that the translation should be 'that which *I* entrusted to God' (God is assumed from the context) and not 'that which God entrusted to me'. But if this is the case then in 2 Tim. 1.14 and 1 Tim. 6.20 the translation must be 'you guard that which you [assumed from the context] entrusted to God'. A more likely translation of 1 Tim. 6.20 and 2 Tim. 1.14 would be 'guard your [good in 1.14] deposit', thus what God has entrusted to Timothy. The use of the personal possessive pronoun, 'my' used in 2 Tim. 1.12 and 'you' used tacitly in 1 Tim. 6.20 and 2 Tim. 1.14, simply stresses that this deposit belongs to Paul and Timothy respectively. Thus it is more likely this *parathēkē* is something which God has entrusted to people since this position makes equal sense in each context.

Fourth, whatever the meaning of *parathēkē* is, it must make sense with the clause 'guard it until that day'. There are two possible meanings of 'that day': the death of Paul or the parousia of Christ. This phrase is found twenty-three times in the NT, most of them being in the Gospels (nineteen times) with the meaning Day of Judgment or Return of the Messiah (cf. the OT usage, Zeph. 1.9; Zech. 14.6). The lone usage in Acts has no theological significance (Acts 8.1). The other two occurrences are located in the Pastorals and both of them have an eschatological meaning (1 Tim. 1.12; 2 Tim. 4.8). Thus it is very doubtful that this phrase indicates the day of Paul's death.

Therefore it is most likely that *parathēkē* in 2 Tim. 1.12 signifies that which God has entrusted to Paul. Is it the gospel? As we saw earlier this meaning seems consistent with 1 Tim. 6.20 since Paul insinuates that Timothy can guard the gospel by turning from godless chatter and objections based on what is falsely called knowledge. But this meaning does not fit the context of 2 Tim. 1.12 and 1.14. Here the context suggests a meaning that has to do with administering the gospel through the role of herald and teacher. So the *paratheke* is most likely the 'administration of the gospel'. This captures both the gospel itself and the orthodox proclamation keeping it free from impure teaching. It is this great gift that God has entrusted to Paul and Timothy. The usage of *paratheke* here is probably parallel to the usage of the term *oikodomia* elsewhere in Paul's letters to mean 'administration'; in Eph. 3.2 Paul refers to the 'administration of grace given to me for your sake, that is the mystery made known to me by revelation' and in Col. 1.25 'the administration of God given to me for your sake, to present the Word of God in its fullness'. In both cases the word refers to the ministry and gospel entrusted to Paul (cf. Tit. 1.7). A final confirmation of this proposition is found in the name that Paul gives elsewhere for these people who are entrusted with the gospel and the ministry of this gospel. They are called 'administrators/stewards' (*oikodomos*) which comes from the cognate of *oikodomia*. Paul refers to them as 'administrators of God's mysteries' (1 Cor. 4.1) who must prove themselves to be 'faithful' (4.2) and as 'administrators of God' (Tit. 1.7).

Paul is firmly persuaded that God will guard this *paratheke* until the Day of the Lord. The middle reflexive ('I have persuaded myself') or passive ('I have been persuaded by God') of the Greek verb 'to persuade' (note that the morphology could go either way; see Rom. 8.38; 14.14; 15.14 for examples of Paul 'being persuaded') suggests that his experience has convinced him or he has been convinced by God that God is able to guard this deposit. The former is more likely. Earlier in the letter Paul expressed the same degree of certainty with respect to the sincerity of Timothy's faith (2 Tim. 1.5). But in what sense does this *paratheke* need to be guarded until the Day of the Lord? Though the exact sense of this clause may be lost to us, Paul probably means that when he is dead God will continue to oversee the process (of which he was a small part) by which the gospel is kept unadulterated and proclaimed well until the return of his Son.

Paul's Appeal for Timothy (1.13-14)

Paul's appeal comes in two parts. He wants Timothy to follow his example and he wants him to guard the administration of the gospel he has received (cf. 1.12). Whereas in 1.6-12 the focus has been on the relationship between Paul and Timothy and their call to suffer for the gospel, the focus shifts slightly, in these two verses, onto the problem of the false teachers and their gangrenous effect on the church. Paul thereby emphasizes the importance of an unadulterated gospel and of being an unalloyed minister. Timothy is to hold up Paul's teaching as a model for himself and others (cf. 2.2). It is not enough to have the right teaching. The teaching of the Christian faith must also be applied. Why? Paul knows that people learn by example and he is certain that they will learn from Timothy's example too, regardless of his age and stature (1 Tim. 4.12).

Hold Fast to Paul's Teaching (1.13)
The idea of 'holding fast' and 'not holding fast' (*prosechō*) is a concept unique to the Pastorals. In 1 Timothy Paul tells Timothy not to hold fast to myths and endless genealogies (1 Tim. 1.4; cf. Tit. 1.14) or wine if a deacon (1 Tim. 3.8). In part, Paul gave these instructions because false teachers were 'holding fast to deceitful spirits and the teachings from demons' (4.1). In contrast to these false teachers, Paul wants Timothy to hold fast to the work of public reading of Scripture, exhortation and teaching (4.13). Similarly in 2 Tim. 1.13 Paul uses a cognate verb (*echō*) to impress upon Timothy the importance of holding onto the pattern which he heard from him.

The idea of presenting a positive example to follow or a negative 'example' (*tupos*) to avoid is quite common in Paul's writings and also among moral philosophers. Paul puts forth his lifestyle as an example to emulate (Phil. 3.17; 1 Thess. 1.7; 2 Thess. 3.9; Tit. 2.7) and the lifestyle of certain others as an example to learn from and reject (1 Cor. 10.6). In 2 Tim. 1.13 Paul utilizes a cognate, *hupotuposis*. With the addition of the prefix, this word becomes an intensive form of *tupos* which is derived from the verb 'to impress or stamp' and means 'paradigm'. In his first letter to Timothy, Paul considers himself to be the paradigm for others to follow with respect to belief in God for eternal life (1 Tim. 1.16; the same noun is used). In 2 Tim. 1.13 Paul understands his teaching to be the paradigm for Timothy to follow and to which he must hold fast (cf. 1 Tim. 4.16). Paul does not say this out of pride or arrogance but rather from a deep conviction that he is following Jesus (1 Cor. 11.1). This teaching is based on the words Timothy has heard from Paul. It is this teaching Timothy is to pass on to others (2 Tim. 2.2).

Scholars have raised concern over the awkwardness it produces in translation because of the lack of an article before *hupotupōsis*. The text literally says, 'hold fast *a* pattern/paradigm' instead of 'hold fast *the* pattern/paradigm' as they prefer. Some think the omission is due to the poor style of the author of the Pastorals who frequently omits the article. But it is more likely that the author omits the article in the same way the author of Hebrews omits the article with the word 'son'. When the author of Hebrews refers to Christ as 'son' he omits the article even though one might expect the text to say 'the Son' (Heb. 5.8, 'although he was son, he learned obedience'). He does this to stress the quality of God's son in contrast to other mediators and to show his superiority over them (prophets, 1.2; Moses, 3.6; Aaron, 5.8; Melchizedek, 7.28). Similarly Paul stresses the quality of the pattern or paradigm that he has left Timothy, thus emphasizing the importance of heeding it.

Some scholars understand the meaning of *hupotupōsis* to be 'outline' and therefore interpret Paul to be saying that Timothy is to hold fast to the outline of the teaching Paul had shared. To do this is to impose an unnatural meaning on the noun.

Paul does not expand on the content of this teaching, rather he comments on its quality. He draws on medical imagery (cf. Lk. 5.31; 7.10) in much the same way the philosophers of the time would consider their teaching to produce health within the listener. These ancient philosophers considered philosophy to produce health in an individual through enabling an increase in wisdom or virtue etc. depending on their particular brand of philosophy. For Paul his teaching brought health in the areas of faith and love. The word 'healthy' is important in the Pastorals (eight of twelve NT occurrences are found there: 1 Tim. 1.10; 6.3; 2 Tim. 4.3; Titus 1.9, 13; 2.1, 2) because it provides a stark contrast to the teaching of the false teachers. Three times Paul emphasizes for Timothy the importance of 'healthy teaching' (1 Tim. 1.10; 6.3; 2 Tim. 4.3) because false teaching is self-absorbed (2 Tim. 4.3) and erroneous (4.4) and it leads to destructive behaviour (1 Tim. 6.4).

Faith and love have unique connotations for the person who is in relationship to Jesus Christ. The combination of faith and love is found four times in the NT and all of them in the Pauline corpus. In 1 Tim. 1.14 Paul reflects on the grace of God. It was through the grace of God that he received the love and faith which became the bedrock for his conversion and calling. But faith and love are not a one-time experience, they are required for the entirety of one's salvation experience; one must abide in them continually (2.15). In fact they are to be actively sought after (6.11; 2 Tim. 2.22). When describing the armour of God, faith and love comprise the breastplate that is needed to live as 'people of the day', those who are alert and prepared for the return of Christ (1 Thess. 5.8). Faith and love are required to be expressed by the servant of God in order to provide an example for others to follow (1 Tim. 4.12). In 2 Tim. 1.13 Paul wants Timothy to hold fast to the teaching he heard from Paul through the years with faith and love in two ways. First, Paul wants Timothy to remember that the source of faith and love is Christ and therefore the teaching he has received from Paul comes from Christ. In essence Paul is saying: what I received from Christ, I have passed onto you (1 Cor. 15.1-3) and you must hold fast to this teaching since it is the grid by which you evaluate any other teaching. Second, Paul wants Timothy to hold fast to this teaching in the sense that he expresses this teaching in the same way Paul has so that he can be a model for others.

Guard the Good Deposit (1.14)

The backdrop for this command is the problem of the false teachers. Paul has one eye on the problem of false teaching as he asks Timothy to guard the good deposit. We saw in 1.12 that this deposit Timothy received was the administration of the gospel both in terms of the gospel itself and its proclamation. This time Paul qualifies the word for 'deposit' (*paratheke*) with 'good'. Of the forty-one usages of 'good' in the Pauline corpus twenty-four are found in the Pastorals. He speaks of the Law as good in the sense of being a just standard for evaluating behaviour (1 Tim. 1.8). Prayer for others is good because it is appropriate for believers and may carry the connotation of 'effectual' since these prayers may lead to believers living a peaceful life (2.3). Several times good is used with respect to the Christian ministry. To be an overseer is to desire a good work (3.1). Ministers for Christ are to express a good testimony with those outside the church (3.7) and fight the good fight (1.18; 6.12; 2 Tim. 2.3). These aspects of ministry are good because they are pleasing and acceptable to God. In light of these ideas, when Paul tells Timothy to guard the good deposit he does so with the understanding that the gospel and his calling to proclaim this gospel are pleasing and acceptable to God. Timothy has received a trust from God which he must not let be contaminated, as the false teachers have.

Paul knows that guarding this trust will require more than human effort. It will require reliance on the Holy Spirit. Just as the suffering in Asia taught him the need for relying on God, in the same way he has learned that neither his talents, strengths, abilities nor cleverness will be enough for his task. Timothy will need the Holy Spirit. Paul is not limiting the role of the Spirit only to himself and Timothy or even those in the ministry. The Spirit is needed by every believer for all aspects of life (cf. 2 Cor. 3.6; 2 Thess. 2.13). Paul is simply reminding Timothy of the fact the Spirit is in them both and that to remain loyal to the gospel and their respective callings they will need to rely heavily on the Spirit to sustain them through the inevitable times of suffering ahead.

The importance of Timothy guarding this deposit is observed by its threefold emphasis in the Pastorals (1 Tim. 6.20; 2 Tim. 1.12, 14). There may be other reasons too for his urgency. First, Paul's emphasis may be due to the number of defections he has experienced in Rome (2 Tim. 4.9-10, 16) and Asia (1.15). Second, Paul is aware of the antagonists to the gospel he has faced and is certain Timothy will also face (1.17; 4.14-15). Third, the intensity of Paul's imprisonment is heightened from his first Roman incarceration. This reality plus his past experiences may be making him more aware that death is a possibility for him at any moment so he wants to exhort Timothy to carry on his administration of the gospel.

Paul's Two Examples of Servants for Timothy to Consider (1.15-18)

Having presented for Timothy the request to suffer shamelessly with Paul for the gospel, he now presents negative and positive examples of gospel ministers. The structure of argumentation resembles that of Phil. 1.27–3.13 in which he states the appeal (i.e. to live worthy of the gospel which includes suffering) followed by four positive examples of this lifestyle beginning with Jesus, then Timothy, Epaphroditus and finally himself. In this section Paul begins with the negative examples of the Asians, Phygelus and Hermogenes followed by the positive example of Onesiphorus. These individuals illustrate positively and negatively certain aspects of Paul's request in 1.6-14, though the focus is on 1.8, 'not to be ashamed of Paul and his gospel' and 'to suffer for it'. The example of Onesiphorus is followed by the positive example of Paul and then Jesus, the paragon of one who was unashamed of the gospel and for which he was willing to suffer.

The chiastic structure in this section is built on 'know' and 'give'.

1.15, 'you know'
    1.16, 'may the Lord give'
    1.17, 'may the Lord give'
1.18, 'you know'

Negative Examples: Asians and Phygelus and Hermogenes (1.15)

The Asians in general and Phygelus and Hermogenes in particular exemplify those who have been ashamed of Christ, Paul and his gospel. Paul uses a strong word to describe their abandonment of Paul (*apostrephō*). It can mean 'apostasy' in the sense of 'turning away from the orthodox teaching of the gospel' in 2 Tim. 4.4 and Tit. 1.14 (cf. Heb. 12.25). It is used in the Sermon on the Mount where Jesus tells people to give to those who ask and not *turn away from* the one who wants to borrow from you. When Paul refers to people abandoning him (2 Tim. 4.10, 16; cf. Heb. 13.5) he uses a different verb (*egkataleipō*). Because of the specific word choice being made, Paul may be implying that these people have not only abandoned him, refusing to give him aid, but they have rejected his gospel too. For Paul, the appropriation of this salvific gospel and the willingness to suffer for it are so inextricably related that one cannot simply accept the gospel in thought only. A further possible implication from this text is that apostasy cannot simply be understood in terms of doctrine alone but also in practical terms of lifestyle.

Paul says that 'all those in Asia have turned away from me'. Some take this as a hyperbolic statement coming from Paul's depressed state. It is not clear exactly to what situation he is referring but he does say that this turning away from Paul in Asia is something about which Timothy is familiar. It could refer to the tough times Paul endured on his first and second missionary journeys (2 Cor. 1.8), both the rejection he received personally and the rejection of his message. Paul could have in mind the time he was arrested in Troas (2 Tim. 4.13) when he expected the Asians to stand by him, in particular Phygelus and Hermogenes. In both these cases Timothy would have had secondhand knowledge of these experiences. A few scholars suggest that Paul is referring to all the Asians in Rome who did not come to his support during his trial. They suggest that the phrase 'all in Asia' should be read as a Hebraism and thus translated as 'all those from Asia [in Rome]'. This translation is doubtful since the Greek seems quite clear that it is referring to those who are in the area of Asia. From the text it appears that these people have known Paul and his gospel and subsequently rejected both. For this reason Paul may be alluding to the situation Timothy is presently facing in Ephesus and would know full well. The Asians are those people who came to faith during Paul's previous work but have now turned away from him and his gospel during (even because of) his imprisonment in Rome. Paul takes this personally and probably overstates the situation due to his frustration by saying 'all those in Asia have abandoned me'. Probably there have been quite a few who have left the faith and Paul's teaching but what is most painful is to have those closest to you leave, represented by Phygelus and Hermogenes.

Different suggestions have been made with respect to the identity of Phygelus and Hermogenes. They could be *actual characters* whom the pseudonymous author is presently facing, but this position runs contrary to typical pseudonymous writings in which the pseudonymous author seeks to include real characters from the named author's (i.e. Paul's) life. They could be *symbolic names*. Phygelus comes from the Greek word 'flight' which is what he is doing in Paul's eyes. Hermogenes can mean 'born of Hermes', who was the messenger for the gods, and thus he can represent one with a message, albeit a bad one. Thus their names would bring a striking contrast to Onesiphorus, which means 'bringing advantage'. This position takes too much interpretive liberty to make it credible. Some scholars look to the writing of *The Acts of Paul and Thecla* in which Hermogenes appears. They use this to defend pseudonymous authorship and a late date of writing (second century). But the Hermogenes in this writing is called a coppersmith who opposes Paul by declaring that the resurrection had taken place. He along with Demas are said to be 'full of hypocrisy'. The author of this fictional apocryphal book seems to confuse Hermogenes with the characters Alexander, the coppersmith in 2 Tim. 4.14, and Hymenaeus, in 2.17-18. Therefore looking to *The Acts of Paul and Thecla* does not elucidate the identity of Hermogenes. Lastly, I propose that Phygelus and Hermogenes are actual colleagues and friends of Paul and probably fellow workers for the gospel in Asia but have turned away from Paul and his gospel sometime between the time Paul visited Ephesus and the time he was put in Roman imprisonment.

Positive Example: Onesiphorus (1.16-18)

The point of the example of Onesiphorus is to provide for Timothy an example of someone who was not ashamed of the gospel, not cowardly or afraid in sharing in the sufferings of the gospel. Later Paul provides himself and Jesus as examples (2.3, 8). The similarity of Timothy's situation and Onesiphorus's is obvious since Onesiphorus risked danger to visit and help Paul. Timothy must do likewise.

Onesiphorus was not ashamed of Paul as a brother (cf. Jesus' unashamed willingness to call us his brothers and sisters; Heb. 2.14) or as a prisoner, thereby willing to share in this shame by visiting him. He was not cowardly. By associating himself with Paul he risked the possibility of being imprisoned, especially during the time of the Neronian persecution. He shared in Paul's sufferings in two ways. First, he refreshed Paul through practical means in the same way people had helped him before (Phil. 4.14-19). The word used here, *anapsuchō*, is a hapax legomenon though other cognates (Col. 4.11; Lk. 16.24) are used which suggest such means as bringing food and clothing and running errands. Second, and probably more importantly, his presence boosted Paul's morale (cf. Rom. 15.32) just as Epaphroditus's presence did during his earlier Roman imprisonment (Phil. 2.25). We see the human side of Paul here where he allows someone to minister to him. I suspect this may have been difficult for him (cf. Rom. 1.8-9) since he usually considered it necessary for him to give more than others in order to exemplify the gospel.

Onesiphorus exerted a lot of effort (literally 'zealously' or 'earnestly') by means of the Spirit of power to find Paul. Paul was probably not being treated in the same manner he was during his first Roman imprisonment when he appealed to Caesar. It probably took Onesiphorus a significant amount of time and energy to find Paul, probably due to bureaucracy and the lack of privileges afforded to Paul. Also during this time Tigellinus, who was anti-Semitic and anti-Christian, had become the praetorian prefect and was brutal in comparison to the former prefect Burrus who died (poisoned?) in AD 62.

It is likely Onesiphorus's attitude conveyed in Rome characterized his work done in Ephesus. The text says literally 'you know better [than I] how much he served in Ephesus'. This text most likely looks back on the work he did during Paul's and Timothy's ministry in Ephesus or Timothy's present solo ministry. A remote possibility is that it is referring to the time when Onesiphorus—who, according to *The Acts of Paul and Thecla*, was a citizen in Iconium—entertained Paul when he was therein Iconium.

Paul shares two wishes. The first is for Onesiphorus's family and the second for Onesiphorus himself. Both wishes are given in the rare optative mood (there are only 68 cases of this mood in the NT of which thirty-one are in Paul and three in 2 Timothy) which intrinsically carries a lot of contingency. Paul uses the optative (which projects something possible or wished for) here probably because he realizes the bestowal of rewards does not belong to him but to God, who judges justly and with omniscience.

Is Onesiphorus dead? Some suggest that he is not dead but simply apart from his family at the time Paul writes this letter. In support of this they point to 1 Cor. 1.16 in which Stephanus's household is mentioned but he is still alive. But it is worth noting that Paul later addresses Stephanus personally which he does not do in the case of Onesiphorus. Others propose that he is dead since Paul does not address Onesiphorus directly. Paul refers to his household and to Onesiphorus in the third person, and later on in the epistle Paul states his parting greetings to Onesiphorus's household and not to him personally (4.19) which is strange if he helped so much. Furthermore the twofold wish is not for Onesiphorus *now* but rather it is for Onesiphorus at the future Judgment Day. Therefore it is most likely that he is dead.

In the first wish he prays that Onesiphorus's family might receive mercy from the Lord. It is possible that the teaching of Jesus is behind these words, for those who are merciful shall be shown mercy (Mt. 5.7) although it is vicarious (i.e. Onesiphorus's family will be shown mercy for his actions). Similarly those who seek shall find (Mt. 7.7). So just as Onesiphorus sought and found Paul, Onesiphorus's household will find mercy. For those who think Onesiphorus is still alive, Paul is commending his ministry and thanking his family for their understanding and support while he has been absent from them. For those who think Onesiphorus is dead, in addition to commending his ministry and thanking his family for their understanding and support he is asking that they receive tangible expressions of mercy now that he is gone. Mercy plays an important role in 1 and 2 Timothy as it is part of both greetings (1 Tim. 1.2; 2 Tim. 1.2) and was something Paul experienced in the present when Jesus drew him to himself (1 Tim. 1.13, 16). But mercy is also something to be experienced in the future (Jude 21; 2 Tim. 1.18) on the Day of Judgment. Basically Paul is hoping that God will bless Onesiphorus's family in their times of need (Heb. 4.16).

Paul is not espousing a 'works righteousness' in the sense that Onesiphorus's works of mercy are the basis for his household receiving mercy. Rather he is commending Onesiphorus because his works of mercy are proof of a vital relationship with God. This is consistent with Jesus' teaching (Mt. 25.36) and Paul's teaching elsewhere (Eph. 2.8-10; cf. Js. 2.17).

In the second wish, Paul hopes Onesiphorus finds mercy from God (an unusual example of 'Lord' being equivalent to 'God') on the Day of the Lord. Paul's hope is equivalent to his expectation of the athlete receiving the eschatological prize in 2 Tim. 2.5. Structurally this wish (and in 1.16) reflects the LXX usage (Ode. 7.39; Dan. 3.39). Wish prayers using the optative exist in the NT (Rom. 15.13; 1 Thess. 3.11-13; 5.23). For some 2 Tim. 1.18 is deemed to be an example of a prayer for the dead. These ones point to 2 Macc. 12.39-45 as a precedent in which Judas prays and makes atonement for the dead soldiers who had placed tokens of the idols of Jamnia around their necks. *The Acts of Paul and Thecla* §28 records the prayer for a pagan to be delivered to the place of the righteous. Also there are many inscriptions on Roman catacombs which suggests praying for the dead was an established practice among early Christians. In spite of this evidence, there are several reasons why it is unlikely that Paul is praying for the dead. First, the structure of the prayer mitigates against this interpretation. If it is an intercessory prayer it does not follow the typical construction (cf. Eph. 1.17). Second, it seems unlikely that this is a prayer for the dead man Onesiphorus to receive mercy (i.e. salvation) since Paul's purpose for including him in this context is to provide Timothy an example of someone who has clearly lived and embraced the gospel. Third, the evidence is not that pervasive to suggest that there was a widespread acceptance of the practice of praying for the dead. Rather in this passage Paul is simply sharing his hope in the mercy of God as the only means by which anyone can enter heaven on the Day of Judgment.

2 Timothy 2.1-7
Paul's Second Request: Suffer for the Ministry with Him

The second request of Paul in 2.1-7 is interconnected with the first request (1.6-14) and the examples given in 1.15-18. This exhortatory material continues to build on the advice given in 1.13-14 about guarding the deposit Timothy received and following Paul's example. Some scholars think that the material in this wider section (1.15–2.7) is a disconnected, illogical hodgepodge of ideas and that the personal examples serve no purpose and are creations of a pseudonymous writer. Nothing could be further from the truth. It is vital not to miss the importance of the two examples given in 1.15-18. These examples serve two purposes. First, though these examples seem to be a digression, they actually function as a transition from the first request to the second request. Second, the imperatives of 2.1-3 given to Timothy are to be read in light of 1.15-18 in order to set up the contrast of characters. Paul's purpose for 2.1-7 is to exhort Timothy to choose between two examples of service (negative = Asians and positive = Onesiphorus). Paul is certain of Timothy's faith and character (1.5) so he knows that he will opt for the latter. In true rhetorical fashion, Paul presents the examples of Onesiphorus (1.16-18), Paul (2.2, 9-10) and Jesus (2.8) in order to show that a true servant is characterized by single-minded devotion, willingness to share in suffering with others and for others, and confidence of a future reward for doing so.

The structure of this section (2.1-7) is easily identifiable. Paul begins the section (in 2.1-3) by offering three imperatives (i.e. 'be strengthened', 'entrust' and 'suffer with') that all believers need to appropriate but which are particularly addressed to the situation Timothy is facing. On the one hand, Timothy is facing tough circumstances and therefore needs to be strengthened by God's grace in Christ in order to endure suffering for the gospel. On the other hand, Paul is asking Timothy to join him in Rome and thus there is a particular urgency that Timothy entrust the gospel to reliable people so that when he is gone the gospel will not be tainted by the ideas of the false teachers. Therefore the order of the three imperatives may reflect an intentional progression. Strengthening by the grace of God is necessary before discerning to whom the gospel should be entrusted and before one can suffer with and for others with respect to the gospel. Just as Paul found suffering in Rome, he is expecting Timothy will face the same. Paul's premonitions were not unfounded as the writer of Hebrews states (Heb. 13.23) that Timothy is arrested in Rome. Few details of his later life exist except that possibly he became the first bishop of Ephesus (*HE* 3.4).

Each imperative is important in its own right and the emphasis is not on the last imperative as many scholars assume. Rather each exhortation reiterates an aspect Timothy will need in order to fulfill his ministry. Power through grace (cf. 1.8-9) is needed for both of the following tasks of entrusting the gospel to others and suffering for the gospel. Entrusting others with Paul's teaching is necessary to combat the false teachers (2.16-17) and to replace them (1 Tim. 1.3-4). Suffering for the gospel is necessary for the godly life (2 Tim. 3.12) and to be expected by Christ's evangelists (1.8). These imperatives are followed by three metaphors (i.e. military, athletic and agricultural) that further develop the three imperatives. The thread, which unites the three metaphors, is the steadfast wholehearted perseverance necessary to overcome and succeed in their respective areas. Yet there is a unique nuance in each example, which Paul draws out, and I will discuss these later.

Paul shifts figures to the paradigm of Jesus (2.8-10) who is the paragon of suffering servanthood (cf. Phil. 2.5-11) and the one whom Paul seeks to emulate. Jesus is presented in terms of a low Christology which makes him easier for Timothy to identify with.

Finally, Paul closes the section (in 2.11-13) with a 'faithful saying', a particular literary form unique to Paul though probably rooted in the tradition of Jesus. This is the first and only 'faithful saying' in this epistle though there are three in 1 Timothy (1.15; 3.1; 4.9) and one in Titus (3.8). The short pericope comprised of nine lines reinforces the idea of God's grace for those suffering for the gospel in terms of being able to count on God's reward for faithfulness and the provision of his faithfulness even amidst human unfaithfulness.

The structure of this section looks like this:

Paul's Second Request: Suffer for the Ministry with Paul (2.1-7)
    Threefold Exhortation (2.1-3)
    Three Metaphors (2.4-7)
Basis for Suffering for the Gospel: Examples of Jesus and Paul (2.8-10)
Trustworthy Saying on Ministry (2.11-13)

Threefold Exhortation (2.1-3)

The three imperatives—'be strengthened', 'entrust' and 'join in suffering'—together articulate the essence of 1.6-14 though there are particular ideas within vv. 6-14 that Paul wants to develop. The following correlations can be seen:

'Be strengthened'	1.7, 9 (power of Spirit and grace of Christ)
'Entrust the gospel to others'	1.11 (teach as Paul did)
'Join in suffering together'	1.8, 12 (suffering for gospel and with others)

'Be Strengthened' (2.1)

In 2.1-3 Paul is drawing an inference from 1.6-14, introducing it with the words 'therefore you, my son'. Paul begins the section with an intensive form of the personal pronoun 'you'. He uses this same literary device three times more in 2 Timothy (3.10, 14; 4.5) when he wants to emphasize the importance for Timothy to heed his advice. In each instance the emphasis is on some aspect of Timothy's own ministry which Paul wants him to pay attention to, whether it is following or abiding in Paul's teaching (3.10, 14), fulfilling his different ministries (4.5) or refining his character (cf. 1 Tim. 6.11). He combines this intensive pronoun with 'my child', thereby emphasizing the intimacy and teacher/student relationship they have (cf. 2 Tim. 1.2) and thus Paul's confidence in Timothy's obedience, which is in stark contrast with the false teachers's lack of power and willingness to obey (3.5).

It is out of Paul's concern for Timothy in his difficult circumstances that Paul tells him to be strengthened in the grace, which is in Christ Jesus. There is some confusion on how to translate the verse since the imperative could be rendered in the middle voice ('strengthen yourself in the grace...') or the passive ('be strengthened'). It is likely that the passive voice is meant here to be consistent with the usage elsewhere. But is Timothy to be strengthened by God (the personal agent omitted in the text) in the grace of Christ (i.e. locative of sphere) or is he to be strengthened by the grace of Christ (i.e. instrumental)? The evidence from parallel texts (Rom. 4.20; Eph. 6.10) is not conclusive.

It is possible that Paul is telling Timothy to be strengthened by the grace of Christ directly. This instrumental usage is found in Eph. 6.10 where Paul exhorts the Ephesians to be strengthened by his mighty strength (i.e. impersonal agent). The idea of grace as power is found in the classics (Hom. *Od.* 4.235–36), OT (Gen. 39.21; Exod. 3.21; 11.3; Ps. 44.2) and extra-biblical material (*T. Jud.* 2.1) and often refers to power being given by God to a person. The same idea is observed in the NT. Grace is seen as an active force in salvation (Tit. 2.11) and in justification (3.7) through the Father and Son respectively. The idea here would be parallel to 2 Tim. 1.7-8 in which the Spirit of power is needed when suffering for the gospel. On the other hand the locative usage is found in Rom. 4.20. If Paul is telling Timothy to be strengthened by God in the sphere of grace that is in Christ Jesus then this ties in well with his thoughts that Jesus is the source of grace (1.9) and that grace is the basis of their salvation and calling. The strengthening from God is there in the form of grace that is available to those who belong to and are in relationship to Christ Jesus. Paul may use grace here because from his theological perspective suffering for Christ is an expression of grace, in the sense that it is something freely received to be experienced on his behalf (Phil. 1.29) but knowing that the grace will be provided to endure it (2 Cor. 12.9). In the end the meanings of the instrumental and locative usages are similar. So the meaning of the imperative is possibly 'allow yourself to be strengthened by God in the grace which comes from being in Christ Jesus'. With God's empowerment and Christ's grace Timothy can fulfill the next two commands: entrust reliable people with the gospel and suffer for it.

Paul understands that God's power is most effective in a person's weakness (2 Cor. 12.9). He learned this lesson early, shortly after his conversion, when he confounded the Jews in Damascus with his teaching about Jesus as Messiah (Acts 9.22). He saw this principle in Abraham's life, observing that though he grew older and physically weaker, yet he grew stronger through his faith (Rom. 4.20). From personal experience he knew that people are powerless before Satan and his demons so they need to be strengthened by the Lord and his power in order to hold their position in Christ (Eph. 6.10). On a physical level Paul experienced both times of need and times of plenty. Yet in both of these extremes and every situation in between, he experienced the power that enabled him to be content (Phil. 4.13). Now, in his present situation in prison and as he has stood on trial, with the abandonment of his friends, he feels the presence of the Lord empowering him to speak the gospel boldly. It is from this experience that Paul commends Timothy to the power of God and the grace of Christ.

What Paul means by the phrase 'the grace which is in Christ Jesus' needs a little more unpacking. Paul understands that the source of this grace is Christ Jesus himself. This grace was expressed tangibly in Jesus' death and resurrection and this became the means by which one is saved (Eph. 2.8). It is also the basis of one's calling and life (2 Tim. 1.9). But grace in this context may mean something very close to the presence and fellowship of Christ that the believer appropriates through faith and experiences in love (1 Tim. 1.14) and through tangible unsolicited provisions of God done on behalf of his children. Timothy will certainly need this for the days ahead as he suffers for the gospel (1.8; 2.3), guards the deposit (1.12, 14), fulfills his obligations (4.5) and remains unashamed of the gospel (1.8).

'Entrust the Teaching to Trustworthy People' (2.2)
It is easy to see the connection between 'be strengthened' (2.1) and 'suffer as a good soldier of Christ' (2.3). But the second exhortation for Timothy to 'entrust the teachings' from Paul almost seems out of place following the preceding exhortation to be strengthened. One might expect Paul to have said 'be discerning' in v. 1 and 'entrust these teachings' in v. 2. There are two reasons for the order of the imperatives here. First, Paul is looking

ahead to the fact that later in the letter he will be asking Timothy to join him in Rome. For this reason Paul knows that Timothy will have to find people to continue his work in Ephesus before Tychicus (4.12) comes to replace him. This will take effort. Second, finding trustworthy people will be difficult and it will require God's strength and Christ's grace. Some of the false teachers have infiltrated the Ephesian church but others have come from within their own ranks (Acts 20.29-30). Paul is aware that it might be difficult for Timothy in choosing people to carry on the responsibility of teaching since it will require showing no favouritism (cf. 1 Tim. 5.21) and because of his age and stature (4.12). Timothy will certainly need discernment found in the grace of Christ Jesus to assist him in choosing well. But in selecting he will certainly upset people who think they deserve to teach or who think that they are capable of teaching, just as he unquestionably angered those he commanded not to teach false doctrines (1 Tim. 1.3). Strength and grace will be needed in abundance for Timothy during this upcoming transitional period, thus the order is appropriate.

The verb used for this command (*paratithēmi*) in 2.2 has a few meanings. It can refer to 'setting something before someone' just as Jesus set before the disciples his teaching about the Kingdom of God through parables (Mt. 13.24, 31; cf. Acts 17.3). It can also refer to 'entrusting someone to someone else' as Paul and Barnabas do when they set the elders apart for the Lord (Acts 14.23). Finally it can depict 'entrusting something to someone else for safekeeping' as is the case here. Yet the idea of entrusting these people to the Lord is not in the too distant background, for to be entrusted with the transmission of the gospel is to be entrusted to the Lord. Moreover to be entrusted with much means more will be asked of them (Lk. 12.48), and thus they will have to prove themselves worthy.

The content of what Timothy is to pass on is 'that which [Timothy] has heard from [Paul]'. This same expression is found in 1.13 which Paul calls 'the healthy teaching'. Because the content refers to 'that which [Timothy] heard', this suggests that oral teaching was still the primary form of instruction and could explain some of the disparity over Paul's teaching (2 Thess. 2.2). Having the testimony of many witnesses may reduce this problem. It is important to remember that oral communication was still the preferred mode of communication even in the first century AD. In fact many contemporary Graeco-Roman letter-writers often trusted the most important material to the courier to pass on to the recipients verbally rather than include it in the letter. There is also a Jewish flavour to this command, reminiscent of the *Shema* (Deut. 6.7-9), in which one is to pass on orally the traditional teaching to others.

The message Timothy is to pass on involves many witnesses. Several attempts have been postulated to explain their role. Chrysostom (AD 354–407) proposed the translation 'the things you heard from me *in the presence of many witnesses*' (*Hom. on 2 Timothy* IV). Translating the preposition *dia* as 'in the presence of' is unusual but not unheard of. Plutarch (*Mor.* 338F) refers to Darius invoking the gods *as witnesses* to the event when Alexander took his seat on the throne of Cyrus. Similarly Philo, when describing the man who greeted them with news of Gaius's intentions of erecting a statue of himself in the temple, states he wept in the presence of many witnesses. Chrysostom and others who follow this reading of the text propose the context of the many witnesses is Timothy's baptism or ordination at which time a formalized transfer of apostolic tradition took place. There are two problems with this position. First, it is not a natural reading of the preposition and therefore the text. Second, it is reading too much into the text (or at least reading the present into the past) to support the idea of a formal ceremony.

Typically the preposition *dia* (with the genitive) is understood to convey the meaning of 'through' or 'by means of'. Some reject this position since they feel it raises a contradiction in the text. For them it sounds like Timothy did not hear Paul's message directly but rather it was mediated through many witnesses. But this is to miss the intention of the text and to apply too rigidly the meaning of the preposition. The things that Timothy has heard from Paul have been shared over an extended period of time. Elsewhere Paul emphasizes the longevity of their relationship and the student/teacher rapport they have had (1.5-6, 13-14; 3.10, 14) which is more than enough time for Timothy to hear the things from Paul. But Timothy, throughout his sixteen years as Paul's traveling companion, has watched, heard and seen the effectiveness of Paul's teaching. The emphasis in this phrase is on the witness of many to the integrity and 'soundness' (cf. 1.13) of Paul's teaching. This is especially important in light of the prevalence of different false teachings, the quantity of teachers floating about Ephesus and the substantial number of defectors from the faith in Asia (1.15; 4.10).

Not only the content *of what* is being entrusted is important to Paul but also *to whom* this teaching is being entrusted. Paul exhorts Timothy to find 'faithful people'. The word (*pistos*) used to describe the character of these people is 'faithful' or 'reliable'. This word is important in the Pastorals, accounting for almost one third of the total occurrences in the NT (17 of 62). The same word is used nine verses later in reference to the 'faithful sayings' (cf. 1 Tim. 1.15; 3.1; 4.9; Tit. 3.8) describing the reliability of this teaching (cf. Tit. 1.9). Elsewhere this word is utilized more generally to refer to a believer (1 Tim. 4.10; 5.16; 6.2). But more specifically he employs it to describe the qualitative nature of people who are in service to God. It is this word that Paul applies to describe himself (2 Tim. 1.12), the reliable slave-masters (1 Tim. 6.2b) and the female deacons (3.11). Paul founds this virtue for believers—and specifically in this case, teachers—on the paradigm of Jesus who is the paragon of faithfulness (2 Tim. 2.13).

Who are these faithful ones to whom this teaching is to be entrusted? Traditionally commentators have agreed that Paul is commanding Timothy to entrust this teaching to men only. Typically they base this on the text concerning overseers (1 Tim. 3.1-7) assuming it refers exclusively to men. It is beyond the scope of this commentary to deal with this huge issue but there are a couple of important points that need to be made which suggest that he is referring to men and women. First, the term used to describe these people, *anthrōpos*, when found in the plural refers to people in general, that is male and female (1 Tim. 2.1, 4, 5; 4.10; 2 Tim. 3.2). Second, when Paul left Timothy with the task to 'command certain people not to teach false doctrine' (1 Tim. 1.3) he was not referring exclusively to men since the indefinite relative pronoun (*tisin*) refers to both male and female. It is likely that the false teachers who initially infiltrated the Ephesians's ranks or those existing elders who had become corrupt were probably male (Acts 20.29-30). The character of these men is described in 2 Tim. 3.6-8 and one important aspect is that they take advantage of women who are not discerning with respect to doctrinal truth. These are the women who were disseminating their teaching and by association are also false teachers. Third, Paul requires women leaders to be faithful leaders too since he uses the same word 'faithful' (*pistos*) in 1 Tim. 3.11. Fourth, he expects that women will teach other people too (Acts 18.19, 26). Therefore Paul's exhortation to entrust his teaching to faithful people probably includes women. He realizes that some men and some women have been deceived by the false teachers and injured by their false teaching. So Paul begins by having Timothy get new teachers who embrace his sound teaching (2 Tim. 1.13) but who are also able to teach others.

The final qualification he gives Timothy for these teachers is that they are 'worthy to teach others'. Paul has already had bad experiences of people passing on his tradition without accuracy (2 Thess. 2.2) or intentionally misrepresenting him (Phil. 1.15-18). He is looking for people like Tychicus (Eph. 6.21; Col. 4.7) or Timothy (1 Cor. 4.17) who will accurately pass on his teaching in the same way Jewish elders were expected to preserve the traditions used in the synagogue. But what does Paul mean by being 'worthy to teach'? This term has a specific meaning for Paul. He understands it within the framework of hamartiology, God's glory and his calling. Paul considers himself the least of all disciples and does not think he is worthy to be called an apostle since he persecuted the church (1 Cor. 15.9). In comparison to God's glory he feels inadequate as a sinner to be used as a vessel of God to communicate the gospel, which for some is life but for others is death (2 Cor. 2.16). Paul knows that his suitability and acceptability to be God's spokesperson comes from God, otherwise it is presumption. For Paul, to be worthy to teach means to have a healthy self-understanding as a sinner before God who has been saved by grace, and to have a firm confidence of being called to preach and teach on behalf of God. Elsewhere

Paul stresses some of the necessary characteristics needed to be a teacher (careful orthodox interpreter of Scripture, 2.14-15; able to teach with gentleness and firmness, 2.24-25; wise from lifelong study, 3.14-17; 4.2).

Some scholars have tried to find a basis for apostolic succession in this verse, sometimes looking to 1 Clem. 42.1-4; 44.2 and Irenaeus *Adv. Haer* 3.3-4 for support, particularly the latter, which lists several men through whom the succession of the episcopate passed. But the emphasis in 2 Tim. 2.2 is not on the succession of people but rather the transmission of teaching albeit using faithful people to do so. The point is: just as Timothy received a trust, in the same way he is to entrust this to others. To see in this text the earliest formation of theological schools (cf. Acts 19.9), as some have, is presumptuous.

'Join Together in Suffering as a Good Soldier' (2.3)

This exhortation is a reiteration of what was said in 1.8 except with the added qualification 'as a good soldier of Christ Jesus' and provides the second and possibly the most important reason why Timothy needs to be strengthened with the grace of Christ (note that for this reason some manuscripts add '*therefore you* suffer together'). The word 'soldier' (*stratiōtēs*) is not used in the NT to refer to a minister of Christ, although the word 'fellow soldier' (*sustratiōtēs*) is used in this manner (Phil. 2.25; Philemon 2). There are plenty of references in the Pauline corpus that draw on some element of the military metaphor. For example, the soldier's armour is used to describe the character believers need to withstand spiritual warfare (Eph. 6.10 ff.) or to be ready for the return of Christ (1 Thess. 5.8). But in this text Paul draws upon the imagery of the soldier in the field in order to draw out two points. First, the soldier in the field willingly expects and accepts he will have to endure inconvenience and hardship (note that Tertullian in *Ad Mart.* 3.2-4 writes, 'no soldier comes out to the campaign laden with luxuries…where every kind of unpleasantness must be put up with'). Second, a soldier has a single-minded focus on obeying his commander, who is Christ. This part of the metaphor is developed in the next verse. Possessing these two attributes is what makes a person a 'good' soldier and is what will make Timothy an effective servant for Christ. Elsewhere Paul uses 'good' in the moral sense (cf. 1 Tim. 1.7; 2 Tim. 4.7) but this is absent here.

The call is to suffer together with other believers. Timothy is familiar with the difficulties Paul has endured: beatings, shipwrecks, floggings, imprisonments and worries about the churches (2 Cor. 11.24-28) and others (e.g. Epaphroditus, Phil. 2.25-30). So he is probably all too aware of what Paul is asking of him: total commitment at any cost.

As I said above, Paul utilizes the image of the foot soldiers and not the superior officer since he is stressing their inconvenience and hardship, which is not so much the experience of the commanding officer. The reference to a 'soldier of Christ Jesus' suggests that Jesus is the military commander which sets up the following metaphor but also looks ahead to Jesus as the paragon of the suffering servant in 2.8-13 and thus of an even lower status than a soldier.

Three Metaphors (2.4-7)

Several scholars believe that the three metaphors are connected only with the final exhortation, 'suffer together as a good soldier of Christ Jesus'. There is some merit to this idea since each metaphor (i.e. the soldier, the athlete and the farmer) either tacitly or explicitly calls a person to endure hardship. But I believe that there is also a subtle relationship between the exhortations of 2.1-3 and the metaphors of 2.4-6. The relationship is seen through the chiastic structure (ABCCBA).

   A Be Strengthened in Grace (2.1)
      B Entrust Teaching to Worthy, Responsible People (2.2)
         C Suffer Together as a Good Soldier (2.3)
         C Military Metaphor: Single-minded Devotion (2.4)
      B Athletic Metaphor: Compete by the Rules (2.5)
   A Agricultural Metaphor: Share in the Fruit (2.6)

Figure 4. *Chiastic Structure of 2 Tim. 2.1-6*

The correlation between these strophes will be made clear as I explain the different metaphors. What is important to notice from the outset is that the emphasis is upon the call to suffer together with other believers since it stands in the middle of the chiasm.

Paul has grouped all three metaphors (i.e. military, athletic and agricultural) previously in chap. 9 of 1 Corinthians (cf. 1 Cor. 9.7, 24) although with a different application than in 2 Tim. 2. In 1 Cor. 9.7 Paul refers to a soldier and farmer to illustrate how Christian ministers have the right to financial benefit from their ministry. He uses the athletic image of a runner to show the necessity of preparation for the ministry and the promise of a reward. This might show some dependence of the author of 2 Timothy on the passage in 1 Corinthians and has been used in defence of Pauline authorship though more likely these are common metaphors that can be adapted accordingly, depending on the context.

Metaphor #1: Military (2.4)

Paul seamlessly develops this metaphor from the previous verse (2.3) in which he urges Timothy to suffer together with others for the gospel. In this verse the focus shifts from the soldier's commitment to accept hardship to the soldier's single-minded focus and desire to please his enlisting officer. Some manuscripts have 'no one serving as a soldier for God…' in an attempt to make the connection between a Roman soldier and a Christian soldier more obvious. This is not necessary since the correlation is easily recognized and therefore the variant reading should not be accepted.

The single-minded perspective of the soldier is expressed in two ways: first, by not 'being involved' in the 'activities of life', and second, by pleasing his enlisting officer. 'Involved' (NIV) is probably not a vivid enough translation. The Greek word used here, *emplekō*, literally means 'to entangle'. This verb is used literally of sheep grazing among thorns and thistles and getting entangled (Herm. *Sim*. 62.7). But the usage of this verb here is metaphorical and is similar to the idea in Prov. 28.18, 'the one who walks uprightly is safe, but the one who walks the crooked paths *will be entangled*'. The point of the text is that the soldier's priority is to focus on the battle at hand and not to be entangled with other things that can distract from his first concern.

This idea for single-minded devotion of disciples is found in the moral philosophers. Epictetus (AD 55–135), the slave taught by Musonius Rufus, states with respect to philosophy that 'When you have considered all these things [i.e. the cost and the need for single-mindedness] completely, then, if you think it proper, approach to philosophy' (Epictetus, *Diss.* 3.15). The same commitment is found between the laity and the presbyters in 1 Clem. 54.1–57.3. But nowhere is it more explicit than in the Gospels. Jesus calls his disciples to lay down their lives, pick up their cross and follow him wherever he leads (Mk 8.34). Paul is drawing from this model of devotion.

The things from which Timothy is to stay clear are called the *pragmateia biou*, 'the activities of life' (lit.). The first word, a hapax legomenon, is used in the LXX to describe the King's matters over which Daniel had control (Dan. 6.4). The exact phrase, *pragmateia biou*, is found in Philo (*Spec. leg.* 2.65) where it refers to 'everyday affairs' though the idea of the passage may be very similar to Hermas, *Man.* 10.1.4, 'they have been mixed up in *business activities* and wealth and pagan friendships, and the many other *activities* of this world'. The context of the text suggests that the contrast is between the military life and the civilian life and the two should not be mixed together. Likewise Paul does not want Timothy to be distracted by the affairs of this world probably for the same reason Jesus said, in the parable of the sower, that 'the concerns of life' keep the good seed from growing (Lk. 8.14; literally 'they choke the seed').

Some have tried to define more narrowly what are these affairs in which Timothy should not involve himself. Most scholars see these in economics terms of making money or earning a livelihood. This may seem odd, even contradictory, since in Corinth Paul earned his living as a leather worker (Acts 18.3) so that he could offer the gospel free of charge. He did this so that he would not be indebted to any of the Corinthians, some of whom had the perspective that Paul was like a sophist to whom they should pay money as a sign of allegiance. Paul's general rule is that 'the Lord has commanded that those who preach the gospel should receive their living from the gospel' (1 Cor. 9.13). So Paul expects Timothy to earn his living from the gospel but not to seek wealth beyond what he needs; contentment with his circumstances is important (cf. Phil. 4.13).

The reason for this command may in part be influenced by the actions of the false teachers since they had a love for money which was plunging them into destruction, even abandoning their faith (1 Tim. 6.3-10). Paul wants Timothy to have his attention on fulfilling all the responsibilities of his calling (2 Tim. 4.5) and have his focus on the future when he will be rewarded just as every soldier is rewarded after victory (4.8).

The single-minded perspective of the soldier is expressed in a second way, by pleasing his enlisting officer. One might expect the text to say, 'please his commanding officer' but instead the word used is a hapax legomenon meaning 'to enlist soldiers' or 'to gather an army' (Dionysius Hal., *Ant. rom.* 11.24; Diodorus Siculus, 12.67.5; 14.54.6). To say that this is a reference to election is to go too far. But the metaphor may have been used with respect to Timothy for two reasons. First, there is a direct reference to Christ who summoned him to the ministry as a soldier of Christ (2 Tim. 2.3). It may have taken place at an early age or later in life (cf. 2 Tim. 1.13); the particulars of this calling are lost to the reader although his calling is confirmed by others (1 Tim. 1.18). Second, there may be an indirect reference to Paul who in some sense 'enlisted' Timothy when he passed through Lystra since the believers there and at Iconium spoke well of him. The subtext may be saying that Timothy is to be loyal to Paul and this is to be shown by suffering and having a single-minded devotion to Christ.

To follow Christ encompasses a certain amount of shame that in the Graeco-Roman culture is significant. To please a crucified criminal of the state and associate with Paul who is in a Roman prison does not help one's social status. But as Christ said earlier, 'no one can serve two masters... God or money' (Mt. 6.24), and the same choice is being laid before Timothy. Only by seeing his life through the lens of Christ does suffering and following Christ make sense for Timothy. The choice is given in stark terms and it requires a focused life and not being caught up in the world.

Metaphor #2: Athletic (2.5)

This verse begins with 'and also' (*de kai*). Some scholars put a lot of stock into this double conjunction, suggesting that v. 5 is simply a continuation, even a repetition of the same point made in v. 4. But this is to put too much weight on the meaning and usage of these conjunctions. This combination of conjunctions is used thirty-three times in the Pauline corpus and six times in the Pastorals. Sometimes it is used to string together different ideas in a compound sentence (1 Cor. 1.16). But most of the usages of this phrase express an element of contrast in the sense of 'but also'. Thus in 1 Cor. 14.15 Paul writes, 'I pray by means of the Spirit but also I pray by means of my mind'. This usage is found most commonly in the Pastorals (1 Tim. 3.7; 5.13, 24). The contrast is subtle between the example of the soldier and the athlete and the idea can be paraphrased thus: 'I have exhorted you to be like a soldier who does not get entangled with civilian affairs *but* I am *also* exhorting you to be like an athlete who competes according to the rules if you want to get the crown'.

Nowhere else in the NT does Paul or anyone else use the verb *athleō*, which means 'to compete in a contest'. The cognate noun (*athlēsis*) is used only once in Heb. 10.32 in the metaphorical sense of a 'great struggle'. Typically Paul employs the word '*agōn*', which also means 'contest', when drawing upon athletic imagery. The only other letter in which this word is found is in the *Epistle to the Hebrews* where the word clearly refers to a running race (Heb. 12.1). When Paul applies the word, he uses it as a general reference to 'a struggle' (Phil. 1.30; Col. 2.1; 1 Thess. 2.2) with no particular contest in mind except possibly in 1 Tim. 6.12 and 2 Tim. 4.7 where the imagery is most likely 'a fight' (i.e. boxing) or 'a wrestling match' (both of which were events in the Graeco-Roman athletic games). In this context the emphasis of the image is only partially on the struggle and more pointedly on the need for an athlete to abide by the rules.

The goal of any contest is to win the crown, which in the case of the Olympiad is a wreath made up of olive branches called a *kotinos*. In the earliest days of the Olympiad the olive branches were taken from the sacred olive tree which tradition says Hercules planted behind the Temple of Zeus. Paul certainly would have come into contact with some athletic games since the Olympiad was held every four years, beginning in 786 BC and continuing until AD 394 when Emperor Theodosius banned it because he said it was a 'pagan cult', and the Isthmian games were held every two years outside Corinth, in Isthmus, in honour of Poseidon, the god of the sea and water (and less known as the god of horses and earthquakes).

The verb 'to crown' (stephanoō) is only found two other times in the NT, once referring to the glory of humankind (Heb. 2.7) and once referring to the crowning of Jesus with glory and honour because of his sacrificial death (Heb. 2.9). The cognate noun is used with different meanings. Most commonly it refers to a literal crown made of gold (Rev. 4.4, 10; 6.2), or of thorns placed on Jesus' head (Mt. 27.29 and parallels). There are two meanings for 'crown' used in the Pauline Epistles. First, a crown is synonymous for 'source of legitimate pride'. Paul calls the Thessalonians his crown (1 Thess. 2.19) for they will be his source of pride when Christ returns because of how they have embraced and lived the gospel (1 Thess.

1.3). The same idea is found in Phil. 4.1 though without the eschatological perspective. Second, a crown is associated with the eternal reward bestowed when Christ returns (1 Cor. 9.25, 'imperishable crown'). Other NT authors share this usage (Js 1.12, 'crown of life'; 1 Pet. 5.4, 'crown of glory'). The usage of the metaphor of crowning in 2 Tim. 2.5 is tied together with receiving a reward at the return of Christ. This passage sets up the next passage about the farmer and the example of Paul (2 Tim. 2.10-12a) who suffers for the elect so that they too may obtain eternal life in Christ and reign with him forever. Paul continues this theme again in 2 Tim. 4.8 where he expects that the reward of a single-minded steadfast life for Christ will result in a 'crown of righteousness' for him and for those who follow his example.

As in all competitions, to win a crown is only available for those who compete according to the rules. Scholars have sought to establish to what rules Paul was referring. One option is that he is referring to the *rules of the contest* whether it was running or wrestling. This would mean that Paul is asking Timothy to embrace the rule of ministers of the gospel, namely the willingness to share in suffering. Thus, the athletic metaphor is a continuation of the military metaphor and expresses the same idea, single-minded devotion to suffer as a minister.

The second option is that the rules refer to the *rules of training*. Many scholars are quick to turn to the quote from Pausanias 'that for ten successive months they have strictly followed the regulations for training' (Pausanias, *Graec. descr.* 5.24.9b). This idea relates well with Paul's earlier idea in 1 Tim. 4.8 for the need of exercise and training in godliness because of its promise of life in the present and in the future. In 1 Cor. 9.27 he stresses the importance of training in order to fulfill his calling and win the prize. Similarly, Paul is asking Timothy to embrace the struggles of ministry as a refining tool to prepare him better for the future and for the final reward in heaven.

The third option, my position, is that Timothy is a minister according to the rules of ministry in contradistinction to the false teachers. The word, which is often translated 'according to the rules', literally means 'lawfully'. An athlete is not crowned unless he competes lawfully. The same word is found in 1 Tim. 1.8: 'the Law is good if one uses it lawfully'. Paul's point in that passage (1 Tim. 1.8-11) is that the false teachers have not been using the Law 'lawfully' nor have they been living 'lawfully' (i.e. according to the Word of God). But the Law when used 'lawfully' can and will expose their lawlessness and immorality. So in 2 Tim. 2.5 Paul is stressing for Timothy that he must be a minister of the gospel who lives according to the gospel and not the rules of the false teachers who show favouritism and use their teaching to get rich (1 Tim. 5, 6). The standard and paradigm found in the gospel is Jesus whom Paul implores Timothy to remember just two short verses later (2 Tim. 2.8). Timothy (or any minister of the gospel) must be committed to being a servant with integrity even in the midst of suffering. This makes even better sense than suffering being the 'rule' since suffering is a consequence of participating whereas the 'gospel' can provide parameters for the contestant and expose cheaters.

The third option also makes sense with respect to Pausanias's quotation. Many scholars quote him because of the oath to train but fail to note the significant first half of the verse. In *Graec. descr.* 5.24.9a, Pausanias refers to Zeus as the Oath-god whose 'image it is the custom for athletes, their fathers and their brothers, as well as their trainers, to swear an oath upon slices of boar's flesh that in nothing will they sin against the Olympic games'. Similarly Paul expects Timothy not to sin against God in the manner that the false teachers have but rather present himself as an example for others to emulate. This idea is developed in 2.14–3.16 where Paul underscores the importance of his disposition (2.15) and actions (2.16) in order to be an instrument for noble purposes (2.21). In this way the exhortation to entrust the gospel to worthy, responsible people is connected to the need to compete by the rules. If Timothy lives in a manner worthy of the gospel then he will be able to attract and appoint people of like kind to replace the false teachers in the church.

Metaphor #3: Agricultural (2.6)

The use of the farmer metaphor is quite common among the contemporary moral philosophers (Epictetus, *Diss.* 4.8.35-40; he describes the farmer who plants too early and the seed freezes, likewise the young philosopher should not state who he is until he has had time to develop more) and in the Gospels (fifteen times), and it is even used to describe God the Father (Jn 15.1). But outside the Gospels it is found twice: here and in Js 5.7 where it depicts the farmer waiting patiently for the Autumn and Spring rains just as believers should wait patiently for the return of Christ. 1 Cor. 9.7 includes an agricultural metaphor, which is based on different agricultural workers (i.e. the vinedresser and the shepherd), whose meaning is similar to the meaning of the farmer metaphor in 2 Tim. 2.6.

The author uses a present participle to stress the durative aspect of a farmer who works hard, literally 'the farmer who consistently labours'. Elsewhere in Paul's letters the same verb is employed, describing workers for the Lord (Rom. 16.12; 1 Thess. 5.12) or those who labour for the work of the kingdom of God (1 Cor. 4.12; 15.10). Paul may have the role of teacher in mind when he gives Timothy this advice since he says earlier 'those elders who lead well in the church are worthy of double honour, especially those who *labour* in the word and teaching' (1 Tim. 5.17). Thus, Paul may be saying, 'just as the hardworking farmer shares in the fruits of his labour so too should you, Timothy, as servant of the gospel, in particular a teacher for the faith, share in the fruit of your labours'.

It is not clear where the adverb 'first' fits into the Greek of the sentence. It is possible to take 'first' with 'labour' and translate this text as 'the farmer must labour hard *first* before expecting to enjoy the fruits'. Although this translation is possible it is unlikely because of the proximity of the adverb to the verb 'to share' and because the emphasis seems to be on the sharing in the fruits. Therefore the most likely translation is 'it is necessary that the hardworking farmer should share *first* of the fruits'.

But what fruits does the author have in mind? When are these fruits to be realized? As one would expect, there are different positions. First, some scholars believe that the fruits refer to the remuneration the Christian worker is entitled to while serving the church. These people look to 1 Cor. 9.7 and 1 Tim. 5.17 as parallels since ministers of the gospel are to expect to receive their pay and support from those to whom they minister. This statement may serve to counterbalance the previous statement of not getting involved in 'civilian/business affairs' to assure Timothy or any Christian worker that they should expect to receive some material harvest in the present for their work.

Second, some scholars understand that the fruits look forward to the eschatological reward to be received when Christ returns. This idea is alluded to in 2.12a and explicitly stated in 4.8. Under this position, commentators see a direct connection to the athletic imagery in the previous verse and therefore a reiteration of the idea that just as the contestant can expect a crown at the end of the contest likewise the farmer can expect a reward at harvest time.

Third, my position is that there are two things in the text that strongly suggest a present participation in the fruits: the present tense of the Greek verb (*metalambanō*) is used suggesting an ongoing sharing in the fruits and the prominence of 'first' suggests that the farmer/Christian worker should receive this benefit before others. Nowhere in Scripture is there a suggestion that faithful workers receive their eternal reward before others. Only in the rapture text (1 Thess. 4.17) and the resurrection texts (1 Cor. 15.23; 2 Cor. 5.1-5) is there a suggestion of an order of reward but this is based on whether a believer is dead or alive at Christ's return and not on the basis of whether one is a leader or not. Therefore it is most likely that the predominate idea is that the Christian minister, like the farmer, can expect to enjoy some of the fruits of ministry. These fruits could, in part, be monetary which he receives for ministering but more likely Paul is referring to non-monetary fruit. Before going further it is important to note that Paul says that he expects the Christian disciple to share in 'fruits' (plural). This implies that there may be more than one type of fruit that the Christian minister can expect to share in. Certainly one kind of fruit he has in mind is participating in the harvest of souls and changed lives. In Rom. 1.13 Paul expresses his expectation to have fruit among the Romans, particularly in terms of an increase in numbers of Gentile converts as he has had in other places. In Phil. 1.22 Paul feels compelled to minister on earth and share in the fruit among the Philippians in terms of their 'advancement and joy in the faith' (Phil. 1.25). But there is another way in which Paul envisions the Christian worker sharing first in the fruit and that is in terms of the internal experience he or she undergoes. This idea is tied in with the command given in 2 Tim. 2.1; the Christian worker experiences the grace of God. The grace of God is needed first in order for the servant to fulfill his or her task. The grace of God is felt as the servants watch people being transformed. The experience of this grace (particularly in suffering; cf. Phil. 1.29; see comments on 1.11-12) continues until it is fully realized when the servant leader is resurrected and he or she receives an eschatological reward.

There is a sense of urgency with respect to this teaching since Paul says, 'it is necessary'. This same phrase is used to describe the qualities necessary to be a servant of the Lord (2 Tim. 2.24) and an elder (1 Tim. 3.2, 7), how to conduct oneself in the house of God (1 Tim. 3.15), how to live a pleasing life before God (1 Thess. 4.1) etc. This urgency may be due to the fact that the false teachers have so badly skewed this idea in the way they have lived. They have sought their reward now in terms of wealth (1 Tim. 6.3-10) and human-centered teaching (1 Tim. 1.3) instead of humble submission before God in dependence on his grace.

Need for Reflective Insight (2.7)

This section closes with an imperative from Paul to Timothy: he asks him to consider what he has said in the three imperatives and the three metaphors. Literally the Greek text (e.g. original Codex Sinaiticus (a), Codex Alexandrinus (A)) says, 'consider that which [singular] I have said'. Several other manuscripts (e.g. corrected version of Codex Sinaiticus, Codex Claromontaus (D)) include the plural (i.e. 'those things which'). It is easy to understand how this textual variant arose. The plural is included to be consistent with the 'all things' at the end of the sentence (i.e. 'the Lord will give you insight into *all* these things') and the number of points made in vv. 1-6. Nevertheless the manuscript evidence is better for the singular referent and this variant reading is simply the 'collective' usage of the relative pronoun referring to the six previous verses.

It is worth noting that v. 7 could be forward-referring and thus Paul would be commanding Timothy to consider that which follows in 2.8-10. Although this is grammatically possible it is syntactically doubtful since v. 8 begins with the imperative 'remember' and v. 7 is drawing a conclusion through the use of 'therefore' (*gar*).

The translation 'consider' for the verb (*noei*) is probably inadequate. A better translation might be 'understand through reflection' since this verb has the meaning of contemplating an idea in order to gain insight into it or to understand it. Thus Jesus asks if the disciples have understood through reflecting on his teaching about what defiles a person (Mt. 15.17) or what the Feeding of the 5,000 means (Mt. 16.9, 11). In a few instances where this verb is found, there is also the sense that additional outside help is needed in order to understand. Thus the person with a hardened heart cannot understand the meaning of the Feeding of the 5,000 (Mk 8.17; cf. Jn 12.40), the Holy Spirit is needed to understand the mystery of Christ (Eph. 3.4, 5) and faith is required in order to understand how the universe was created (Heb. 11.3).

In this text Paul wants Timothy to reflect on the imperatives and metaphors that he has given him. But there is a tacit understanding that Timothy is expected to be prayerfully considering Paul's teaching with the expectation that the Lord Jesus will be faithful to give him insight into this material. There is a textual variant in this half of the verse. Some manuscripts have '*may* the Lord give you insight into all these things'. The manuscript support is weak and should be rejected for the reading 'for the Lord *will* give you insight into all these things'. By using the future tense Paul is expressing his confidence that Timothy can expect Jesus (note an action typically attributed to Yahweh; see Prov. 2.6) to give him deeper insight into these truths (probably through prayer and reading) just as he is certain that God will empower him with the grace of Christ (2 Tim. 2.1) since all things come from him.

But why does Paul give Timothy this command? It is possible that Paul thinks Timothy lacks insight into these issues and therefore needs additional help. This seems doubtful considering Timothy's history, a joint writer of several Epistles with Paul and trusted emissary in very tough situations on behalf of Paul. No, it is more likely that Paul is simply encouraging Timothy to continue doing what he would naturally do: read, pray and wrestle with the issues just as the wise son does in Prov. 2.6. But there is another reason for this exhortation and it has to do with the false teachers. In 1 Tim. 1.7 Paul states 'although the false teachers want to be teachers of the Law, they do not *understand* what they are talking about or what they so confidently affirm'. Paul wants to ensure Timothy is not like the false teachers but rather understands what he is talking about and affirms and thereby will be a positive example and role model for others to follow.

2 Timothy 2.8-13
Paul's Basis for Suffering for the Gospel

Overview

The purpose of 2.8-13 is to show Timothy Paul's reasons for suffering, thereby providing a firm basis he can hold onto when times get tough. In the two previous sections (1.6-18; 2.1-7) Paul highlighted the importance for Timothy to continue to suffer for the gospel with Paul. Personal examples play a significant role in those sections and are continued into this next section (2.8-13). The majority of the examples to emulate are positive though there are some negative ones too. Note that he begins and ends the list of examples with his own testimony but it is Jesus' example which is foundational with respect to the matter of suffering. To suffer for the gospel is consistent with the paradigm of Jesus whom Paul emulates.

```
Paul (1.11-14)
    Phygelus & Hermogenes (1.15; negative)
Onesiphorus (1.16-18)
    Illustrations (2.1-7)
        soldier
        athlete
        farmer
Jesus (2.8)
Paul (2.9-10)
```

Paul recognizes in the first section (1.6-18) particularly that suffering may look to outsiders as a sign of shame, but he assures Timothy that this is not true (1.8, 12, 16). The second section identifies the need for grace and steadfast endurance in order for Timothy to fulfill his calling. With these two ideas in mind Paul builds his case for suffering.

Paul begins his case by presenting Jesus, the resurrected one and son of David, as the paragon of suffering for the gospel and himself as Christ's servant and fellow-sufferer in order to dispel any sense that suffering is a sign of shame. In fact suffering is to be considered a sign of approval (cf. 2 Cor. 6.4; 1 Pet. 2.20), a necessary concomitant of ministry to the elect (2 Tim. 2.10) and the assurance of a reward (2.12).

The second point in Paul's defence of the need for suffering in ministry is based on a 'faithful saying' (2.11-13). Paul knows that suffering could lead to two very different paths: death in Christ and perseverance leading to eternal life (2.11b-12a) *or* denial and faithlessness leading to destruction (2.12b-13). Therefore he includes this faithful saying to motivate Timothy to follow the way of Christ, which has a present and future reward.

Call to Imitate Jesus the Paragon of Suffering (2.8)

Paul begins his theological basis for suffering as a minister with a present ongoing imperative calling on Timothy to remember Jesus Christ. The intentional rearrangement of the names as 'Jesus Christ' instead of the typical 'Christ Jesus' suggests that Paul is orienting Timothy's attention on the historical human Jesus who lived on earth as the suffering servant. The injunction to remember fits into the 'remembrance theme' running through this letter. Timothy has been told to remember his spiritual heritage (1.5; 3.14-15), his experience of the Holy Spirit (1.6) and the sound teaching he has received from Paul (1.13; 2.2), but here Paul reminds Timothy of the person who is the bedrock of the gospel, his being and his ministry. In other contexts Paul has had to remind people of the fundamentals of the faith (Eph. 2.11-13; 2 Thess. 2.5) because people forget. But nothing creates theological amnesia in a believer as much as suffering so Paul has Timothy fix his eyes on Jesus (cf. Heb. 12.2).

There are two aspects of Jesus' life according to the gospel to which Paul wants to draw Timothy's attention: *he was raised from among the dead ones* (literally 'dead ones' is a common expression in the Gospels [Mt. 17.9; Mk 9.9; Lk. 24.46; Jn 20.9] and in the Pauline corpus [Rom. 4.24; 6.9; 1 Cor. 15.20]) and *he is from the seed of David*. Clearly there is more to Paul's understanding of the gospel but for his argument he focuses on only these two aspects. The Greek (perfect passive participle) used to describe Jesus being raised presupposes that he was dead and was raised by the Father and that he is alive and presently reigns.

Christ's death and resurrection provides the theological basis for suffering since it was only through suffering and rising that Jesus could fulfill God's calling to provide redemption for humankind. However, Paul's interest in Christ's suffering for Timothy and other readers is not the redemptive salvific element but rather the pattern he provides on how to live as servant of God (Mk 10.45). Timothy must follow Christ's pattern of living, which assumes that suffering precedes glory (cf. 1 Pet. 2.21-23). Surprisingly there is no mention of 'death' or the 'crucifixion' in this verse; rather Paul focuses on Christ being raised. There are two reasons for this. First, it keeps Timothy's eyes focused on the eschatological victory of Jesus instead of the suffering thereby stressing victory over suffering and death. This emphasis provides encouragement, courage and hope of life now though fully realized later (cf. 1.10 which emphasizes the victory over death and promise of life). Second, by emphasizing that Jesus exists in the state of being raised, Paul can assure Timothy that the reward after death is secure and certain just as there was a reward for the athlete (2.5-6). This idea also sets up the similar idea in 2.12a in which the one, who endures, reigns with Christ and later in 4.8 where the crown is reserved for the overcomer. Third, it affirms Paul's certainty of the resurrection and the role that the resurrection serves as the foundation of the gospel contra the false teachers who were stating that the resurrection had already come (2.18).

Several different views have been espoused concerning the statement 'from the seed of David'. Some scholars attach very little significance to the statement, suggesting that its inclusion is due simply to the fact it belonged in the original creed; the important phrase is 'he was raised'. Most scholars see a greater intentionality on the part of the author to include this phrase. One option is that this is a Jewish Christian formula about David which points to the process of discipleship in terms of initially believing in the risen Lord and then subsequently identifying with the Davidic Messiah. Certainly discipleship is part of the reason for its inclusion but certainly not the whole reason. Another option is that there is a twofold reference to the birth of Jesus: born of David's lineage (i.e. seed of David) and his rebirth in the spiritual realm at the resurrection. The idea is that Timothy (the believer) will follow suit, which would give him confidence amidst a difficult situation. But, the order of the phrases mitigates against this position. A more likely option is that the phrase is used as a reference to the faithfulness of God (1.3, 5; 3.14-17) to fulfill his promise and the expectation of his people. This is consistent with its usage in Rom. 1.3 where Jesus is the fulfillment of 2 Sam. 7.12-16. Although this option is attractive it lacks cohesion with the literary context. I propose that 'seed of David' is incorporated because it points to Jesus' fulfillment of his calling (2 Sam. 7.12-16), which included suffering *unlike what the people expected*. Thus the first stanza (i.e. he was raised) accentuates Christ's victory in death but the second stanza demonstrates Christ's suffering in life (Is. 53.11). Likewise, Paul has learned to suffer for the elect in life to fulfill his calling before reigning with Christ (cf. 2.12; 4.8). Timothy is being asked to do the same.

Timothy's Invitation to Imitate Paul in Suffering (2.9-10)

After focusing Timothy on Jesus, Paul now draws his attention to his own example. This is the second time in the letter Paul has used himself as an example (see 1.8-13) and in both cases the point of the example is the willingness to suffer. It is not clear in the Greek in 2.9, if Paul is referring back to *Jesus* or to the *gospel* as that for whom or which he is suffering as a criminal. The reference to the gospel has two strengths: first, it is consistent with 1.11 where Paul refers backs to the gospel in 1.10 and second, the word 'gospel' is the closest antecedent. The reference to Jesus is also attractive since in 2.8 Paul has just told Timothy to refocus his attention on the person of Jesus since Paul is looking at the issue of suffering from a personal experiential perspective. In favour of this position is the fact the text literally says 'in whom/which' which clearly makes more sense to think of suffering in Christ (cf. Col. 1.24), not in the gospel. Even if the referent is the gospel it is probably not wise to make too big a distinction between the gospel and Jesus. Elsewhere Paul has made the connection that the gospel is Jesus, his life, teachings, death and resurrection (Rom. 1.2-4) just as the author of Mark has done ('the beginning of the gospel which is Jesus, the Christ, the Son of God', Mk 1.1).

The weight of this verse is on the willingness of Paul to 'suffer hardship' and by inference Timothy is to do the same. The etymology of the verb used in 2.9 may not be too far off the mark in terms of meaning. It is a compound verb made up of 'suffer' (*paschō*) and 'bad' (*kakos*). Paul's hardship and suffering is due to his relationship with Jesus and his gospel which tacitly means that there is and will be resistance to his message and Lord (cf. 2 Cor. 2.14-16). Later in the letter in a context dealing with the unwillingness of people to hear sound teaching, Paul uses the same verb to exhort Timothy specifically to suffer hardship (4.5). At some level for Paul, suffering hardship legitimizes one's ministry and may make people open to hear the gospel. Therefore Timothy needs to continue to suffer hardship for the gospel and his King. The only other use of this verb is in Js 5.13, 'who is suffering hardship, let him or her pray'. Though in this context Paul does not mention the need for prayer he would certainly aver as he does elsewhere (cf. Eph. 6.20-21).

Paul describes the extent to which he is suffering through two phrases: 'until chains' and 'as a criminal'. The word for 'chain' is used metaphorically for the *bondage* of sickness (a chain on a tongue of a mute man; Mk 7.35) or bondage of Satan causing a sickness (Lk. 13.16). More typically it is used metaphorically in the plural to refer to *imprisonment*, especially in the Pauline letters (Acts 20.23; Phil. 1.7, 14, 17; Col. 4.18; Philemon 10, 13). It is also used literally to refer to the actual *chains* put around prisoners (Acts 16.26; 26.29). If Luke is the author of 2 Timothy with Paul as I assume then it is possible to take this term literally or at least to describe the heightened security Paul is under. Since Paul's imprisonment is taking place during the Neronian persecution (*circa* AD 64–67) it may be that Paul, a Christian, is in chains or it may be a reference to his first trial (2 Tim. 4.16) in which he addressed his accusers bound with chains as he had done earlier in Caesarea (Acts 26.29).

The second term Paul uses to describe the extent of his hardship is *kakourgos*. Literally it means an 'evil-doer' though typically it refers to criminals of the state who have committed a serious crime. This term is used of pirates (Diodorus Siculus 20.81.3) and the thieves crucified next to Jesus (Lk. 23.32-39). But in one text (*Ep. Socr.* 30.6) it is found with the word *paranomos*, which means 'proposing unconstitutional measures'. If *paranomos* does inform the meaning of *kakourgos* then it may mean in this context that Paul's imprisonment is due to his message being understood as contrary to the Roman constitution. Certainly this is how Paul's ministry and message was understood when he was arrested in Philippi (Acts 16.20-21). By calling himself a criminal, Paul is expressing some of his indignation since he knows that he is innocent and as a Roman citizen he is being improperly treated.

Paul's joy amidst the suffering comes from knowing that the 'word of God is not chained' even if he is. There is a play on words with 'chains' in 2.9a and 'not chained' in 2.9b as they come from the same root. The point that Paul is making for Timothy is that neither suffering nor imprisonment can stop the progress of the gospel and its effectiveness. Paul reaches a similar conclusion in Phil. 1.12-18. He takes courage from knowing that his imprisonment actually helped the gospel because people realized he was innocent and in prison for Christ's sake so that many fellow prisoners were emboldened to preach even more fearlessly. The messenger can be chained but no power, human or spiritual, can chain the message.

A friend of mine was a missionary during the Vietnam War. One day a number of Viet Cong soldiers found and killed a group of Christians praying and reading Scripture. Then they dragged the whole village to the grisly site for them to witness what would happen if they did the same. But when the townspeople saw the dead bodies holding the Scriptures they got down on their knees and began to read them. The Word of God cannot be chained.

Paul makes an inference in 2.10 though the referent is not clear. It literally says 'because of this I endure all things for the sake of the elect that they might obtain salvation in Christ Jesus with eternal glory'. It is possible that 'because of this' is pointing forward (as some think it does in 1 Tim. 1.16) to 'the elect' or to 'they might obtain...eternal glory', thus meaning he endures all things for the elect because he knows they might obtain salvation. This option is doubtful for three reasons: first, the phrase 'because of this' is better taken as referring *back* to the 'faithful saying' as in 1 Tim. 1.15-16; second, typically *dia touto* ('because of this') is not forward-referring in the NT; and third, 'because of this' seems superfluous if it is forward-referring. Therefore 'because of this' is probably referring to a preceding statement, most likely 'the word of God is not chained' (note that it could refer to Christ and the gospel). Paul draws on the truth that the word of God cannot be chained. This fact serves as his hope in the midst of suffering and his motivation for enduring all things.

Paul changes verbs from 'suffer' (2.9) to 'endure' (2.10) in order to move the focus from isolated sufferings or death, as was the case of Jesus (2.8) and is the present possible situation for Paul, to the ongoing need for endurance. The necessity of endurance has been underscored elsewhere in Paul's letters (Rom. 12.12; 1 Cor. 13.7) and something he repeats two verses later (2 Tim. 2.12). Paul wants Timothy to embrace 'always' the mindset of perseverance necessary to run a long distance race, without which there will be no crown (2.12a; 4.8; cf. Acts 20.24); this teaching is consistent with Jesus' (Mt. 24.13). To endure will also set Timothy apart from the false teachers who are not willing to suffer or persevere for their faith (1 Tim. 1.6; 6.10, 21; 2 Tim. 2.17-18; 4.4).

Scholars spend a large amount of effort in trying to determine 'who are the elect?' and less effort on what it means for Paul 'to endure everything for their sake?' With respect to the first question, one option is that Paul is referring to those who are not believers but are predestined to become believers. He is certain that his suffering and preaching for the sake of the unredeemed will result in them responding affirmatively when they hear the gospel. This is probably to read too much into the text. It is not certain that the 'elect' refers in the NT to those 'predestined' to believe and certainly it does not in this context since the 'faithful saying' (2.11-13) depicts salvation as conditional on one's willingness to die with Christ, endure and remain faithful. Another issue is that it seems odd that the believers are excluded among the elect. A second common option is that it refers to those who are presently believers and a third option is that it refers to both believers and future believers.

The term 'elect' has unfortunately been equated with those predestined to believe. Rather the term 'elect' is a term imported from the OT, for the people of God or Israel (Ps. 105.6, 43; Is 43.20), a usage which the church took over (Mt. 22.14; Mk 13.27; Rom. 8.33; Col. 3.12). As I said above, there is nothing in the context that suggests bringing together the terms of election and predestination in the sense of predetermining who will believe. When Paul does refer to predestination elsewhere it has to do with the kind of people God has foreseen they will be (i.e. the Church); people conformed to the image of Christ (Rom. 8.29), holy and blameless (Eph. 1.4). It is therefore interesting to note that when Paul speaks of the elect in Col. 3.12 he refers to them in terms of their qualities ('holy, loved, compassionate, kind') as he does in Tit. 1.1 ('according to the faith of the elect'). Therefore when Paul speaks of the 'elect' in 2 Tim. 2.10 he is simply referring to God's people whose heritage reaches back into the OT covenants and he is not using this term to distinguish between those who are predestined to believe and those who are not.

The relationship between Paul's sufferings and how they function for the sake of the elect is not made clear in the text. Clearly his sufferings do not obtain salvation for the elect or have any efficacious element. Only Christ's sacrifice can do this (note that he says 'the salvation which is in/through Christ Jesus'), which he has made clear elsewhere (Rom. 3.21-27). Some scholars understand Paul's statement in light of Mt. 24.6-31 supposing that there is a set amount of suffering which must precede Christ's second coming (Mt. 24.6ff.). The suffering, which Paul is now enduring, will mean less suffering for the elect and therefore will make it less difficult for these people to obtain salvation. Though this position is doubtful it does raise an important point: Paul's sufferings have a supplemental function, helping the gospel do its work. There are two other texts in which Paul refers to his sufferings functioning in this way (2 Cor. 1.6; Col. 1.24). In these texts, Paul understands that his sufferings are completing the sufferings of Christ in the sense that in each hardship he is representing and acting on behalf of Christ (who is now in heaven) with the hope that these trials will help someone in their pursuit of salvation (by seeing faith in action). There is also the sense that through suffering on behalf of others Paul is attempting not to put any stumbling block before his people so that they can reach the prize at the end of life (2 Cor. 6.3-13). In this context, salvation is primarily a future benefit (thus the inclusion of 'with eternal glory in 2.10) which is conditional on a person enduring to the end (2.12a). Paul's point is that he wants Timothy to follow his example of enduring suffering because in doing so he will be showing others the way to receive the prize and thereby indirectly helping God's people obtain the eschatological goal of salvation, eternal glory (cf. 1 Tim. 1.11). This is something which cannot be received through achievement or merit but rather is given in the future based on grace and faith (cf. Lk. 20.35; Heb. 11.35).

Scholars have looked primarily to Rom. 1.3-4 as the source or at least the background for the material found in 2 Tim. 2.8-10. The main reason is the similarity of the material—seed of David, resurrection of Jesus—even though different words are used and the order of the material is reversed (note that seed of David is placed before resurrection in Romans). One way to account for the similarity of this material is Lukan authorship. Luke may possibly have drawn this material from memory, which would account for the odd order of the material. Also Lukan authorship may explain the use of *kakourgos* ('criminal') found only in Luke's Gospel (Lk. 23.32, 33, 39) thereby stressing Paul's identification with Jesus and the thieves and his desire for Timothy to do likewise. The example of Jesus' death demonstrates the effectiveness of enduring all things for the elect since through this event one thief comes to faith and enters into eternal glory.

Faithful Saying: Support for Paul's Thesis to Suffer (2.11-13)
Faithful Sayings
The final piece of support for Paul's mandate to suffer is what has been generally labeled 'a faithful saying'. There are five 'faithful sayings' in the NT,

introduced by the simple phrase *pistos ho logos* and all five are found in the Pastoral Epistles (1 Tim. 1.15; 3.1; 4.9; 2 Tim. 2.11; Tit. 3.8). Some scholars identify these sayings as examples of a particular literary form called 'a quotation-commendation formula'. This conclusion may possibly be too hasty. A literary form has to have an established identifiable structure that is found in different sources outside of the one being considered, otherwise it is simply a unique form born out of the creativity of the author. If indeed the same author has written the Pastorals then it is likely that the latter would be the most likely case. The exact form found in the Pastorals is not found elsewhere (particularly important is that it is missing from the LXX). There are some examples which closely resemble this form inside the NT (Rev. 21.5; 22.6) and outside the NT (Dionysius Hal. *Ant. rom.* 3, 23, 17; Dio Chrys. 28 [45], 3) but they do not resemble the function of a faithful saying which is to introduce an important saying or message.

The following (Figure 5) is the structure of the Faithful Sayings. I am using 1 Tim. 4.9-10 as an example.

Introductory Formula	'This saying is trustworthy and worthy of all acceptance
Statement of Emphasis	'For this we labour and struggle
Content of Saying	'That we hope in the living God, who is the saviour of all people
Explanatory or Clarifying Comment	'Especially believers'

Figure 5. *Structure of a Faithful Saying*

The *Introductory Formula* always includes *pistos ho logos* and in two instances *pasēs apodochēs axios*, 'worthy of all acceptance' is added for emphasis (1 Tim. 1.15; 4.9). The purpose of this formula is to assure the reader that the subsequent word is reliable and trustworthy. If these sayings are a Pauline creation, utilized by Luke in 2 Timothy, then there is likely a correlation between these statements and the faithfulness-of-God statements (*pistos ho theos*, 'God is faithful') made elsewhere in the Pauline corpus (1 Cor. 1.9; 10.13; 2 Cor. 1.18; cf. 1 Thess. 5.24; 2 Thess. 3.3; Heb. 10.23 for similar ideas). The point is, just as God is reliable, in the same way this saying is reliable and trustworthy. Theodore of Mopsuestia, an early church father (AD 350–428), understood these sayings in the same way as Jesus used the 'truly I say to you' sayings in the Gospels.

The purpose of the *statement of emphasis* is typically to express the importance of the saying or its significance for the author. This statement is not found in every Faithful Saying and indeed it is not found in the example of 2 Tim. 2.11-13.

Surprisingly the *content of the saying* section is not comprised of direct quotations from the Gospel tradition or Pauline tradition. Rather, the material appears to be short statements summarizing teaching found in both traditions. For example, in 1 Tim. 1.15 the faithful saying reads, 'Christ came into the world to save sinners'. There is material close in meaning in Luke's Gospel ('the Son of Man came to seek and *to save* the lost', Lk. 19.10), Mark's Gospel ('I did not come to call the righteous but *sinners*', Mk 2.17), John's Gospel ('*came into the world*', Jn 1.9; 3.19; 6.14; 16.28; 18.37) and Paul's experience ('the worst of *sinners*', 1 Tim. 1.16). The *content of the saying* section in 2 Tim. 2.11-13 seems to consist of material largely drawn from the Pauline tradition. For example, the content of the clause in 2.11, 'if we have died together [with Christ], then we shall live together [with him]', is very similar to what is written in Rom. 6.8: 'if we have died together with Christ, then we believe that we shall also live together with him'. I will look at the source of the material in 2.11b-13 in more detail below. It is also important to observe that the *content of the saying* in 2.11b-13 is comprised of four conditional clauses, which is significantly different from the content of other faithful sayings (cf. 1 Tim. 1.15; 3.1, 16; 4.10; Tit. 3.8). The significance of this will be subsequently treated.

The purpose of the *explanatory or clarifying statement* section, though not included in all the faithful sayings (note 1 Tim. 3.16), is to elaborate on a particular element of the saying, which may be significant to the audience's situation or may need further explanation so that the readers do not misunderstand the saying. It is most likely that 2 Tim. 2.13b ('for it is impossible [for him] to deny himself') is an explanatory or clarifying statement written for the sake of the audience to assure them of Christ's faithfulness amidst their unfaithfulness.

Scholars have sometimes struggled ascertaining whether the content of the faithful saying is the material that precedes or follows the introductory formula. Some cases are quite clear. The *content of the saying* in 1 Tim. 1.15 is most certainly what follows the *introductory formula*, 'Christ Jesus came into the world to save sinners', since it is introduced with the conjunction *hoti*, 'that'. But it is less certain as to what the content of the saying is in 1 Tim. 3.1. It could refer backwards to the statement about women being saved through childbirth or to the subsequent saying 'if someone seeks to be an overseer, he or she desires a good work'. The latter is more likely since all the other faithful sayings point forward but its content, when compared to other faithful sayings, does not seem important enough to warrant being called a 'faithful saying'. Some point to 1 Tim. 3.16 as the content of the saying which has been separated from its formula in 3.1 by blocks of teaching material or simply a digression in the author's thoughts.

General Observations on the Faithful Saying in 2 Tim. 2.11-13

There has been some debate whether the *content of the saying* precedes or follows the *introductory formula*. It is doubtful that the *content of the saying* precedes the saying since there is no clear referent unless one considers 'the Word of God is not chained', but it is quite far removed. The main reason for thinking the *content of the saying* does not refer to the material which follows in 2.11b-13 is the inclusion of *gar*, 'therefore/for', in 2.11b. Scholars believe that it seems out of place. Some have said it was part of the original block of material that has been imported wholesale without editing. Others understand it as a 'connective' in order to emphasize what follows in the saying and have translated it as either 'here' or 'namely, if…' or 'for as you remember'. Most likely, the author has included it intentionally as an *explanatory conjunction* in order to elucidate what has been said in 2.1-10. Paul is concerned to explain especially the needed mindset and theological perspective if one is going to suffer hardship (2.9) and endure all things (2.10). Therefore the *content of the saying* most likely is the material in 2.11b-13, which follows the *introductory formula* in 2.11a.

Paul uses 'we' throughout this saying in two ways: first, in the collective sense as those who are the people of God and therefore including Paul and Timothy (thus the antecedent of 'we' is the 'elect' in 2.10); second, in the partitive sense that the 'we' must endure to the end in order to be considered the people of God which may suggest some will not. The plural greeting at the end of 2 Timothy indicates that people other than Timothy will be reading the letter. So it is likely that these sayings are to encourage some to follow Christ and to warn them if they do not.

The saying is comprised of four stanzas. The first two stanzas refer to positive experiences one will enjoy (i.e. life and eternal glory) if one fulfills the conditions of enduring for Christ and dying together with Christ. The second two stanzas refer to the negative consequences people will experience if they fulfill the condition of denying God and apostasize. All the stanzas are conditional which suggests that they are dependent on the will of the person cooperating with God.

It is possible to spot a progression of thought in the saying. It begins with conversion (possibly baptism) and continues with the life of discipleship (which requires perseverance), the potential danger of apostasy and the constant availability of hope because of God's faithfulness.

Stanza One: Death and Life (2.11b)

There is no mention in the text with whom the death takes place and with whom life is lived though it is tacitly understood to refer to Christ as it does in the clear source of this teaching, Rom. 6.8. Traditionally scholars have pointed to conversion as the event to which Paul is referring, particularly since the Greek aorist tense is used which they consider to be past-referring. Certainly Paul is referring to the spiritual death that takes place at conversion. He he is probably using the aorist tense of 'die together' in order to look at death to sin as the ongoing process of dying and rising 'in Christ' which begins at conversion and culminates at physical death (cf. Rom. 6.11-12; Col. 3.1-11). Thus dying together with Christ is both a positional and an experiential phenomenon. Paul uses the future tense of 'live together' to underline what Timothy and the people of God, who have died with Christ, can expect to experience. The emphasis is on the promise of a qualitatively better life now in the present as it is in Rom. 6.8 and in the Pastorals (1 Tim. 4.8; 6.19; 2 Tim. 1.1). This life also includes the eschatological reward of eternal life in the future (1 Tim. 1.16; 6.12). In order to continue to experience this life in the present and one day in the future, Paul, Timothy and others need endurance, which is dealt with in the following stanza.

These two verbs, 'die together' and 'live together', are found juxtaposed in two other Pauline texts (Rom. 6.8 and 2 Cor. 7.3). The first instance is the same usage as here. The second instance uses the words literally in the sense of dying physically and living together physically (cf. Mk 14.31, Peter's bold claim that he would die together with Christ and never deny him). This literal interpretation has led some scholars to understand this stanza within the broader framework of martyrdom, meaning that Paul is giving Timothy assurance that if he should be martyred he will be alive with Christ and experience eternal life. The context of suffering and Paul's constant possibility of death supports this position though this idea is second to the primary idea stated above.

Stanza Two: Enduring and Reigning (2.12a)

In this stanza Paul reiterates the requirement of endurance by using the same verb (*hupomenō*) that was used in 2.10. The repetition of this verb suggests the importance of endurance for a faithful minister like Timothy since it was the focus in 2.8-10. Although *hupomenō* is not a 'together' verb like the surrounding verbs 'die together', 'live together' and 'reign together' in 2.11b and 2.12a, the idea is that God's people are to endure together with Christ and his grace (cf. 2.1). The point of the stanza is that steadfast endurance precedes glory and is necessary to attain glory.

To live with Christ requires persevering and enduring the hard stuff of life and ministry. The paradigm for endurance is Christ himself who spent a lifetime suffering at the hands of sinners (Heb. 12.2) and in particular the most demeaning hardship, the cross (Heb. 12.3). Later in the letter Paul presents himself as an example, for Timothy, of one who has shown endurance (2 Tim. 3.10; cf. 1 Pet. 2.21). Jesus taught that only those who endure to the end would be saved (Mt. 10.22; 24.13). Scripture lists many different types of trials a believer might face in which endurance is needed; a few include betrayal (Mt. 10.21), hatred (Mt. 24.10), reproach and personal loss (Heb. 10.32), temptation (Js 1.12) and physical harm (1 Pet. 2.20). Paul exhorts Timothy in his previous letter to 'pursue endurance' (1 Tim. 6.11) and expects it from elders (Tit. 2.2). This implies that endurance requires an act of the will and a humble submission to Christ's power and grace through prayer to receive the gift to endure (Rom. 15.5; 2 Thess. 3.5; 2 Tim. 2.1).

Although enduring hardship is painful and unpleasant, Paul proposes that it has a redeeming value and thus the need to pursue it. The very nature of struggles requires endurance to overcome them (Rom. 5.3). If believers (and Timothy in particular) endure these struggles they will experience a transformed character that has been tried and tested which in turn will lead to a greater hope in God when subsequent struggles come. The best benefit of enduring is the reward of ruling with Christ.

Paul says for the benefit of Timothy and other readers that if they endure they will also 'rule with Christ'. Traditionally scholars have understood this to refer to the time in the future when Christ establishes his messianic kingdom in which believers will rule with him. The main support for this position comes from the Gospels where Jesus says 'you, who have followed me, will also sit on twelve thrones, judging the twelve tribes of Israel' (Mt. 19.28) and Lk. 22.30, 'I confer on you a kingdom...so that you may eat and drink at my table in my kingdom and sit on thrones, judging the twelve tribes', which some think is the source for this saying. There is support in the Pauline literature too: Paul believes that at the consummation of the ages, the believers will be part of the judgment of the world and the angels (1 Cor. 6.2). One reference from the Church Fathers (Polycarp, *Phil.* 5.2), states that the believers, who have lived as worthy citizens of Christ, will rule with him after the return of Christ. In 1 Cor. 4.8, Paul rebukes the Corinthians because they think they are reigning with Christ already, the assumption being that this reign will not take place until after the return of Christ.

Just as Paul uses the future tense in stanza one to express the idea that the believers are to expect to live in the present and the future, in the same way the future tense is employed to aver that those who endure with Christ in the present can expect to rule together with Christ in the present and after the return of Christ. Paul states in Rom. 5.17 that Christ's death and resurrection results in believers being able to rule in life through Christ. Similarly the author of Rev. 5.10 points out how God, through Christ, has created believers to be a kingdom and priests to rule on the earth. Both authors understand that through Christ the requirements of the Adamic Covenant are now able to be fulfilled in part, namely 'they are to rule over the earth' (Gen. 1.26, 28). When Paul gives his instructions to the Corinthians with respect to women participating in worship, he does so by relating it to creation (1 Cor. 11.7-10). The point there is, just as men and women were expected to rule together over creation, in the same way men and women are to lead worship together for the church. In conclusion, believers rule imperfectly now with Christ with the help of the Holy Spirit but after the return of Christ and the consummation of the ages they will rule perfectly with Christ.

Stanza Three: Denying Christ and Being Denied by Christ (2.12b)

The third stanza stands in stark contrast with the previous two stanzas. This part of the saying certainly is based on Jesus' teaching in the Gospels (Mt. 10.33) although the issue of 'denial' is treated several times in the NT (cf. 1 Jn 2.22-23). There are two types of denial in the Gospels: positive and negative. The positive form of denial, which Jesus expects of his followers, is denial of oneself for him and his kingdom (Mk 8.34). Stanzas one and two are clear examples of self-denial: death and life with Christ coupled with enduring with Christ. The negative form of denial explained in the Gospels is denial of Christ and his kingdom teaching (often for self-preservation; Mt. 10.33). It is this denial Paul is concerned with here. Paul spells out, for Timothy, the consequences for those who actively deny Christ, which is the antithesis of enduring in Christ and self-denial for Christ's sake.

This stanza uses the rare case of a future condition (lit. 'if we will deny [him] then he will deny us') which projects what is expected will happen. Therefore it is likely that Paul is expecting some people will deny Jesus. Paul probably has the secondary readers in mind, not Timothy (cf. 1.5) and he writes this especially in light of some of those who have denied Christ (Hymenaeus and Alexander in 1 Tim. 1.20, 2 Tim. 4.14; Phygelus and Hermogenes in 2 Tim. 1.15, 2.17-18). The main function of this stanza is to act as a warning (cf. Lk. 12.9) so that Paul's readers will hold fast and endure in Christ and secondarily it functions as a judgment.

Denial comes in different forms, both in terms of belief and action. The NT includes several specific acts of denial and particularly those who profess to know God but their actions deny it (Tit. 1.16). Paul says that those who refuse to look after their family members and the household of God deny their faith and in doing so act worse than unbelievers (1 Tim. 5.8). Later in 2 Tim. 3.5, Paul describes the people of the Last Days as those who outwardly look like they have the power of godliness but inwardly they deny its power. But people can deny Christ through what they believe. In very stark strident language John states that a person is a 'liar' and an 'antichrist' if they deny Jesus is the Messiah because in doing so they deny the Father and the Son (1 Jn 2.22-23).

The second half of the stanza states that Christ will deny the one who denies him. The future tense is used in the second half of the conditional clause (apodosis) projecting what action can be expected for those who deny Christ. It is important to know the moment when Christ will deny this person and for what. The time of the denial is the Last Judgment when God will judge the hearts of all people, which is consistent with the references in the Gospels. More important is the latter question, 'for what will they be denied?' The examples of Peter and Judas are good examples of those who denied Christ. Progressively and increasingly Peter denies Jesus at Caiaphas's courtyard (Mt. 26.69-75). First, he denies *being with Jesus*. Second, he moves from the fire to the gateway (thus trying to escape) and denies *knowing Jesus*. Third, now cornered by several people, Peter calls curses down either on Jesus or on himself, emphatically denying knowing Jesus. Then he goes outside and weeps prodigiously which is the beginning of his repentance. Judas also denies Jesus unequivocally through his actions. But subsequently he repents (note that the same word for 'repent' is used with respect to Judas in Mt. 27.3—*metamelomai*—as is used to describe the tax collectors and prostitutes who repented and received the kingdom of God) by returning the money to the priests and oddly by taking his own life as a demonstration of the guilt and shame he felt (Mt. 27.3, 5; for a fuller explanation of this point see ch. 11 in Craig A. Smith, *At the Cross, At the Crossroads: Loving our Enemies in the 21st Century* [Manila: OMF Literature, 2007]). The point is that the denial of Christ has to be a set, established and entrenched disposition within the individual; such a person has consciously and consistently rejected Christ (Jude 4). Therefore the denial of Christ at the final judgment to which Paul is referring is not based on specific acts, which have been repented of, but rather a hardened, unrepentant, determined rejection of Christ.

Stanza Four: Refusal to Believe and Christ's Faithfulness (2.13a)

The difficulty interpreting this stanza largely revolves around determining the meaning of the verb used, *apistoumen*, in the first half of the clause (protasis). Does it mean 'if we are unfaithful' or 'if we choose to disbelieve' or 'if we apostasize'? This verb is used seven other times in the NT. In six of the examples the verb clearly means 'to disbelieve' (Mk 16.11, 16; Lk. 24.11, 41; Acts 28.24; 1 Pet. 3.7); only Rom. 3.3 is debatable though the consensus among scholars is that it means 'to be unfaithful'. Most scholars agree that the second half of the clause (apodosis) means 'that one [Jesus] remains faithful' though there is some disagreement concerning what he is remaining faithful to. It is also important to notice that in this stanza the verbs are in the present tense and not in the future tense as in the preceding stanza.

The first option is 'if we are unfaithful, then that one remains faithful'. Romans 3.3 is used as support for the translation 'unfaithful' since the same verb and noun are found juxtaposed and the contrast appears to be between the unfaithfulness of God's people and the faithfulness of God. Some scholars look at the stanza from a personal individualized perspective. Paul is seeking to comfort Timothy and all believers by assuring them that if one should be temporarily unfaithful, like Peter, God will continue to be faithful to that person(s) in order that they will be saved and receive the crown of salvation (cf. 2 Tim. 1.12: God guards Paul's good deposit in the same way). Other scholars look at this text from a corporate perspective (particularly in light of Rom. 3.3). Their point is that human unfaithfulness cannot nullify God's faithfulness to save others (i.e. his gracious gift of eschatological salvation for his people). The purpose of the final strophe 'for he is unable to deny himself' roots the truth of this stanza in the character of God: he is faithful and must always remain true to his character. The main problem with this position is that this is not the typical meaning for the verb and it is questionable that 'unfaithful' is the best translation in Rom. 3.3 (see discussion below).

The second option takes the verb to mean 'to apostasize'. For some scholars stanza four is parallel with stanza three though the language has changed from denial to apostasy. Under this position, Paul is giving out a warning that for those who apostasize, God will be faithful to mete out the proper punishment. There are two problems with this position. First, it is doubtful that the faithfulness of Christ should be taken negatively as a reference to judgment since the context does not warrant it. Second, the meaning of the verb does not mean 'to apostasize' but 'to disbelieve' or possibly 'to refuse to believe'. Sometimes this disbelief continues to the end of a person's life and ends in condemnation (Mk 16.16; 1 Pet. 2.7). But the majority of occurrences of this verb depict either 'disbelief' or 'refusal to believe' based on the information or circumstances. Some Jews in Rome were convinced by Paul's words but others refused to believe (Acts 28.24). The disciples disbelieved or refused to believe the women who returned from the tomb (Mk 16.11; Lk. 24.11). They even disbelieved when Jesus appeared to them after the resurrection (Lk. 24.41). The disbelief of the persons in each instance is momentary and in most cases it gives way to belief. For example, after Jesus ate the bread and opened the disciples's minds they believed (Lk. 24.43, 45). As I stated above, the example of Rom. 3.3 could mean that some Jews were unfaithful. It is just as likely, possibly more likely, that Paul is saying that even though certain Jews did not believe the words of God (this comes from the context, Rom. 3.2) their refusal to believe did not nullify or render ineffective God's faithfulness.

The third option reads, 'if we *disbelieve*, then he will remain faithful', which maintains the typical meaning of the verb. Stanza four is therefore parallel with stanza three but looking at the situation from the perspective of disbelief. This saying helps Timothy in two ways. First, it encourages Timothy and believers like him who may struggle with momentary bouts of disbelief. Since Timothy is facing much hardship, he may struggle at times in his faith (cf. 1.6-7). This word is given to comfort him that God will always be there for him just as he was for Peter or the demoniac's father (Mk 9.24). Second, it gives Timothy hope that God will continue to be faithful to those who disbelieve presently and have turned away from the faith in a deliberate manner. In the subsequent verse (2.14) Paul tells Timothy to remind his readers about these things. This suggests that this faithful saying is for their benefit too since the following verses in 2.14-21 deal with false teaching and its negative effects on people's faith resulting in some even losing their faith (2.18) which can only be restored through repentance. Drawing hope from 'stanza four' Timothy can gently instruct his opponents (2.25), who have wandered from the faith (1 Tim. 6.21), because he knows and they now know that they can escape the trap of the devil (2 Tim. 2.26). If they remain hardened and their disbelief moves to denial then Christ's denial is inevitable.

Explanatory Comment: Christ Cannot Deny Himself (2.13b)
A great deal of debate has centered on whether this verse was part of the original hymn which is included here or a subsequent addition by Paul or some later editor. If my understanding of the structure of faithful sayings is correct then it is quite likely that it was part of the original material and functions as the *explanatory or clarifying comment* in the saying form. This statement, through the use of 'for' (*gar*), clarifies the final stanza. Christ is and will remain faithful within the context of people's disbelief because he is quintessentially faithful and it is impossible for him to act contrary to his character. As I said above, both Timothy, who is ministering to people who disbelieve, and certain readers, who disbelieve, need to know that God will remain faithful should some lose their faith.

2 Timothy 2.14–3.17
Paul's Concern with the False Teachers

2 Timothy 2.14–3.17 constitutes the fourth major section in the body of the letter. The focus of this section of the letter is on dealing with the problem of the false teachers. Paul left Timothy in Ephesus to quell false teachers (1 Tim. 1.3) by removing some and appointing others (1 Tim. 5.17; 2 Tim. 2.2). This problem has not gone away and it is still in the forefront of Paul's mind even while he sits in a Roman prison. He begins this block of material outlining for Timothy the things he needs to do with respect to the false teachers (2.14-26). The series of imperatives in this section are concerned with two areas: Timothy's character and Timothy's actions. The goal of these commands is to ensure that Timothy continues to distinguish himself from the false teachers so that he might present himself as the model of an orthodox teacher, who shares sound teaching (1.13). The next section (3.1-9) describes the false teachers in terms of their character and actions, which condemn themselves and make themselves easily identifiable. In 3.10-17 Paul returns to an appeal he has made before: he wants Timothy to remain loyal to him and his gospel, and be willing to suffer for it. The difference in this appeal is that he looks at this appeal with the false teachers forming the backdrop. If Timothy holds fast to the gospel and Christ in suffering he will be readily identifiable by others as a true servant of the Lord. To help in this task he has the examples of Paul and others (e.g. Timothy's mother and grandmother), and the Scriptures from which he can draw strength and encouragement.

These instructions are as much for Timothy's sake as they are for Tychicus. As I said in the introduction (see p. ?), it is most likely that Tychicus is the carrier of this letter to Timothy and the replacement for Timothy in Ephesus. So these instructions, on how to deal with the false teachers, are given for Timothy to help train Tychicus and prepare him to take over the situation in Ephesus with the goal that Timothy might get to Paul before winter.

Structure of 2.14–3.17:

Paul's Charge to Timothy Against False Teachers (2.14-26)
Denunciation of the False Teachers (3.1-9)
Paul's Appeal to Timothy for his Commitment to Him and the Gospel (3.10-17)

Paul's Charge to Timothy against False Teachers (2.14-26)

Introduction

The material presented in this section is *paraenetic* in nature, not *protrepic*, since Paul exhorts Timothy to live in a particular manner and do specific things in order to deal with the false teachers who are still alive and well in Ephesus. Paul contrasts the true worker of God, which he refers to as the unashamed worker (2.15) and the servant of the Lord (2.24), with the false teachers whose character is dishonourable (2.20) and whose work is unprofitable and destructive. Timothy is to provide the example of the good worker. Hymenaeus and Philetus already stand as examples of bad workers/teachers. The effects of false teaching are graphically portrayed in terms of gangrene. To drive home the point of the difference between types of workers, Paul provides an illustration about the different kinds of vessels in a large house.

Figure 6 below outlines the structure of Paul's argument. Notice the symmetry of this section, whereby three commands at either end function like bookends stating Timothy's responsibilities. Bracketed in the middle lies the problem of the false teachers and the contrast of good and bad teachers.

Three Commands: Act and Live Differently from False Teachers (2.14-16a)
Remind and Warn Listeners
Be Eager to Demonstrate Personal Integrity as a Minister
Avoid Godless Talk

    Two Effects of False Teaching (2.16b-17a)
    Two Examples of False Teachers: Hymenaeus and Philetus (2.17b-18)
    Two Kinds of Workers: God's Foundation and the Illustration of the Great
        House (2.19-21)

Three Commands: Be a Model of Mature Christian Virtue (2.22-26)
Flee Youthful Passions
Pursue Godly Virtues
Avoid Fruitless Arguments

Figure 6. *Structure of Paul's Argument in 2 Tim. 2.14-26*

Three Commands: Act and Live Differently from False Teachers (2.14-16a)

a. *Remind and Warn Listeners (2.14)*
It is not clear in the text, who is being reminded, since there is no object stated. One possible reading is 'call to mind these things' with Timothy being the person addressed. This is doubtful since the translation of the

verb *hupomimnēskō* as 'call to remind or remember' is rare and because it does not make sense to have the warning in the latter half of the verse addressed to Timothy. The parallel in Tit. 3.1 makes it quite certain that Paul is asking Timothy to remind and warn a particular group. For these reasons the reminder and warning are for either the false teachers specifically (2.2) or the Ephesian church in general (2.10). The latter seems possible since the injunction against fruitless arguments could apply generally. Nevertheless, it is most likely that the reminder and warning are for the false teachers only since the entire section (2.14-26) is focused on the contrast between good teachers and bad teachers and on Timothy's need to confront them.

What Timothy is to remind them of is not immediately obvious (literally 'these things') but most likely it refers to the gospel Timothy received from Paul (2.2) and the summary of which is given in 2.11-13. The best offence against a gangrenous false teaching is the constant reinforcement of the healthy teaching of the gospel.

The flipside of the reminder is the warning against arguing about words. The seriousness of this aspect of the false teachers's *modus operandi* is seen through Paul's use of the *charge form*. Paul gives the command by the authority of God (note that some manuscripts have 'Lord' and one manuscript has 'Christ') thereby stressing the importance for Timothy to confront this problem. The exact nature of the problem is somewhat elusive since the word to describe it is a hapax legomenon and is not found in the LXX or the Church Fathers. Typically it is translated 'to argue about words'. Thus part of the problem may be the 'content' of what the false teachers are saying. Some clues to this problem may be found in 1 Timothy where Paul describes how these false teachers devoted themselves to 'myths and endless genealogies...foolish talk' (1 Tim. 1.4, 6) and are in essence misinterpreters of the Law (1.7; cf. 4.3). The result of their arguing about words has led the false teachers to deny the resurrection (2 Tim. 2.18). Part of the problem and therefore the strong adjuration may be the penchant of the false teachers to argue. In 1 Tim. 6.4 the cognate noun is used in a context describing how these false teachers are 'sick' with the need to fight over words. It is possible that these false teachers are similar to the sophists of the day who made their living through public speaking and engaging in arguments. Clement of Alexandria (AD 160–215) later spoke of this type of people as those who 'speak about everything unjustly and who shout forth all kinds of names and words decorously...hunters of paltry sayings...toiling their whole life about the division of names and the nature of the composition and conjunction of sentences' (*Strom.* 1.2.21.2–3.24.4; the latter part demonstrates their desire to argue over words). Therefore Paul may be concerned about both the content of the quibbling over words and the manner of arguing. Paul had only marginal success when he entered into public debate (Acts 17.34) but at least in this context the hearers had an open mind to his message. Apollos had more success as a public debater (Acts 18.27-28). Later in 2 Tim. 2.24-25 Paul exhorts Timothy to correct with humility and gentleness those who oppose their message and to endure evil without resentment. The point of this passage is that Timothy is not to stoop to the level of the false teachers when defending the gospel and Timothy is to avoid them altogether if he deems he is laying pearls before swine (cf. Mt. 7.6).

Two reasons are cited by Paul for why one should not argue about words: it profits nothing and destroys those who listen. Paul's concern at this moment is not for the false teachers but for those who hear them. From Paul's perspective listening to people engage in arguments of this nature does not further his cause (cf. 2 Macc. 12.12) or the growth of the kingdom of God, nor does it aid the listeners's personal development (cf. Wis. 8.7; embracing wisdom is useful for life). There may be a play on words with the cognate used in 2.21: a useful worker (2.21) will bring a useful message. But in fact just the opposite is true of the false teachers: listening to their message is destructive. The extent of this destruction is seen in the metaphorical usage of the word in 2 Pet. 2.6 in which it refers to the destruction of Sodom and Gomorrah. Typically this word is used in the LXX together with 'sinners' or 'ungodly', thus referring to the destruction of sinners, but here the destruction comes upon those unaware of the invidious nature of the false teaching.

b. *Be Eager to Demonstrate Personal Integrity as a Minister (2.15)*
Paul turns his attention directly to Timothy's demeanour. He wants to make sure that Timothy stands out from the false teachers in terms of his conduct as a teacher. Timothy is implored to present himself as a model of a Christian worker for the Ephesians just as Paul has been a model for Timothy (1.11, 13; 3.14). Christ, of course, has been the model Paul has been emulating and provides the paradigm for all believers (1 Cor. 11.1). Timothy is to pursue this eagerly. The verb 'to be eager' is found seven times in all the Pauline letters. Two of these seven occurrences deal with an important aspect of the Christian calling as does 2 Tim. 2.15: remembering to care for the poor (Gal. 2.10) and seeking the unity of the Spirit through peaceful relationships (Eph. 4.3). The other four deal with Paul's desire to see someone (1 Thess. 2.17; 2 Tim. 4.9, 21; Tit. 3.12; cf. 2 Tim. 1.17).

The imagery here is of a soldier presenting himself before God to review his record in order to prove himself sufficient for the next needed task. In this sense there is some continuity with the metaphor in 2 Tim. 2.4 where the soldier seeks to please his enlisting officer. Paul makes great use, in his letters, of the transitive usage of the verb 'to present' (*paristēmi*). Fundamentally, believers are to present themselves wholly to God in a sacrificial act of surrender (Rom. 12.1) and obedience (Rom. 6.16) so that they might, in an ongoing process, present themselves to God as workers of righteousness

(Rom. 6.13, 19). This issue of purity is significant to the Ephesian situation since the false teachers have lacked purity so Timothy cannot make the same mistake (cf. 1 Tim. 5.2). Similarly Timothy is to present himself to God as one who is approved, an unashamed worker and who correctly handles the Word of God.

A person who is approved is one who has been tested and refined (1 Pet. 1.7). Paul sees tribulations and hardships (Rom. 5.3-4) as the means by which a person develops endurance (cf. 2 Tim. 2.12: the same cognate) and depth of character (the same cognate as in 2 Tim. 2.15). Through this process believers are approved by God but not in the salvific sense since their ministry is judged on the basis of their faithfulness to the task (1 Cor. 4.2). For this reason deacons are to be 'tested' before they are approved to serve in the church (1 Tim. 3.10). Tested and refined believers express the glory of God (Rom. 5.2; 2 Cor. 3.18). Timothy must continue to embrace the hardships and sufferings of being a worker for God and as he does, he will be a model for the Ephesians and express this glory. God alone has the right to bestow approval and only his approval counts. Yet the false teachers are seeking the approval of people (2 Tim. 4.3-4) in order to reap financial gain (1 Tim. 6.6-10); thus they are rejected and unapproved by God.

It is not exactly clear what Paul means when he asks Timothy to present himself as an unashamed worker. A worker in the Gospels primarily refers to someone who is an agricultural hired hand (Mt. 20.1, 8; cf. Acts 19.25) though metaphorically it refers to a worker for the Kingdom of God (Mt. 9.37-38 and parallels). In this context Paul has a worker for the kingdom (1 Tim. 5.18) in mind (cf. 2 Cor. 11.13; Phil. 3.2 for the opposite). The source of shame is uncertain and different options exist: Timothy is not to be ashamed of his calling, which was founded by a crucified criminal and espoused by an imprisoned friend (2 Tim. 1.8); Timothy is not to be ashamed to face God for how he has fulfilled his ministry—results are not the issue, faithfulness is (1 Cor. 4.2); Timothy is not to be ashamed of his task of preaching the gospel and reproving false teachers; or, taking a passive understanding of 'ashamed', Timothy is to work in such a way that God or Christ would not be ashamed of him (Mk 8.38). There is merit to each position. Most likely Paul wants Timothy to have the same perspective he shares with the Philippians (Phil. 1.20) that he has conducted himself in such a way and handled the Word of Truth in a correct manner so that he can stand unashamed should he hypothetically meet God now and certainly at the last judgment. In contrast, the false teachers should be ashamed to present themselves to God now (but are not) and will be later.

Finally, Timothy is to be eager to present himself as one who correctly handles the Word of Truth. Teaching in this way would distinguish himself from the false teachers who are not correctly handling the Word of Truth; although they desire to be teachers of the Law, instead they create fanciful, doubtful interpretations (1 Tim. 1.3-7) or like Elymas the sorcerer they 'twist the straight paths of the Lord' (Acts 13.10) through their teaching. But this is only one of several ways this verb (*orthotomeō*) can be translated. Its rich metaphorical usage has led to different interpretations of this participial phrase.

Some scholars associate this word with a similar word (*orthopodeō*), which means 'walk straight or [metaphorically] uprightly'. Paul rebukes Peter and others for not walking uprightly according to the truth of the gospel (Gal. 2.14). In this context, Paul would not be focusing on Timothy's teaching but rather on his conduct, which must come in compliance with the gospel. This emphasis is certainly one maintained in 2.14-26 but the fact is the verbs have different meanings and the close connection with 'worker' in the previous phrase suggests this verb has something do with the work he does which brings him no shame.

Etymologically this verb means *ortho* ('straight') *tomaō* ('cut'). For this reason and the verb's usage in Prov. 11.5, some understand the metaphor in terms of a mason cutting stones straight in accordance with a set pattern. From this perspective, Paul would be telling Timothy to be eager to teach according to the pattern that has been presented in the Word of Truth.

Most commonly this verb is used in the sense of clearing a straight path for something so that it can be guided along a straight and direct path. Typically this meant clearing trees and obstacles in order to create a road or path (e.g. Archelaus King of Macedonia built straight roads: Thucydides, *Hist. Pelop.* 2.100.2). Metaphorically it is used to refer to God making straight paths and guiding those who trust in him along this path (Prov. 3.7). The point in this text most likely is that Timothy is to hold fast to the teaching he has received and not to be derailed by the false teachers and their finesounding arguments.

The Word of Truth is not the OT but rather the gospel (see Col. 1.15; cf. 'gospel of salvation', Eph. 1.13). Paul's emphasis on the gospel is not surprising in light of the context of false teaching for he knows that it is God's desire for everyone to be saved through this word, even the false teachers (1 Tim. 2.4).

c. *Avoid Godless Talk (2.16)*
Paul readdresses an issue he dealt with in 2.14 concerning the false teachers's propensity to argue which shows the gravity of this problem in Ephesus. Onesiphorus has probably reported back to Paul the problem in this area (2 Tim. 2.16, 18; 4.19). In the Greek text the phrase 'word of truth' is juxtaposed with 'godless empty' thereby presenting a stark contrast of content of the two types of messages. The content and results of the false teachers's message (of which Hymenaeus and Philetus are examples) show that they are not handling the word of truth correctly and thereby are not approved by God.

The imperative Paul gives, to avoid godless empty talk, is directed specifically at Timothy though indirectly at the Ephesians because of its destructive nature upon the listeners. Literally the verb *periistēmi* means 'to stand around or beside' and is found outside the NT in the sense of 'reject' or 'shun' (e.g. people shun oaths in Josephus, *War* 2.135). Thus this command carries a similar meaning to those found in 2 Tim. 2.23 (reject foolish uninstructed debates) and 1 Tim. 6.20 (turn away from godless chatter). The image created by this word is a little more graphic and might be paraphrased 'avoid getting into the thick of these arguments with these false teachers'.

The content of their teaching is godless empty talk. There is a poorly attested (and should be rejected) variant *kainophōnia* ('new talk') instead of *kenophōnia* ('empty talk') which may simply be an error due to phonetic similarity or an intentional change to reflect the idea that the false teachers's teaching was considered 'contemporary' or 'trendy'. The phrase 'godless empty talk' is found also in 1 Tim. 6.20 and a similar idea 'godless myths' in 1 Tim. 4.7. It is godless in the sense that it does not focus on true godliness, which is the life, death and resurrection of Jesus Christ (1 Tim. 3.14-16). There may also be an allusion to it being profane in its expression and source (1 Tim. 1.9; Heb. 12.16). It is empty talk because it lacks logical defendable substance (2 Tim. 2.23), it is based on fanciful speculations (1 Tim. 4.7; Tit. 3.9) and though it sounds like knowledge, in the end it better resembles hollow chatter (1 Tim. 6.20).

Two Effects of False Teaching (2.16b, 17a)

Paul roots his warning against godless empty talk in two destructive consequences: it advances ungodliness and its infectious nature debilitates listeners. There is no subject stated, so the text could say '*these arguments* advance ungodliness' or '*these false teachers* advance ungodliness'. The immediate context (2.14-21) is generally dealing with teachers (good and bad) and the personal pronoun in 2.17, 'their teaching', suggests that the subject is the false teachers. But the restricted context of 2.16a suggests that Paul is referring to the specific teaching of the false teachers, which he calls 'godless empty talk'. Though the latter idea is most likely, it is probably not necessary to split hairs since the godless character of the false teachers (1 Tim. 1.9) and their message are miscible; they are what they say. What is most concerning for Paul is that these teachers and their teaching will result in even more ungodliness. The false teachers think their teaching is leading to what they call 'advancement' for their listeners. Paul takes their term and turns it back on them (cf. 1 Cor. 6.12 for a similar action) saying that their teaching advances only ungodliness. From personal experience, Paul knows what it means to advance in a worldly manner (Gal. 1.14) and he has seen how people have advanced in ungodliness (2 Tim. 3.13; cf. *T. Jud.* 21.8 for an advancement in immorality). But he also realizes the importance for believers and non-believers to see someone advance in godliness (1 Tim. 4.15). It is not clear from the Greek text how this ungodliness will advance since the modifying phrase is somewhat ambiguous. Here are a few options depending on what is the subject: the false teachers will become more and more ungodly; they will lead many people into ungodliness; or godless empty talk will spread ungodliness among their hearers (cf. Acts 4.17). The latter is the most likely option since the following verse speaks of how their message is like a gangrenous pasture.

Paul describes the second detrimental consequence of this godless empty talk through a mixed metaphor. This teaching can spread out like an open field in the wrong direction if it is not abated. But this teaching is also infectious and potentially deadly to those who come in contact with it and if they see Timothy involved in these arguments they may be emboldened to join in (cf. 1 Cor. 8.10). The effects of their message include destroying the faith of some (2 Tim. 2.18), producing quarrels (2.23) and entrapping listeners for the devil (2.26). The teaching of the false teachers is an unhealthy teaching in comparison to the word of truth, which is a healthy teaching (1 Tim. 1.10). Philosophers used the image of a pasture to express metaphorically the spread of flames (Polybius, *Hist.* 1.48.5) or a disease (Galen, *De Mat. Med.* 9) and gangrene to depict the effect of false accusations (Plutarch, *Mor.* 24). Although this teaching is destructive like gangrene, Timothy does not have to fear for it cannot erode or displace the firm foundation of the church (2 Tim. 2.19).

Two Examples of False Teachers: Hymenaeus and Philetus (2.17b, 18)
As Paul has done elsewhere, he drives home his point with an example (cf. 1 Tim. 1.20; 2 Tim. 1.15 where the same phrase is used, 'among whom is'). In this case he uses two false teachers, Hymenaeus and Philetus, as representative of those who have spread this gangrenous teaching. Philetus is a fairly uncommon name and no other mention is made of him in the Pastoral Epistles or in the NT. Hymenaeus is mentioned in 1 Tim. 1.20 as one of those who had rejected the faith and was fighting against the faith so that Paul excommunicated him by handing him over to Satan. This was certainly a public rebuke in accordance with 1 Tim. 5.20 and now Paul does so again via writing. Some scholars struggle to understand how Hymenaeus was still able to function after this excommunication. This, in turn, has led them to believe that 2 Timothy was written before 1 Timothy in order to remove this tension. But there is no need for such drastic measures, it is more likely the situation is so bad in Ephesus that, despite Paul's ban, Hymenaeus continued to teach and be active among the congregants. Because of their persistence, it might be that Hymenaeus and Philetus (probably Alexander too: 1 Tim. 1.20) are the leaders of this aberrant movement and therefore the need for Timothy not to engage them.

The error of their teaching is that they have deviated from the truth. Literally the word *astocheō* means 'to miss the mark', drawing upon the imagery of an archer shooting for a target or 'to deviate from the course' drawing on the imagery of someone veering off the set path. Twice in 1 Timothy, Paul uses this word to describe those who have veered off from having a sincere faith and good conscience (1.6) and those who have embraced godless chatter instead of the true faith (6.21). Paul utilizes this term again to describe Hymenaeus and Philetus, along with the other false teachers who have shot wide of the word of truth (note the intentional reference back to 2.15 by the use of 'truth') with their teaching.

The proof that Hymenaeus and Philetus have deviated from the truth is because they are saying (note that *legontes* is a causal participle) that the resurrection has already happened. There is some uncertainty among the different manuscripts whether the text is '*a* resurrection has already happened' or '*the* resurrection has already happened'. The majority of the manuscripts (and many good ones like Codex Alexandrinus) support the latter reading. Although fewer manuscripts support the former reading, one of them is Codex Vaticanus, which is an excellent manuscript. The attraction of 'a resurrection' is that it seems difficult to imagine the Ephesians believing that they had missed the resurrection at the end of the age (but cf. 1 Thess. 4.13-18). It is possible that they are referring to a smaller resurrection, as in Mt. 27.51-53. But as I will show below, there are more likely explanations of 'the resurrection having already happened'.

Paul is greatly disturbed by this teaching since he considers the resurrection of Christ and the future resurrection of believers to be foundational to the Christian faith. Without the resurrection of Christ, he says elsewhere, 'our faith is futile and we are still in our sins' (1 Cor. 15.17) and therefore 'we have hope only in this life' (1 Cor. 15.19).

There are several different ways scholars have interpreted how these false teachers surmised the resurrection had already come. First, as elsewhere (1 Cor. 15.12) some thought there was no resurrection of the dead. This idea may be culturally influenced by Greek thought which held to the idea of the immortality of the soul and therefore no need for a resurrection body. The false teachers may have surmised that the resurrection of the body was an anathema to the Greek mind. Second, only Christ has risen from the dead and there is no future resurrection of the dead. Through the resurrection of Jesus, believers are swept into the future era of salvation which the false teachers interpret to mean that there is no marriage (since they are like the angels; cf. Mk 12.25) and abstinence from certain foods (1 Tim. 4.3) both of which are contradictions of the commands given in the Garden of Eden (Gen. 1.30; 2.20-25). Third, the false teachers have spiritualized the resurrection in terms of conversion. They may have twisted Paul's understanding of conversion into the new life in Christ, which he describes in terms of resurrection and baptism language (Rom. 6.1-11) and cosmological language (Eph. 2.6; Col. 3.1). The false teachers's understanding of the resurrection having already taken place is most likely a combination of the latter two positions. They have denied the future bodily resurrection of believers and understood the resurrection solely in spiritualized terms thereby resulting in a skewed spirituality (cf. *Acts of Paul and Thecla* 14). There is nothing in the epistle that suggests the false teachers were acting as Menander, the gnostic follower of Simon Magus (Acts 8.9), who taught his followers that when they were baptized by him they received salvation, the resurrection and immortal youth (Irenaeus, *Adv. haer.* 1.23.5). It is likely in light of this confusion that the creeds of the early church emphasized the resurrection of the flesh (see Apostles's Creed).

Bad doctrine has devastating results. Paul concludes that the false teachers have overthrown the faith of certain believers by leaving out godliness (2 Tim. 2.11-13) in their godless facile arguments. They have also destroyed the believers's hope in the present and future by rejecting the resurrection of the dead (1 Cor. 15.17, 19). Paul's hope is that as Timothy avoids arguments with the false teachers they will grow to be silent (cf. Tit. 1.11), though he realizes some may need a direct confrontation (1 Tim. 5.20). In doing this Timothy will be guarding God's foundation, which he will show is secure even if a few stones in God's building are being shaken loose.

Two Kinds of Workers: God's Foundation and the Illustration of the Great House (2.19-21)

a. *God's Foundation (2.19)*
In dedicating so much time to the false teachers and their destructive teaching, Paul does not want to give Timothy the impression that the church (though he does not use this word) is at risk of crumbling or the word of truth cannot withstand false teachers and false teaching. So through different metaphors he assures Timothy that he is standing on a firm foundation and that even though there are counterfeit teachers out there, they are easily recognizable. Paul also wants to assure Timothy that there are genuine teachers out there too, whom he will find, who can continue to build on this sure foundation.

This section begins with a strong adversative conjunction *mentoi* (cf. Jn 4.27; 7.13; 12.42; 20.5; 21.4), 'nevertheless' (i.e. despite the false teachers's existence), to draw attention to God's foundation and away from the false teachers's feeble attempts to build a movement based on teachings contrary to the gospel.

Different postulations about the identity of the foundation have been put forward. The word for 'foundation' is used fifteen times in the NT. It refers literally to the foundation of a building (Lk. 6.48-50; Rev. 21.14, 19) but metaphorically it has a more diverse usage. Paul talks about the foundation of good works that the rich can build up for themselves (1 Tim. 6.19) which clearly does not fit this context. This word is used to refer to the foundation of teaching that is laid ('gospel' in Rom. 15.20; 'elementary teachings of Christ' in Heb. 6.1). Given the preceding context on false teaching this position has some merit. But it is doubtful since the subsequent clause about the 'seal' which says 'God knows his own' suggests that this foundation is composed of people. In Eph. 1.20 Paul records that the universal church is built upon the foundation of the apostles, prophets and Christ, who is the cornerstone. In 1 Cor. 3.10-12 he describes the local church as being erected on the foundation of Christ and the work of his fellow-workers. These latter images are based on Isa. 28.16, 'See, I lay a stone in Zion, a tested stone, a precious cornerstone for a sure foundation', which the early church saw being fulfilled by Christ (1 Pet. 2.4; cf. Jn 2.19-22). Therefore most likely the sure foundation Paul has in mind here is the universal church of which Christ is the cornerstone. The parallel statement he makes in 1 Tim. 3.15, 'the house of God...which is the church of the living God, the pillar and foundation of truth', makes this almost certain. Paul describes this foundation as 'solid' in the sense that it is immovable (note that the use of the perfect tense of 'stand' suggests this foundation has stood and continues to stand in the present) because it is based on solid teaching (the same word as used in Heb. 5.12, 14) and a great God who helps people hold fast (cf. 1 Pet. 5.9). Although Paul has in mind the universal church, Timothy would apply this to this local church situation to bring him hope and encouragement as he faces the false teachers.

In an unusual mix of metaphors, Paul says that this building has a seal with two statements written on it (cf. Exod. 28.11): 'the Lord knows those who are his' and 'let everyone who names the name of the Lord turn away from wickedness'. Seals typically had three functions in the ancient world. First, they were used as a sign of authority or authentication by kings when issuing a decree (Est. 8.8-10; 1 Kgs 21.8). Second, witnesses of a purchase (Jer. 32.11-14) or covenant (Neh. 9.38) would place their seal on the document. Third, seals were placed on things (e.g. scrolls, tombs) for security so that only persons with authority were permitted to open them. The concept of sealing is also used metaphorically in the NT. Paul speaks of sealing the Gentiles's offering possibly as his guarantee it will be done (Rom. 15.28). In 1 Cor. 9.2 Paul refers to the conversion of the Corinthians as a seal of his apostleship in the sense that their conversion authenticates his apostleship. His usage in Rom. 4.11 is probably similar in meaning where he refers to Abraham's circumcision as a seal of righteousness, authenticating his inclusion into the covenant. Finally, a seal is used occasionally to denote ownership of property (Hag. 2.23 [LXX]; Rev. 9.4; 21.14), which is the sense in this passage. God has his seal on those who are his (cf. Num. 6.27 where it is the name of God which is placed on his people as a sign of blessing). The subsequent illustration about the two types of household vessels expands on this idea but with the further reality that some do not have this seal and therefore are excluded.

But there is more significance to this seal. The image of putting a seal on the foundation (cf. Exod. 28.11) is probably also an intentional device of Paul to get the reader to reflect on Exod. 28.36. The context of that text is a description of the clothing of Aaron the high priest and, of particular importance, the seal on his forehead, which reads 'Holy to the Lord'. That text stresses the importance of holiness and who is allowed to be a priest and minister before God in the Holy of Holies. In the sayings that follow, Paul will develop this theme of different types of leaders and the responsibility to be holy (2.21) and to separate from wickedness.

The first quotation is almost a direct quotation from the story of Korah, Dothan and Abiram (Num. 16.5; cf. *Apost. Const.* 2.54) except that Paul replaces 'God' with 'Lord'. There are two reasons for the substitution: first, to bring a clear connection with Jesus the Lord (cf. 2 Tim. 1.2), who was raised from the dead (2 Tim. 2.8, 18) and is the cornerstone of this foundation; and second, to emphasize the need to belong to Christ in order to receive salvation (2.10b). Paul includes this OT quotation because he sees a parallel situation, namely, just as God knew who were his (i.e. who sided with Moses and not corrupt leaders like Korah) likewise Paul assures Timothy that God knows who are his true teachers, leaders and followers in Ephesus (e.g. Onesiphorus, 2 Tim. 1.16-18). It is doubtful that 'knowing' carries the idea of foreknowledge (cf. Rom. 8.29) in spite of how alluring the quotation from *Odes* 8.15-16 might be: 'for I do not turn away my face from them that are mine; for I know them, and before they came into being I took knowledge of them, and on their faces I set my seal'. Paul's point is that God recognizes who are his in the present by their holy confession and actions. But for those who lack these and therefore do not have the seal (i.e. the false teachers and their followers) there is dishonour (2.20). Since the Korah story deals with the rejection of Moses's authority and his subsequent vindication, Paul may have also chosen this story because it vindicates his apostleship and his message.

The second saying does not appear to be a direct quotation from any one particular OT text. Some scholars see it as a conglomeration of several OT texts (Lev. 24.16; Isa. 26.13; 52.1; Ps. 34.14; Prov. 3.7; Job 36.10; Sir. 17.26) though this is probably not necessary. Paul is probably alluding to the Korah story (but keeping in mind the necessity of exclusive loyalty to God in Is. 26.13, for fear of blasphemy in Lev. 24.16), summarizing the moment when God tells the people to separate themselves from Korah, Dothan and Abiram before he condemns them to death (Num. 16.26-35). Paul's point is that just as God told Moses and his followers to withdraw from Korah, in the same way the Ephesians are to withdraw from the false teachers. For this reason, it is most likely that 'wickedness' is referring to 'false teachers' and not specifically to 'false teaching' though they are not mutually exclusive. The irony is that the false teachers are turning away from the faith (1 Tim. 4.2) whereas the righteous should turn away from wickedness. There are many gods who can be named in this world (Eph. 1.21) but believers are to name (which is equivalent to worshipping; cf. 2 Tim. 2.22) only one name, Jesus. The Ephesian church is to follow only those teachers who have Jesus as the central focus of their teaching and therefore not the fanciful teachings of the false teachers.

b. *Illustration of the Great House (2.20-21)*
Through the use of the illustration of two types of vessels found in a large house, Paul drives home his point in 2.18-19 that there are two different types of teachers and followers. In 2.18 he states that there are those teachers who teach false doctrine and thereby lead their listeners astray in their faith. In 2.19 he shares that there are good teachers and followers who follow Jesus and reject the wicked teachers and their teaching. Paul follows this illustration with an application in 2.21, on how to become an honourable vessel.

(i) *Two Types of Vessels* (2.20). A great deal of discussion has revolved around determining what kind of house the author has in mind. Some see a reference to the *temple* because it is called the 'house of God' in the NT (Mk 2.26) based on the OT usage ('House of the Lord', Ps. 23.6; 'House of God', Ps. 42.4) and because the word for 'vessels' in 2.20 is used of utensils found in the temple (Heb. 9.21). Others see a reference to the *church* since it is called 'his house' in Heb. 3.1-6 (cf. Eph. 2.19-22: though 'house' is not used, there are six cognates of 'house' in that pericope) but in this context Paul refers to a 'large house', not God's house. So, many think that Paul has in mind the house of a wealthy person since there is no reference to God. Yet, because this metaphor is found within the context of architectural language referring to the church (cf. 'foundation' in 2.19), and because he refers to the church as 'house of God' in 1 Tim. 3.15, it is likely that Paul wants Timothy to understand this story about a large house through the lens of the church in Ephesus.

The focus of the metaphor is on the two kinds of vessels in a large house. The vessels are grouped according to value and function:

gold/silver		wood/clay
expensive	vs.	*inexpensive*
honour	vs.	*dishonour*

The wood and clay vessels (cf. 2 Cor. 4.7) are made out of inexpensive materials and would be used for common and menial tasks like holding water or refuse. The gold and silver instruments are made from expensive materials and because of their value they were esteemed and used for public functions, ornamentation and sacred situations. Paul makes a summary statement at the end of v. 20, based on his description of the different vessels, that there are two groups: those vessels appointed for honour and those for dishonour.

The word for 'vessel' is used generally of things (Mt. 12.29) or household items (Lk. 17.31). More specifically it refers to objects used in the temple (Mk 3.27; Heb. 9.21) but it is also used figuratively of people (Rom. 9.23; 2 Cor. 4.7; 1 Thess. 4.4). In fact Luke refers to Paul as a 'chosen vessel' (Acts 9.15). Most scholars understand that Paul is applying this metaphor to different types of people. Some scholars are attracted to Rom. 9.21 since the same categories of honour and dishonour are applied and see a reference to the predestination of believers and non-believers, who are appointed to mercy and wrath respectively. Other scholars look to 1 Cor. 12.12-24 for help, suggesting that there are different kinds of people within the church with different functions. Finally, some read this metaphor through the lens of the Parable of the Weeds (Mt. 13.24) proposing that different types of people will be found in the church and should be left to coexist until the final judgment. All of these interpretations are doubtful.

Drawing on his point in v. 19 (i.e. God knows who are his), Paul is saying that there are different types of people in a church. There are those who are appointed for honour, like Paul and Timothy, whose name ironically means 'honour'. These are 'approved workers' (2 Tim. 2.15), 'servants of the Lord' (2 Tim. 2.24) whose actions and faith make themselves readily identifiable. But there are also those in the church who will experience dishonour (i.e. they are not approved by God), presently and finally at judgment. This group of people covers a broad spectrum. There are those like Hymenaeus and Philetus (2 Tim. 2.17; cf. 3.1-8), who have firmly rejected Christ, his gospel and his kingdom. On the other end of the spectrum, there are also those who are misled by false teaching, who can be redeemed. Then there are those in the middle. Paul is setting the stage for his application in v. 21.

(ii) *Application (2.21)*. While stressing the importance of avoiding false teaching and even some false teachers, Paul does not want to give Timothy the impression that all of these false teachers and those who are deceived by them are beyond redemption. Therefore Paul assures Timothy that they can be cleansed from being a vessel of dishonour but it is conditional on them choosing to become a vessel of honour and heeding Timothy's instructions on teaching and behaviour (2.23, 25).

The text can be read as either 'if people cleanse themselves from *these things*' or '*these people*'. In 1 Cor. 5.7 Paul exhorts the Corinthian church to become a new batch of dough by cleansing itself (note the same verb), which meant the Corinthians staying away from the immoral brother, probably throwing him out of the church. Paul could have this meaning here since he admonishes Timothy earlier to avoid certain false teachers (2 Tim. 2.17) and because keeping away from these false teachers is proving harder than it looks since some still seem to be hanging around even after Paul excommunicated them (note that Hymenaeus appears to be active still in Ephesus; 1 Tim. 1.20). If the reference is to 'these things' then Paul is exhorting these people to reject the false teaching (godless chatter, 2.16; denial of the resurrection, 2.18) and ungodly behaviour associated with this teaching (3.2-5). The reference is probably nebulous and refers to both since bad company corrupts good character and bad teaching corrupts good minds.

Paul's point is that those people in the church, who are vessels of dishonour, can change to become vessels of honour. Clearly it is a process. Paul does not elaborate on this process. He only leaves Timothy and his readers with the general exhortation he gave in 2 Tim. 2.19 that they must turn away from wickedness. Instead of elaborating on the process, Paul chooses to focus on what these people can become, thereby providing them with a hope and a goal to seek after. He offers three statements to show what they will become as vessels of honour: *sanctified*, *useful to the Master* and *prepared for every good work*.

The word that Paul uses for 'sanctified' has two meanings. First, it can mean 'set apart'. Even though the members of the church in Corinth are anything but appropriate in the manner they are living, Paul can still say that they are 'set apart by Christ' (1 Cor. 1.2) as his people since he believes that they have not crossed the line from 'fleshly' to 'natural (i.e. those without the Spirit). Second, it can be used in the sense of 'make holy' or 'sanctify'. This meaning is found with respect to Corinthians whom God has 'washed' and 'justified' (1 Cor. 6.11). The participle in 2 Tim. 2.21 could be translated in the middle voice, 'a vessel who has sanctified himself or herself', or in the passive voice, 'a vessel who has been sanctified by God' (cf. Rom. 15.16). The latter is most logical since the person is 'set apart' by God *after* having changed from being a vessel of dishonour to one of honour. In conclusion the meaning in this this verse is most likely that the person is 'set apart' by God. But in what sense is he or she set apart? This person is set apart in terms of *allegiance to God and his kingdom*. He or she is set apart in terms of *teaching* (i.e. set apart *to* the gospel of Christ and set apart *from* the false teaching). He or she is set apart in terms of *behaviour* (i.e. set apart *to* become like Christ and set apart *from* ungodliness).

Paul describes the person of honour as 'useful to the Master'. 'Master' is used in the secular sense of the *head of a house*, who owns slaves (1 Tim. 6.1, 2; Tit. 2.9; 1 Pet. 2.18). Several other passages refer to 'master' as *sovereign Lord* (Lk. 2.29; Acts 4.24; 2 Pet. 2.1; Jude 4; Rev. 6.10). In this context Paul refers to the master of a large house, which Timothy should understand metaphorically as the sovereign Lord. To be useful a person has to undergo a transformation of character as Onesimus did (cf. Philemon 11) but also one who has submitted himself or herself to the authority of Christ and his teachings (cf. Mt. 10.38). Because the false teachers failed to do this, Paul deems them not useful. In fact, they are quite the opposite; they are destructive (2 Tim. 2.14).

Finally, the vessel of honour is prepared for every good work. The emphasis is on 'preparation' or, in the language of the Gospels, 'discipleship'. Paul's subtext for Timothy is that it might take a great deal of effort to straighten out some of these people, who are vessels of dishonour, in order for them to become effective servants of the Lord. The challenge will be to correct their false teaching with the wholesome gospel (2 Tim. 3.17) and match this with godly living (1 Tim. 4.8; 2 Tim. 3.12). What makes their works 'good' is that they are done in the name of the one 'who is good' (Rom. 2.7), on behalf of others (Acts 9.36) and in obedience to the one who has prepared in advance these works (Eph. 2.10).

This text should not be used to propose that God is limited in whom he can use for his purposes. Clearly God has used dishonourable vessels to accomplish his purposes. Jethro, the Midianite priest and not a Jew, is used to advise Moses, his son-in-law. Cyrus is called 'God's anointed one' (Is. 45.1) and frees Israel. Judas fulfills a significant role though he does repent later (Mt. 27.3). Most of these exceptions are found in the OT with respect to Israel. But in the NT, God typically seeks cleansed/honourable vessels (Rom. 6.13) to do his work and certainly these are the kind he desires within his church.

It is possible that Paul may have in mind the example of Moses when he writes this verse because of its close proximity to the story of Moses in 2 Tim. 3.8. But more to the point, Moses had to cleanse himself of his Egyptian pagan background (Exod. 2.11-25) and separate himself from the false teachers and their lies (Num. 16.3). Through the wilderness experience (Exod. 2), God set him apart, made him into a useful tool and prepared him for a good work, leading the people out of Egypt (Exod. 12.31-42).

Three Commands in Order to Be a Model of Mature Christian Virtue (2.22-26)

In the previous section Paul explained that there are certain people who will remain vessels of dishonour but also those who will be able to change and become vessels of honour within the church. Drawing on this discussion, Paul outlines specific requirements of Timothy in light of the false teachers. He does this by addressing Timothy specifically through three commands (second person singular): flee youthful desires, pursue godly virtues and avoid arguments. Paul does not give these commands because he fears Timothy is a vessel of dishonour or will become one. Rather, he assumes that

Timothy is cleansed and prepared to confront false teachers and exhorts him to continue in this orthodox path. The first two imperatives, then, are more concerned with how Timothy will continue to remain pure amidst the battle with the false teachers. The third command is directed at a particular issue, the false teachers's penchant for arguing. Therefore Paul's concern is geared towards *how* Timothy ministers and confronts the false teachers. First, Timothy must model godly behaviour characteristic of those who call on the name of the Lord (2.22-23) and avoid the devil's traps (2.26). Second, he must maintain a godly attitude in spite of resistance, continually minister with a gentle spirit and have restoration as his goal since the real enemy is Satan of which the false teachers and their followers are only his victims (2.23-26).

Paul's argument changes from specific commands directed to Timothy (2.22-23), to a more general discussion on characteristics and the duties of a 'servant of the Lord' (2.24-26). Paul does this because, although he is focusing on Timothy, he can see some false teachers in his periphery whom he believes can be restored as true servants of the Lord. So to some degree this section is for their sake too.

a. *Flee Youthful Passions (2.22)*
In this verse, Paul exhorts Timothy to be a model of mature Christian virtue. To do this requires turning away *from* ungodliness and turning *towards* godliness along with other orthodox believers. Some insight can be gained from 1 Tim. 6.11 since the same combination of 'flee' and 'pursue' is found there. To 'flee' suggests a decision to reject and separate oneself from something, which is typically dangerous or destructive, and at the same time move towards a place of safety. Sometimes this danger is physical: the angel tells Joseph to take Mary and Jesus away from Bethlehem (because of Herod) and go to Egypt (Mt. 2.13; other examples are Jn 10.12; Lk. 21.21). But this danger can refer to those things which are detrimental to the soul, so Paul exhorts the Corinthians to flee from sexual immorality (1 Cor. 6.18; cf. Gen. 39.12) and idolatry (1 Cor. 10.14) to holiness. This is the meaning here.

Timothy is to flee from the 'youthful desires' though there is some difference of opinion about the meaning of the two words. The word for 'desires' (*epithumias*) can be taken in the positive sense of 'longing'. At the Last Supper, Jesus says he has longed (lit. 'desired with longing') to eat the Passover meal with the disciples. But this word can also to taken in a negative sense of desiring something forbidden or destructive. Examples include sinful desires (Rom. 1.24; 6.12) like deceit (Eph. 4.22) and lust (Col. 3.5), which are contrary to the Spirit's desires (Gal. 5.16, 24). Paul is referring to bad desires, which is consistent with his usage elsewhere in the Pastorals (1 Tim. 6.9; 2 Tim. 3.6; 4.3; Tit. 2.12; 3.3).

Paul qualifies these desires as 'youthful' (*neoterikas*), which is the typical meaning (Jos., *Ant.* 16. 399; *3 Macc.* 4.8). So for some scholars, the command is focused on Timothy's youthfulness (cf. 1 Tim. 4.12) and the folly associated with it. Timothy is to reject these. This interpretation is doubtful since the attraction to youthful desires is not Timothy's problem since Paul believes he is a genuine believer (2 Tim. 1.5). Rather the command is given because of the false teachers and their adherents who are succumbing to their evil desires.

A couple of scholars look for the meaning of this noun in the use of the cognate verb *neoterizein*, which can mean 'to make innovations' or 'to change entirely' (i.e. 'to revolutionize'; *4 Macc.* 3.21) often in the context of violence. According to this position, Paul is requiring Timothy to flee from the desire to create novel innovations of the gospel as the false teachers have done (and who violently defend it). This position should be rejected on the basis that this meaning of the noun is not likely.

The youthful desires are most likely those which are commonly associated with youth and which the false teachers and their followers have embraced. Generally these would include desires born out of immaturity like lack of self-control (cf. 2 Tim. 1.7), favouritism (1 Tim. 5.21), and the desire for arguing and foolish discussions typical of the false teachers (2.23; 4.3). Specifically, Paul may have in mind particular lusts associated with the false teachers: their inappropriate dealings with women (1 Tim. 5.2; 2 Tim. 3.6) and their inordinate attachment to money (1 Tim. 6.9). Timothy is a single man and he must show himself to be above board in these areas.

It is important when fleeing from something that you have something to pursue in the opposite direction (cf. Epictetus, *Discourses* 3.2.1-10). Therefore Paul commands Timothy to pursue a list of godly virtues, which are diametrically opposed to the youthful desires. There are twenty-one occurrences of 'pursue' in the Pauline corpus. It means to seek passionately in a negative manner (i.e. to persecute; Phil. 3.6) or to seek in a positive manner after some virtuous goal (Phil. 3.12, 14) or characteristic (1 Cor. 14.1; 2 Clem. 10.1). The moral philosophers used this term to express how the philosopher would dedicate himself to the moral life (Dio Chrysostom, *Or.* 77.26-28). In the same way, Timothy is to continue to dedicate himself to seeking godliness in the hope that others will be inspired to emulate his lifestyle since the lifestyle of the false teachers has betrayed them (cf. Tit. 1.16) and ensnared them (2 Tim. 2.25-26). Martin Luther captures the intensity of this verb in his German translation by using the verb *jagen* which means 'to hunt or chase' after these virtues.

Lists of vices or sought-after virtues were common among moral philosophers (cf. Epictetus, *Diss.* 3.15.21). In the Pastorals, typically *singular* nouns are used in the virtue lists (1 Tim. 1.5; 4.12; 6.11; 2 Tim. 3.10) and *plural* nouns in the vice lists (1 Tim. 6.4-5; Tit. 3.9). Paul offers a shorter list of virtues here than in 1 Tim. 6.11 although there is a significant overlap ('righteousness', 'faith' and 'love'); only 'peace' is unique to this list. This suggests that the problems when 1 Timothy was written still exist among the false teachers when the second letter is written, with the added issue of lack of peace (i.e. reconciliation). Furthermore these virtues Paul wants Timothy to continue to emulate are those Timothy has seen demonstrated by Paul throughout their time together (2 Tim. 3.12; in particular are love and faith).

Paul lists four virtues. The first virtue mentioned is 'righteousness'. In the Pauline corpus this term often means 'justification' but this meaning is doubtful in this context. More likely it refers generally to 'righteousness' in terms of right actions or specifically to 'justice' in contradistinction to the false teachers's behaviour, which has not been just (cf. 1 Tim. 5). The second virtue is 'faith'. Some see an allusion to 'trustworthiness' in this word, but more probably Paul is using this word as a general term for the content of faith (2 Tim. 3.8; 1 Tim. 2.7) and the act of believing (2 Tim. 3.15; 1 Tim. 1.14). Timothy is to express a genuine faith (2 Tim. 1.5) in the midst of his opponents based upon orthodox belief (1.13). The third virtue is 'love', which entails practical demonstrations (cf. 1 Tim. 2.13) inspired by Christ (2 Tim. 1.13) and not necessarily the feeling. Displays of love (especially in how Timothy deals with the false teachers) will distinguish Timothy from the false teachers who are characterized by fighting and self-centeredness. The fourth virtue is 'peace' in the sense of reconciliation. The penchant of the false teachers for fighting and arguing (2 Tim. 2.23) will require Timothy to be an instrument of peace in order to get them to listen and eventually lead them to repentance. The characteristic of peace is related to the ability to endure suffering (2.24) in the sense that the person who is adept at enduring suffering will be able to keep himself in a state of peace and therefore will be able to bring others back into a state of peace.

It is possible to read the text as 'pursue...peace with those who call upon the Lord' (cf. Heb. 12.14 where seeing God is connected with peace among believers). This would suggest that there is tension between Timothy and those other members in the Ephesian church but nothing in the letter suggests this. Even though syntactically this option is attractive since peace is juxtaposed with this phrase, a more probable reading is 'pursue, with those who call upon the Lord, righteousness...peace'. Paul includes this phrase for two reasons. First, he is reassuring Timothy that what he is asking of Timothy is necessary and asked of all God's people. Second, he is assuring Timothy that he is not alone in this pursuit and that he needs this fellowship.

The phrase 'those who call upon the Lord' has an OT background (Joel 2.32) which Paul has used elsewhere (Rom. 10.12-13; 1 Cor. 1.2) and applies to Jesus. There are two variant readings of this phrase. The first variant, 'all those who call...', expands the scope of believers to the universal church but it is poorly attested (Coptic, Chrysostom). The second variant, 'with all those who love the Lord', which is attested only by Codex Alexandrinus, is probably an intentional change based on Christ's second commandment (Mt. 22.37). Both should be rejected but the former underscores the intention of the phrase.

Paul adds that those who call on the Lord must do so from a pure heart (cf. 2 Tim. 1.3). A pure heart has been cleansed and has gone through the process of being purified from being a vessel of dishonour to becoming a vessel of honour (note that the cognate verb is used in 2 Tim. 2.21). This type of heart has unadulterated motives and is contrary to the false teachers's hearts which have been tainted by sin and the world (e.g. their use of money; 1 Tim. 6.6-10).

b. *Avoid Fruitless Arguments (2.23-26)*
Paul now gives his third command on how to be a model of mature Christian virtue. This command, like the one in v. 22a ('flee'), requires movement from something dangerous and detrimental to something virtuous for Timothy personally and the church corporately. This command is rooted in the greater context of being a 'servant of the Lord' which has its own requirements and characteristics (2.24-25a). The goal of this command is restoration and deliverance from the Devil's traps to which the false teachers and their adherents have succumbed.

Paul alerts Timothy to the danger of falling into the same trap as the false teachers so he exhorts him to 'avoid' these arguments. It appears that the problem of the false teachers arguing has continued since the writing of 1 Timothy, where Paul gave a similar command (1 Tim. 4.7; cf. 1 Tim. 5.11). Though addressed to Timothy, the warning is probably more for the sake of the false teachers and may have some relation to a future disciplinary action, if necessary (note that the same verb is used in Tit. 3.10). Paul gives two reasons why arguments are to be avoided: they are foolish and uninstructed, and they lead to fights not transformation.

There are two possible meanings for the word for 'argument' (*zētēsis*). It can mean 'investigation' (Acts 25.20: Festus was at a loss how to make an investigation concerning the charges against Paul) and derivatively 'speculation' which is consistent with the meaning of the cognate, *ekzētēsis*, used in 1 Tim. 1.4. It can also mean 'controversy' (Acts 15.2, 7: the controversy between Paul and some Jews over the issue of circumcision). The two meanings probably merge with the connotation of 'controversial speculation'.

The false teachers's arguments are foolish because they are based on myths, endless genealogies, word-battles and misinterpretations of the Law (1 Tim. 1.4, 7; 6.4; Tit. 3.9). These arguments are 'uninstructed' (a word frequently used in Proverbs and Sirach to refer to those who are uninstructed or uneducated: Prov. 8.5; 15.14; Sir. 51.23) because the false teachers, who have created them, are uninstructed and poorly informed teachers of the Law (1 Tim. 1.7).

The problem with these arguments is that they literally 'give birth' (cf. 1 Cor. 4.15; Philemon 10) to fights. Clearly, Paul is willing to confront an issue or person and not back down (Gal. 2.11-14; 2 Tim. 4.7). But he does so only when the issue warrants it and he perceives that there will be a positive outcome. Paul is asking Timothy to walk the fine line of confronting the false teachers but not get sucked into their fruitless speculative arguments since they only breed more arguments.

Paul expands on the last command (not to argue) insisting that Timothy not enter into the fray because it is not consistent with the behaviour of a servant of the Lord. The metaphor has changed from a vessel used in a house (2.20) to a slave serving in a house. Paul refers to himself as a *slave of God* (Tit. 1.1) and a *slave of Christ* (Rom. 1.1; Gal. 1.10; Phil. 1.1). For Paul, to be a slave of Christ (or Lord in this case) was a term of honour, in direct contrast to the secular culture of shame associated with being a slave, because Jesus was a slave (Phil. 2.6-11).

Most scholars suggest the background for 'servant of the Lord' comes from the Isaian servant songs (Isa. 42.1-9; 49.1-7; 50.4-9; 52.13–53.12). In support of this suggestion is Paul's description of Jesus as a servant (Phil. 2.7). In this context the allusion to the Isaian servant-of-the-Lord songs is made to draw attention to the character of this servant who does not retaliate with force or speech (Isa. 42.2-3; 50.6; 53.7) not Jesus per se. Though these songs find their ultimate fulfillment in Jesus Christ, different NT writers would apply them to others. Paul alludes to these songs and applies them to himself (Gal. 1.15 and Isa. 49.1; Eph. 6.17 and Is. 49.3). Luke directly applies Isa. 49.6 to Paul in Acts 13.47.

'Servant of the Lord' is found in the LXX referring specifically to leaders like Moses (2 Kgs 18.12), Joshua (Josh. 24.29; Judg. 2.8), David (Ps. 36.1) and generally to a group of the Lord's servants (2 Kgs 9.7; Pss. 134.1; 135.1). There are three good reasons why Paul may have Moses in mind when he refers to the servant of the Lord. First, the term 'servant of the Lord' is used in the LXX to describe Moses (2 Kgs 18.12). Second, the context that precedes (see 2.19, the confrontation of Korah; Num. 16.5) and follows this verse (see 3.8, the confrontation of Jannes and Jambres; Exod. 7.11, 22) is drawn from the life of Moses. Third, Moses was considered a servant of the Lord in the house elsewhere in the NT (Heb. 3.6). Fourth, Moses demonstrates a person who was cleansed and transformed into a vessel of honour. More importantly for this context is that Moses did not quarrel with his opponents. When he got angry with the people he took this anger before God (Num. 16.15). Yet when he was with the people he was gentle, endured wrong, admonished and interceded for them (Num. 16.4).

Traditionally 2 Tim. 2.24 is translated 'it is necessary that the servant of the Lord *not* fight', underlining the necessity that the servant not quarrel. But the Greek is better translated 'it is *not* necessary for the servant of the Lord to fight'. The point is that the false teachers believe being able to argue and fight over words (2 Tim. 2.14) is an admirable quality and necessary for a leader, so much so that they are obsessed (lit. 'sick') with this desire (1 Tim. 6.4). Paul is saying that this type of fighting is not a virtue to be associated with the Lord's servants but is in fact quite the opposite: the Lord's servants should be gentle. As he said earlier to Timothy, as a servant of the Lord, he will have to enter the fray (1 Tim. 1.18), but how he conducts himself is important since people will be watching him (cf. 1 Tim. 3.7).

Paul lists four characteristics that should be associated with a servant of the Lord in place of fighting. The goal of these virtues is redemptive, to woo Timothy's opponents away from Satan's snare to Christ, through the truth and repentance. Two of the four attributes are associated with requirements for bishops (1 Tim. 3.2).

The first characteristic is gentleness. Paul's directive is extensive ('gentle to all'), to guard against the human tendency to exclude those we do not like and wish to avoid (cf. Eph. 4.15). Everyone deserves the same respect (cf. Mt. 5.43-46), even the argumentative ones. 1 and 2 Timothy have a definite thread running through them underscoring the need for believers to be gentle or peaceful in their demeanour (1 Tim. 2.2, 11-12; 2 Tim. 2.22). There is a variant reading in this text which has 'infant' (*nēpion*) instead of 'gentle' (*ēpion*), a variant just like the one in 1 Thess. 2.7. This reading would be using the infant as a metaphor for the manner by which Timothy should approach the false teachers (i.e. like a harmless infant). The lack of reliable manuscripts to support this variant makes this reading highly unlikely.

The second trait of a servant of the Lord is the ability to teach, a quality expected of an overseer (1 Tim. 3.2). Paul is reiterating for Timothy this need (2 Tim. 2.15) because the false teachers need an example of someone who can clearly handle Scripture but more importantly so that through his teaching they might hear the truth and repent. Paul, following the model of Jesus (1 Cor. 11.1), the Rabbi (Mt. 23.8-10), and in the same spirit (Mt. 28.20), wants Timothy to teach well.

The third feature of the Lord's servant is the ability to endure wrong—a rare word in Greek writing, found only here. It means to endure wrong patiently without resentment and to keeps one's composure, just as Jesus did on the cross (Mk 15.29-30). This characteristic is used as a test of the integrity of a righteous person (Wis. 2.19; Mt. 5.12). For Timothy it means to put up patiently with the foolish arguments and taunts of the false teachers, combining grief and anger because of their hard hearts (cf. Mk 3.5) and keeping the hope in front of him that they might repent.

The fourth attribute of a servant of the Lord is the capacity of instructing or correcting with gentleness. There is some confusion over the participle used (*paideuonta*), whether it means 'to instruct/educate' (Acts 7.22) or 'to correct/discipline' (Lk. 23.16) since both meanings are associated with the word. Though this word can have these clear distinct meanings (i.e. Moses is educated in Egypt and Jesus is punished physically by Pilate respectively) quite often the meanings are blurred and the idea is found somewhere in the middle but without using physical force (1 Cor. 11.32). Thus Paul is telling Timothy that he must try to *correct* their false teaching (1 Tim. 1.4) and *instruct* them in the truth (note that their arguments are 'uninstructed', 2 Tim. 2.23) but keeping in mind that he, like Paul, may have to take firmer *disciplinary* action and remove some false teachers and leave it to God to continue the disciplining process (note that the same verb is used in 1 Tim. 1.20; cf. 1 Cor. 5.6). This discipline is to be done with a spirit of gentleness (cf. 1 Cor. 4.21), which is considered one of the fruits of the Spirit (Gal. 5.23), and a characteristic all believers should express (Col. 3.12). Intrinsic to this word is the idea of humility, recognizing that all are sinners who can get caught in sin's web (cf. Gal. 6.1) and thus the need for being gentle with oneself and others as sin is being cast off (Js 1.21). Therefore, Timothy is to share the truth with gentleness (cf. 1 Pet. 3.15-16) in the hope of some being redeemed.

The Greek is not clear about the identity of those being reproved. This text could be read as 'those who oppose Timothy' (middle voice of *antidiathemenous*) referring *specifically* to the false teachers. But it could also be translated as 'those who are being opposed' (passive voice of *antidiathemenous*) corresponding to those who are being taken in by the false teachers. It is probably best to take the participle in the middle voice but referring *generally* to all those who oppose Timothy which includes the false teachers and those who have been duped by their teaching.

The first goal of Timothy's reproof is to lead his opponents to repentance and to accept God's truth (note that the Greek suggests that this a process: 'coming or leading to a knowledge of the truth'). The phrase 'come to a knowledge of the truth' could be restated possibly as 'be saved' (cf. 1 Tim. 2.4; 4.3). Repentance plus coming to knowledge of the truth is equal to conversion. Paul understands repentance as a 'gift' ('lest he give to them'; cf. Rom. 2.4) which consists in turning away from their false teaching (and Satan whom they might not be aware is behind it; 1 Tim. 4.1-2; cf. 1 Jn 3.8) and turning to faith in God and his truth. To do otherwise is to be in danger of denying God and therefore being denied by God (2 Tim. 2.12). The false teachers have built their lives on a crumbling foundation of myths, endless genealogies, and absence of the resurrection, which they have falsely called truth (1 Tim. 6.20). Poor doctrine breeds poor teaching which breeds poor lifestyles and ultimately separation from God.

The second goal of Timothy's reproof is deliverance from the Devil's bondage (lit. 'become sober to the devil's trap'). Just as overseers falling into reproach (1 Tim. 3.7) and those seeking to be rich (1 Tim. 6.9) fall into a trap, likewise those who have embraced false teaching have fallen into the Devil's trap. This metaphor of a 'trap' is expanded in the latter half of the verse: 'those who have been captured alive by him to do the will of that one'. It is possible, though syntactically unlikely, to read this clause as God who has captured these wayward people to do his will or the servant of the Lord who has captured them to do God's will. More likely it refers to the Devil who has captured these opponents through the deception of his teaching to do his will. Metaphorically, these opponents are drunk, unclear in their thinking, and unable to discern what is the truth. Through Timothy's teaching, they may come to their senses and become spiritually sober so that they can see the trap laid for them by the Devil. Elsewhere the word for 'trap' is used in eschatological contexts, stressing the suddenness of judgment and the need for living righteously (Lk. 21.34-35) and Israel's failure to see the truth of God's plan (Rom. 11.9). Given that the following context deals with eschatological realities, it is likely that Paul is emphasizing God's desire for 'all people to be saved and come to a knowledge of the truth' (1 Tim. 2.4) regardless of how far they may have deviated from the truth.

Denunciation of the False Teachers (3.1-9)

a. *Introduction*

This section comprises the second of the three sections dedicated to Paul's concern about the false teachers. In the previous section (2.14-26) Paul gave specific commands to Timothy with respect to the false teachers. In the subsequent section (3.10-17) Paul will appeal to Timothy to be committed to him and the gospel in spite of inevitable trials, which is in direct contrast to the false teachers's pseudo-gospel. But in the middle segment (3.1-9) Paul has a threefold purpose. First, he seeks to describe, indict and denounce the false teachers by examining their character in light of eschatological realities and the effects of their ministry. Second, Paul attempts to temper his statement in 2.24, 'be gentle to all', lest Timothy misunderstand this, causing him to be abused by the false teachers (note the high frequency of terms of abuse in the vice list in 3.2-4). Dealing with the false teachers is tricky business. On the one hand Paul implores staying away from the false teachers (2.19) but on the other hand he calls for gentleness, patience and clear teaching to restore them (2.25). Now Paul returns with a word of caution, calling Timothy to avoid (3.5) those false teachers who are so hard-hearted that there is no chance of their repentance (e.g. Hymenaeus and Alexander, 1 Tim. 1.20) apart from a miracle of divine intervention. Timothy must face the battle in Ephesus with the Spirit of love but also power (1.7). Sometimes a gentle answer does not turn away wrath (cf. Prov. 15.1). So as stated in the commands in Mt. 7.6 and 10.14, Timothy may have to avoid sharing the gospel with some and even avoid them altogether. Third, drawing on the Exodus 7 account, Paul writes forewarning Timothy to expect resistance. These false teachers will not go down quietly or without a fight. The fact that Hymenaeus is still active (2.17) is proof.

The structure of the argument is chiastic.

Character of the False Teachers: Vice List	3.1-5a
Command: Avoid False Teachers	3.5b
Character of the False Teachers: Two Examples	3.6-9

The focal point of the argument is on the command 'to avoid' in 3.5b. On either side of this imperative the false teachers are described. The vice list of 3.1-5a describes the false teachers in terms of depraved people of the Last Days. In 3.6-9 their character is described through the example of their dealings with certain women and the OT example of Jannes and Jambres, Pharaoh's magicians during the time of Moses, who like the false teachers were deceitful charlatans. Structurally these two descriptions of the false teachers provide the framework and they serve as brackets around the main concern of the passage, that Timothy avoid these people as necessary.

b. *Last Days (3.1)*
Paul begins this segment with a strong command, literally 'this know'. 'This' is placed in the emphatic position and refers to what follows, 'in [the] Last Days there will be fierce times'. 'Know' is in the singular and is addressed to Timothy. There is a variant plural reading which would be addressing the Ephesians at large but this reading should be rejected on the grounds of poor manuscript support and because all the preceding imperatives are in the singular (2.14, 15, 16, 19, 22, 23).

When Paul tells Timothy 'know this' it does not mean he is imparting new information to Timothy concerning the last days. Rather, Paul wants Timothy to keep the information concerning the character of people of the last days and the false teachers in the forefront of his mind. Paul lays out this information in order to set the context of ministry for Timothy lest he think the existence of the false teachers is unusual or unexpected. On the contrary their existence is proof of the last days.

The concept of the 'last days' originates from the Jewish apocalyptic tradition. It was believed that the end would be preceded by an increase in immorality and evil after which time the Messiah would come and establish his kingdom reign (Dan. 12.1; 1 En. 80.2-8; 100.1-13). Jesus accepted this tradition but adapted it by extending the length of the last days as the time between his two comings (Mk 13.24-27). Similarly, the early Church embraced the extended last days interpretation as the time between the two parousias of Christ. Luke understands the phenomenon of Pentecost through the Joel 2.28 prophecy as a sign of the last days. The author of Hebrews, in the same way, considers Jesus proclaiming his message as taking place during the last days (Heb. 1.2). Finally, James bemoans that the people have stored up treasures during the last days (Js 5.3). In addition, the early church associated the last days with the prevalence of immorality (1 Cor. 7.26; 2 Pet. 3.3). There is no article attached with 'last days' (lit. 'in last days') which is probably intentional in order to emphasize the character of the days which are subsequently described as evil.

Timothy is to keep in mind that 'evil times *will be present* in the last days'. The future tense of the verb *enistēmi* is not referring to some future time period, like the tribulation, as some suggest. Rather the future tense points to what can be expected in the last days in which they presently live. The use of the present tense to describe the false teachers's present actions (3.5, 6, 8) supports this interpretation.

Paul uses a rare adjective, *chalepoi* (twice in the NT), to describe these times in the last days. This word can mean 'difficult' and it is used to describe 'difficult things to do' (Sir. 3.21) or 'difficult consequences for unrighteous living' (Wis. 3.19). In other contexts it has the meaning of 'harshness' or 'fierceness'; the 'fierceness of the argument' (2 Macc. 4.4) or the 'fierceness of the demonized men of Gadarenes prevented people from passing by' (Mt. 8.28). Finally it can take the meaning of 'evil' as in 'the works of the wicked angel are evil' (Herm., *Man.* 6.2.10) or the 'change from an evil disposition to a good disposition' (M.Pol. 11.1) or 'the beginning of all evil things is the love of money' (Polycarp, *Phil.* 4.1).

It is not exactly clear what 'difficult times' Paul is describing. In light of the context concerning the servant of the Lord, Paul could be suggesting that there will be particularly 'difficult times' ahead for Timothy and others like him during the last days which are considered evil (Eph. 5.16). The subsequent vice list seems to stress the violent nature and actions of these people of the last days which points to the meaning of 'fierce times'. The ferocity could stem from the fact that Satan lies behind their beliefs and behaviour. Paul is stressing the particular fierceness and evil of the last days caused by these false teachers during this time and people like them in the future. The fierceness of these days will result in difficult times for servants of the Lord like Timothy and all those who call on the name of the Lord.

c. *An Introduction to Vice Lists*
It is beyond the scope of this section to explain fully vice lists as a literary form. But I will try to provide a general framework for understanding them as they pertain to the vice lists in the Pastorals and specifically 2 Tim. 3.2-4. Most scholars agree that a vice list is a literary form. What is less

certain for them is its structure and content. Structurally, vice lists are difficult to recognize since they do not have any identifiable introductory or concluding clause or phrase. Although no structurally identifiable phrase or clause exists, vice lists do begin with a particular word or idea, which is then expanded and further defined by a list of words. Thus in Tit. 3.3 the pre-conversion state of people is described through the vice list. Similarly in 1 Tim. 1.9, Paul lists the people for whom the Law is given. The vice list in 2 Tim. 3.2-4 is given to describe the people of the Last Days.

A vice list is comprised of nouns, substantival adjectives or participles. The vice list of 2 Tim. 3.2-4 has all three ('lovers of self [adjective]…boasters [noun]…having a form of godliness [participle]'). It is not certain how many words are needed to make a list though probably four or more is a typical length.

The content of vice lists varies depending on the topic the list is describing. There is no *Urkatalog* from which these lists are drawn. Paul draws upon the Decalogue for some of the content of the vice list in 1 Tim. 1.9-10. The arrangement of the list is dependent on the creativity of the author who composed it though authors draw upon rhetorical categories (e.g. assonance, alliteration, couplets, chiasms).

Different attempts exist to find the background of the vice list in 2 Tim. 3.2-4 but most are unconvincing. Parallels can certainly be found with material in other vice lists. The terms 'lovers of self' and 'lovers of god' are found in Philo (*Fug.* 81) and similarly 'lovers of pleasure' is found in *Agr.* 83. The vice list of Rom. 1.28-31 shares four terms with this list. But there is not enough overlap with either source to account for the list's background. More likely Paul has created his own vice list drawing on the truth of statements found in apocalyptic texts which stress the wickedness of humankind in the last days (*T. Iss.* 6.1-2; Mt. 28.12). The content of the material is fashioned to expose the character of the false teachers. Some items on the list portray the general human condition (e.g. love of money), nevertheless these items are included too because they depict specific characteristics of the false teachers which they may share in a heightened form (e.g. lovers of money, 1 Tim. 6.5).

The structure of the list is unique. Though attempts have been made to group the material in couplets, it is more probable that Paul groups the material on the basis of types of sin and uses alliteration to help group the material. There are nineteen vices listed. The middle vice, 'irreconcilable', is the focus of the list since it is the main reason for the command in 3.5, 'avoid these men'. These men will not change and therefore Timothy is to avoid them and not cast his pearls before swine (Mt. 7.6). The main part of the vice list is bracketed by two alliterative couplets (based on 'love') on either end that point to the major problem with the false teachers: they love themselves and not God. The final vice sums up the character of the false teachers: they profess a form of religion based on appearances and faulty theology but without any internal transformation.

The following figure is an outline of the structure of the vice list:

Perspective: Self-Love
    Love of self
    Love of money
        Speaking sins
            boasting
            arrogance
            abusive
        Behavioural sins
            disobedience to parents
            ungrateful
            unholy
            unloving
            irreconcilable
            abusive
            without self control
            untamed (brutal)
            not lovers of good
            traitors
            reckless
            proud
Perspective: God-Love
    Love of pleasure
    Love of God
Concluding Vice: Powerless religion

Figure 7. *Vice List in 2 Tim. 3.3-5*

d. *Character of the False Teachers (3.2-5a)*
This vice list describes the character of people in the Last Days. Paul's depiction is consistent with the gospel tradition (Mt. 24.10-13) that describes people of the Last Days primarily in terms of 'lovelessness' in which 'self-love' has replaced 'love of God'. The false teachers are the fulfillment and proof of the Last Days. Their preoccupation with themselves contradicts Jesus' greatest commandment (Mt. 22.37-38) and precludes following his second command (Mt. 22.39). It is the character of the false teachers that makes the 'Last Days' so difficult for the servant of the Lord to minister and to endure (Mt. 24.13).

(i) *Lovers of Self and Money.* These two vices are alliterative because they both have the same prefix 'love' (in Greek *phil*). Humankind's preoccupation with self-interest and satisfaction of self with material goods is in contradistinction with loving God. This allegiance to self results in a love of money (cf. the Pharisees in Lk. 16.14) and pleasure (see 2 Tim. 3.4), and also a lack of passion (lit. *love*) for doing good (3.3). Paul in his first correspondence outlined the destructive nature of having an inordinate attachment to money. Love of money is a primary problem among the false teachers. This lust may in part have been fueled by the affluence of Ephesus that surrounded them. They have used their religion for financial gain (1 Tim. 6.5b), which has resulted in many trials even to the point of abandoning their faith (1 Tim. 6.10). The author of *4 Macc.* 1.26 suggests that reason can overcome love of money but Paul suggests true religion (i.e. trust in Christ) with contentment as the solution. But before the false teachers can get there they need to repent first.

(ii) *Speaking Sins*. Boasting is found in the vice list of Rom. 1.30. The author of James considers the sin of boasting as evil (Js 4.16) and the author of the first Johannine epistle proposes that boasting comes not from the Father but from the 'world' (1 Jn 2.16).

Arrogance is also found in the vice list of Rom. 1.30. This is a word frequently found in the Psalms to describe those who speak in a manner of exaggerated self-importance. This vice may reflect the false teachers's over-confidence as teachers of the Law (1 Tim. 1.7). Boasting and arrogance reflect a lack of humility (1 Clem. 2.1) and both are abhorred by God (Ps. 119.21). These people will be humbled (Mt. 23.12) since boasting and arrogance are contrary to the manner in which Jesus lived (cf. 1 Clem. 16.2).

The next vice can mean either 'blasphemers', in the sense of speaking a message contrary to the gospel or Law (Acts 6.11), or 'slanderers/abusers', in the sense of speaking in a derogatory fashion towards others (cf. 2 Pet. 2.11). Paul identifies himself with this term in 1 Tim. 1.13 when he was a non-believer. Both meanings fit the false teachers since they malign the gospel (1 Tim. 1.3-5, 11; 2 Tim. 2.16-18) and they are abusive towards others (2 Tim. 2.24). It is likely Paul has primarily the former in mind since he refers specifically to slander later in the list of vices.

(iii) *Behavioural Sins*. The next five vices begin with the Greek letter alpha. The first sin, 'disobedience to parents', is found in the Rom. 1.28-31 vice list (cf. Eph. 6.1). Disobedience, as a character flaw, is found elsewhere in the Pastorals (Tit. 1.16; 3.3) but here it is focused on disobedience to parents. Paul may have in mind the disobedient son of Deut. 21.18 (note that the same word is used) suggesting that some of these false teachers have been disobedient to their parents and therefore he might have in mind those false teachers who were elders in the church who have gone astray (Acts 20.30). Similarly this vice may have reference to those who have not provided for their parents in their old age (1 Tim. 5.8).

Ungratefulness, which can lead to hopelessness (Wis. 16.29), can pertain to a lack of gratitude for things or people but ultimately God. Elsewhere Paul has addressed the false teachers's lack of gratitude for things created by God, including food and marriage, from which they have abstained. Similarly they have been ungrateful for their parents and the breadth of believers choosing favourites instead (1 Tim. 5.1ff.). This attitude is in direct contrast to what is expected of all believers, 'to give thanks for all people' (Eph. 5.20). In both cases, their theology expresses ingratitude to God.

The word 'unholiness' is used with respect to unholy acts (evil rituals, Wis. 12.4; lewd acts, Ezek. 22.9; unholy tortures, 1 Clem. 6.2) or unholy people, presumably who do unholy acts (2 Macc. 7.34; 8.32; *3 Macc.* 2.2; 1 Tim. 1.9). For the false teachers this may pertain to the unholy manner in which they had been treating women (1 Tim. 5.2). Their unholy external actions (cf. 1 Tim. 2.8, lifting up *holy* hands) reflect the inner impurity of their souls.

The word *astorgos* means to lack all natural affection basic to humankind. Examples of this type of natural love include the affection between a wife and a husband (1 Clem. 1.3) or between parent and child (*4 Macc.* 14.13-14). Interestingly Paul includes *astorgos* in Rom. 1.31 as an example of those men and women who were giving up the intrinsic love found within humankind for the opposite sex in order to pursue homosexual relationships. This lack of love probably accounts for the disobedience of parents mentioned above and their lack of prudence in relationships.

The next vice literally translated is 'without libation'. The imagery is that of a drink offering or libation being poured out at the conclusion of a treaty or at the creation of a covenant (Gen. 35.14). In essence the false teachers refuse to be in a covenant relationship with the orthodox church of Ephesus that Timothy leads and they refuse to be reconciled to the people within it. This is the main reason Timothy is to avoid them (3.5) because they are unwilling to change and therefore will only deplete Timothy's emotional energy when he deals with them. They are parasites.

The next vice, *diabolos*, does not begin with alpha like the five vices which preceded it and the three vices which follow it. Its root meaning is 'slanderous' from the cognate verb, *diaballō*, which means 'to bring charges against someone with evil or unrighteous intent' (Lk. 16.1). The majority of the NT instances are in the substantival form denoting the Devil (1 Tim. 3.6, 7; 2 Tim. 2.26) but here the emphasis is on the act of slandering (1 Tim. 3.11; Tit. 2.3) by the false teachers. Their slander probably comes in the form of blasphemous teaching (1 Tim. 1.20) and because they have fallen into the trap of the Devil (1 Tim. 3.7; 2 Tim. 2.26) they have become like him making backbiting evil attacks on others behind their backs (1 Tim. 2.8).

The next three vices begin with the letter alpha. Lack of self-control heads this section. It is a NT hapax legomenon and is found only once in the LXX (Prov. 27.20b, a text not in the MT). In this text it refers to the lack of control of one's speech, which is certainly an issue for the false teachers. This word can take on the nuance of 'dissolute', one who cannot control his or her sexual temptation, which also fits the false teachers's profile. Both aspects of this vice stand out against the virtue of self-control required of overseers (1 Tim. 3.2; Tit. 1.8). Literally this vice means 'untamed' and shows the extent to which they have lost control. It is a word which is typically associated with animals (Epict., *Discourse* 1.3.7; Dio Chrysostom, *Or.* 12.51). Metaphorically they have become like animals, savage-like in their character in the way they deal with others (cf. *Ep. Arist.* 289). The predatory manner in which they go after women (3.6) and use them may be in mind.

'Not lovers of good', *aphilagathos*, is found only here in the NT and therefore may be a word created by Paul though a similar word, *aphilagathia*, is found in Oxyrhynchus Papyrus 33, 2, 11, 13 (second century AD). This vice is the opposite of what overseers need (Tit. 1.8). It probably has to do with the lack of desire for what is good in terms of thought, word and deed.

Verse 4 begins with two vices with the alliteration '*pro*'. The first vice (*prodotai*) of the two is 'traitor' or 'betrayer'. Luke is the only author to use this word elsewhere in the NT and this may be further proof for Luke's hand in helping to write this letter. He uses this word to describe Judas in the list of disciples (Lk. 6.16) and the Jewish leaders who betrayed Jesus unto crucifixion (Acts 7.52). Paul may have particular false teachers in mind like Alexander who probably betrayed Paul to the authorities in Troas (1 Tim. 1.20; 2 Tim. 4.14). It could also refer more generally to those who are traitors in the church (cf. Hermas, *Sim.* 6.4; 19.1) and specifically to those who abandoned Paul (Demas in 2 Tim. 4.10; those who deserted him at his trial in 2 Tim. 4.16).

The second of the two vices which begin with '*pro*' in 3.4 is also only found elsewhere in Luke. Luke includes the same word in Acts 19.36 when the city clerk addresses the Ephesians who have dragged Paul's travelling companions before him with the intention of acting 'rashly/recklessly' by killing them. The author of Proverbs describes fools as reckless in their speech leading to their ruin and self-destruction (Prov. 10.14; 13.3; cf. Sir. 9.18) because of their lack of self-control. It is probably this latter idea Paul has in mind reflecting the rash manner in which the false teachers have conducted themselves in their speech (2 Tim. 2.16-18) though it could refer to their abusive actions since Luke describes them as 'savage wolves…who drag away disciples unto themselves' (Acts 20.29-30).

People of the Last Days will be conceited. Paul describes these people with a substantival participle instead of a noun or adjective. The verb behind the participle is not found anywhere else in the NT (or LXX, Pseudepigrapha or Apostolic Fathers) except the Pastorals. Overseers are not to be 'conceited' lest they fall into the trap of the Devil because of their immaturity in the faith (1 Tim. 3.6). Paul depicts the false teachers as 'conceited understanding nothing' (1 Tim. 6.4). As this example shows, there is a sense with this word that one's conceit has made one deluded, even blinded to one's folly (cf. Polybius, *Hist.* 3.81.1; Philo, *Conf. Ling.* 106; Dio Chrysostom, *Or.* 6.21) which may explain why they think they have godliness (see the final vice in 3.5a). This vice is like the first, a form of self-love, and provides a natural segue into the next vice, love of pleasure more than love of God.

Frequently philosophers would challenge their followers to resist the love of pleasure (Epictetus, *Discourses* 1.9.19-21; Plutarch, *Mor.* 6b). Sages would exhort similarly in OT wisdom literature (Prov. 21.17; Eccl. 7.4) though the same word is not used. Occasionally philosophers exhorted love of god (Philo, *Agr.* 88; Aristotle, *Rhet.* 2.17.6) but typically their call was to pursue a love of wisdom. In wisdom literature the call is to seek wisdom (Prov. 4.1-8) and fear God (Prov. 1.7). Loving God is an important theme in Deuteronomy (Deut. 6.5; 11.1, 13, 22; 19.9; 30.16, 20). Paul's contrast at the end of v. 4 differs from the contemporary philosophers since he contrasts love of pleasure and love of God. The former is a vice based on self-love which is the vice which began this list (3.2) and endemic to the false teachers.

(iv) *Concluding Vice: Powerless Religion.* The final and concluding vice, 'having a form of godliness but denying its power', sums up the false teachers. There are two ways in which 'form of godliness' can be understood based on the twofold meaning of the word for form, *morphōsis*: 'embodiment' ('the Law is the embodiment of knowledge and truth', Rom. 2.20) or 'appearance' ('certain ones who have the appearance of godliness', Philo, *De Plantatione* 70). First, the vice may point to the arrogant claim of the false teachers as being the embodiment of godliness but the falsehood of this claim is evident in the powerlessness of the manner in which they live their lives. Second, the vice could refer to the deceptive manner in which the false teachers are living, namely giving the appearance of being godly but inwardly they are in rejection of the orthodox healthy teaching of the gospel (1 Tim. 3.14-16). It is hard to imagine, given this vice list, that from Paul's perspective these false teachers had an appearance of godliness. Therefore it is likely that Paul has in mind particular actions like their practice of asceticism (e.g. prohibition of marriage, abstinence from certain foods, 1 Tim. 4.3) and their predilection for discussions though not based on godliness (1 Tim. 6.4). They have confused the gospel with 'being religious' instead of understanding it as something powerful to save sinners (1 Tim. 1.15). They probably resemble those mentioned in Tit. 1.16 who 'confess to know God but deny [him] by their works' or those in Rom. 2.17-24 who considered themselves teachers yet were guilty of blatant sins. The thin veneer of the false teachers's religiosity is not thick enough to cover up their true identity; they are wolves in sheep's clothing (cf. Mt. 7.21).

e. *Command: Avoid False Teachers (3.5b)*
In 3.6-9 Paul expands the preceding vice list which demonstrates the evil character of certain individuals in Ephesus but in particular certain false teachers. This list shows us that in matters of faith and life both doctrine and lifestyle matter. Certainly these people had knowledge but it did not translate into transformed character or love for others (cf. 1 Cor. 8.1). In fact their knowledge, because it was skewed, actually led to aberrant behaviour. This cycle of deception has now gotten to the point that they are almost past redemption (cf. Rom. 1.21-28; 2 Thess. 2.9-12). For this reason Paul exhorts Timothy to avoid these people. Paul's advice corresponds to the advice of the author of Proverbs: 'Do not set foot on the path of the wicked or walk in the way of evildoers. Avoid it, do not travel on it; turn from it and go on your way' (Prov. 4.14-15). Paul's command parallels the command in 2 Tim. 2.19.

f. *Character of the False Teachers: Two Examples (3.6-9)*
Paul uses the vice list to expose the character of the false teachers who exemplify the character of people who belong to the Last Days. In order to emphasize the need to avoid these people, Paul describes the character of the false teachers again through two examples. First, Paul depicts their selfish, ruthless, deceptive nature through the real present situation in which the false teachers were preying upon vulnerable women for their own ends (3.6-7). Second, he rehearses the OT example of two magicians Moses faced before the Exodus of Israel. These men opposed Moses's leadership, his message and the faith. The false teachers are of the same ilk and therefore Timothy is to avoid such people.

(i) *Example #1: Deceptive Dealings with Certain Women (3.6-7)*. Literally 3.6 begins 'from these [types of characteristics of Last Day people] there will be those who...'. Through this structure, Paul makes clear what he has assumed throughout 3.1-5, that the false teachers are a specific group who exemplify the character of people in the Last Days and that these 'evil days' are upon Timothy and the Ephesian Christians. The insidious character of the false teachers is demonstrated through a present-day situation in which the false teachers are exploiting women, preying on their vulnerability and weakness. Though no particular vice is mentioned, this example illustrates various vices on the list (e.g. abusive, savage), which combine to demonstrate their unholy deceitful nature. These men have been 'creeping into women's houses'. The verb *endunō* is translated 'to slip in' (Aelian,

Var. hist. 4.22), sometimes stealthily ('slipping into her breasts', Antigonus, *Hist. mir.* 172) or even figuratively 'slipping into oneself' (Barn. 4.10). But in this context it may suggest 'creeping in deceptively' (possibly in the same way the false teachers did in Jude 4) since it is consistent with Paul's depiction of them elsewhere (1 Tim. 4.2; 2 Tim. 3.13). Therefore, there is a negative connotation here suggesting they came in false pretence in order to exploit these women both financially and sexually.

The false teachers entered '*the* houses' which may suggest that Paul has certain houses in mind. It is possible that he is referring to non-Christian households but more likely the false teachers have preyed upon wealthy women believers who have been sympathetic to, possibly enthralled with, and vulnerable to them and their message.

These false teachers have taken these women captive, *aichmalōtizontes*. There is a poorly attested textual variant (corrector of Codex D and Majority Text), *aichmalōteuontes* (cf. Eph. 4.8), but there is no difference in meaning; they both mean 'to capture in war' (Lk. 21.24). However, the former reading has a figurative meaning of 'making one captive' to something (e.g. the law of sin, Rom. 7.23) or someone (e.g. obedience to Christ, 2 Cor. 10.5). In some instances the capturing is done in conjunction with deception and therefore means to 'mislead' (Judith's beauty deceived Holofernes in Jdt. 16.9; cf. *T. Reub.* 5.3). Though deception may be associated with the manner in which the false teachers prey on these women and correspond to the meaning 'to creep in', it is more likely this word is used to express the way in which they control them and possibly treat them harshly (i.e. like prisoners of war).

Paul uses four descriptive statements to flesh out these women, although unexpectedly the emphasis is not on the women but rather on the false teachers. The expanded description of the women serves two purposes. First, it shows the cruel character of the false teachers by showing how they preyed upon and used a vulnerable, easily duped type of person. Second, it shows the negative impact of the false teacher's ministry upon the people; their teaching is powerless to transform.

First, Paul describes the women with the plural diminutive form of woman, literally 'little women' though it has nothing to do with their stature. Paul uses the word figuratively with respect to their disposition. They are weak in morals, self-control and discernment, and even foolish because of their willingness to be controlled by the false teachers. In this respect they resemble the fools in the book of Proverbs.

Second, these women are 'piled up with sins', thereby creating the image that they are 'weighed down' or 'drowning' in their sins. The only other NT usage of this verb is in Rom. 12.20, which is a quote from Prov. 25.22, in which loving one's enemies is like 'piling up fiery coals on their heads'. The effect of their sinful past continues to cloud their ability to live godly lives in the present (Eph. 4.14). Their conscience has been seared in such a manner that it has made them susceptible to the false teachers who are hypocritical liars and whose teaching comes from demonic deceitful spirits (1 Tim. 4.2). The result is a codependent relationship with the false teachers in which they are unable to leave their life of sin; rather it gets reinforced and legitimized by them.

Third, 'they are led by various kinds of passions' (cf. Tit. 3.3). A few manuscripts (Codex A, 1505) include 'and pleasures'. This is probably an intentional addition in order to coincide the sins of these women with the vice 'love of pleasure' found in the vice list above and because early translators saw a sexual inference with respect to the women and the false teachers. The word for 'passion', *epithumia*, is found mostly in the Pauline letters (19 of 34 occurrences). Paul uses it twice in a positive sense as the 'desire to be with Christ' (Phil. 1.23) and 'longing to see the Thessalonians's (1 Thess. 2.17). But most of the references are negative, referring to the general desires for forbidden things generated from a sinful nature (Gal. 5.24; Eph. 2.3). The women are led by 'various desires' which suggests that their sinful nature is active and that many desires drive them, including love of money (1 Tim. 6.9), pleasure (including sexual, 1 Tim. 5.6) and even knowledge (2 Tim. 3.7). There will always be problems when people are led by their sinful desires instead of the Holy Spirit (Rom. 8.14).

Fourth, these women are 'always learning but never coming to the knowledge of the truth'. This portrayal suggests that their devoted efforts proved futile due to their sin or that they were enamoured with knowledge and the process of learning but there was no transformation. The latter is more likely though both are possible. They suffer the same problem as the false teachers, 'appearance management'. They like the appearance of seeking knowledge and being knowledgeable and open minded but in fact they refuse the truth. Exploring 'godless myths and old wives's tales' are more infatuating than the pursuit of godliness (1 Tim. 4.7-9) and the truth in God's word which does lead to salvation (2 Tim. 3.15). Their relationship with the false teachers is parasitic: the women pay the teachers who in turn feed them a teaching, which never satisfies or brings them freedom. The phrase 'come to the knowledge of the truth' is at the heart of Paul's calling (Tit. 1.1). It can refer to 'repentance' (2 Tim. 2.25) but more generally to an experiential understanding of salvation (1 Tim. 2.4) and the faith (2 Tim. 2.18).

It may appear that Paul is a misogynist, vilifying women as weak, stupid (i.e. unable to come to a knowledge of the truth) and lesser than men. Women were certainly stereotyped as being easily persuaded by religious swindlers (Lucian, *Alex.* 6; second century AD). Paul, as he is portrayed in *The Acts of Paul and Thecla*, is considered to be a charmer of easily influenced young women like Thecla, who was betrothed to Thamyris, and convincing her not to marry (*Acts of Paul and Thecla* 7-11). Among philosophers women were reviled for their attempts to learn (Horace, *Epodes* 8). Juvenal mocks the woman who understands and publically shares philosophy: 'I hate a woman who pours over the "Grammar" of Palaemon, who observes all the rules and laws of language' (Juvenal, *Sat.* 6.434-56). In spite of this background, it is more likely that Paul exposes these women not because of their gender but because of their susceptible disposition as a result of their unrepentant life of sin and their desire to be disciples of men (Xenophon, *Cyr.* 2.2.6). These women are simply one group of the many who are portrayed in 2 Tim. 4.3-4. It is clear that Paul is not biased towards women in his criticism of foolish people since in the next section Paul makes even stronger admonitions against the false teachers who have rejected the truth for some form of 'madness' due to their corrupt minds, which reject the faith (2 Tim. 3.8, 9).

(ii) *Example #2: Jannes and Jambres (3.8-9)*. In this section Paul continues his description of the character of the false teachers but this time with an example from the OT during the time of Moses (Exod. 7.11, 12, 22; 8.7). His point is that these false teachers are charlatans, like Jannes and Jambres, who reject the truth and the leaders, who proclaim the message of truth. Paul continues to draw on the image of Moses (which he began in 2.19) as the servant of the Lord, providing a paradigm of steadfastness amidst opposition for Timothy to emulate so that he will know what to expect. But the good news for Timothy and all other servants of the Lord is that these false teachers will not advance far just as Jannes and Jambres did not. In the Exodus account the magicians receive boils (Exod. 9.11) and no longer stand in opposition to Moses.

The experiences of Israel throughout the Exodus often serve as parallels for the experiences that the early church would experience (1 Cor. 10.1-13). In 3.8-9 Paul draws on the experience of Moses in his confrontations with Pharaoh's magicians, in which Jannes and Jambres form a typological connection (note the use of *tropos*, 'kind' or 'type', in 3.8) with the present-day false teachers. The text reads, '*in the manner which* Jannes and Jambres resisted Moses likewise these [false teachers] are resisting the truth'. Just as Jannes and Jambres were fakes, swindlers and deceivers and resisted Moses and the truth, the false teachers are conducting themselves in the same way. It is not certain how far to take the comparison. Some believe that the false teachers were using sorcery just as the magicians did. There are good reasons for this position: first, the word for 'magician', *pharmacos*, found in Exod. 7.11 of the LXX means 'sorcerer'; second, Paul speaks of 'sorcerers/ swindlers' (*goetēs*) in 3.13; third, magic played a significant role in Ephesus (Acts 19.19-20) and in Graeco-Roman culture (Acts 8.9; 13.8). Against this some understand the parallel more in terms of deception as a swindler or fake just as Lucian uses the term (*goetēs*) to describe sophists as 'cheats [who were] often more convincing than genuine philosophers' (Lucian, *Pisc.* 42). Philo, writing in the same century, describes these people as 'conjurors and enchanters, who attempt to contend against the divine word with their sophistries...increase everything for their own destruction, and while thinking to deceive others they are deceived' (Philo, *On the Migration of Abraham* 83). The false teachers certainly fit the latter description as swindlers and it is difficult to ascertain with certainty if the former description also applies to them.

The names 'Jannes and Jambres' do not appear in the OT texts. They are simply referred to as 'magicians' (similarly Pliny, *Nat. hist.* 30.1.11). These two characters appear in the Dead Sea Scrolls (CD 4.5.17-19) in which it is stated that Jannes and his brother were raised up by Belial, the prince of lights, with his cunning. The Palestinian Targum, *Pal. Tgs. Exod.* 7.11, includes both names ('Janis and Jambres, magicians of Mizraim' [Hebrew for 'Egypt']) and they are referred to as 'sons of Balaam' in *Pal. Targ. Num.* 22.21, 22 (cf. *Targ. Ps.-J.* 40.6). In light of this background, it suggests that Jannes, Jambres and the false teachers share the same penchant for evil.

There may be some significance to the names themselves and thus their inclusion. Jannes is the Greek version of the Hebrew *Janis* which may be derived from the Hebrew verb *'anah* meaning 'to oppose or to do violence'. This verb often translates *anthistemi* ('to resist') in the LXX (Isa. 3.9) which is the verb used twice in 2 Tim. 3.8 to describe how Jannes and Jambres opposed Moses and the false teachers oppose the truth. The change of 'Jambres' to 'Mambres' in the Vulgate and followed by a few Greek copyists of 2 Tim. 3.8 (F, G) is consistent with the Jewish tradition of the name 'Mamrey' which comes from the verb *marah*, 'to rebel'. Therefore, there is some possibility that the names have been included because they express the character of these men and indirectly the false teachers as those who are rebellious and violently oppose and oppress others and the truth.

The focus of this example is upon how Jannes and Jambres opposed Moses and the truth and secondarily on their means of deception. God says to Moses, 'I have made you like God to Pharaoh' (Exod. 7.1). Later in that account Aaron throws down his staff, which becomes a snake. Pharaoh's magicians do likewise but immediately afterwards Aaron's snake eats theirs (Exod. 7.8-12). Paul directly applies this story to Timothy's situation. Timothy is to stand firm like Moses with divine authority before the false teachers. The false teachers correspond to Jannes and Jambres as those who oppose the truth and Timothy the messenger of this truth (*houtos kai*, 'in the same way also', is common in Paul's letters: 28 times but only once in the Pastorals; e.g. Rom. 5.15, 18, 19, 21). Their opposition is reminiscent of Elymas, the deceiver and sorcerer, who opposed Paul (note that the same verb is used: *anthistēmi*) and his message (Acts 13.1-12). Later in 2 Timothy, Paul points out Alexander (a false teacher; cf. Hymanaeus and Philetus,

2.17-18) as someone for Timothy to guard against since he vehemently resists the message of truth (2 Tim. 4.15). The difference between the false teachers and the women just mentioned is that the false teachers actively reject and stand against the gospel whereas the women simply fail to appropriate it. It is no wonder the women cannot come to knowledge of the truth, since their teachers reject it and do not possess the faculties to embrace it.

Paul lists two reasons for the false teachers's resistance: corrupt minds and worthless faith. Their minds have been corrupted by their teaching, which in turn has a destructive corrupting effect on others (cf. 1 Tim. 6.5). In the same way the people became corrupt (note that the same verb is used: *kataphtheirō*) during Noah's time by 'corrupting God's way' (Gen. 6.12), so the false teachers have corrupted themselves by ignoring or misusing the Scriptures (2 Tim. 3.15-16). The debilitating nature of their corrupt minds functions in the same way as their seared consciences (1 Tim. 4.2) which inhibit them from appropriating and teaching the truth. They are 'disqualified concerning the faith'. The noun used, *adokimos*, suggests that the false teachers are rejected by God as those who have failed the test of faith (cf. Tit. 1.16) and are therefore the opposite to those who are 'approved' (*dokimos*, 2 Tim. 2.15). They have failed with respect to both the *content* of their faith, because of its heterodox nature, and the *expression* their faith.

Paul closes this section on a positive note reaffirming God's sovereignty and faithfulness, and claiming that 'these people will not advance far'. The Greek could be read 'not advance anymore' (Acts 24.4) or 'not advance even more' (Acts 4.17). It is clear that Paul does not believe that the false teachers will be stopped entirely (former position) since he states later in the letter that they will continue to deceive and be deceived (2 Tim. 3.13) which is in contrast to the Exodus scenario and where the application of the Exodus text breaks down (Exod. 9.11). Archelaus later uses the Jannes–Jambres text in the same way Paul does (note that he even quotes from 2 Timothy) to refer to a false teacher named Manes thereby showing that this type of false teacher is still in existence years later (Archelaus, *Disp. Man.* 36, 25). Paul is probably picking up the false teachers's slogan of 'advancement' (cf. 1 Tim. 4.15). They believe that their teaching and religion advance 'godliness' (2 Tim. 2.16) possibly drawing upon the Stoics' use of the term and their concomitant emphasis on asceticism. Paul is saying that their ministry and teaching will not ultimately triumph since both are built on a sandy foundation in contrast to the gospel, which has a sure foundation (2 Tim. 2.19; 1 Tim. 3.15-16). As Paul said earlier, there are two types of vessels. Those made of wood and clay will not succeed; the false teachers are these types of vessels.

An interesting textual variant exists in the latter half of the verse. This variant reads 'their thoughts [or possibly 'plans', *dianoia*] will be quite evident to all'. Only Codex Alexandrinus supports this reading. Though Codex

A is a good manuscript it is likely *dianoia* is an intentional change to the text. The more likely translation is 'their 'madness [or 'folly' (*anoia*)] will be quite evident to all'. 'Madness', found elsewhere in the NT only in Luke, describes the response of the Pharisees and Scribes to kill Jesus because he healed the man with the withered hand on the Sabbath (Lk. 6.11). The word also has a more muted meaning of 'folly' as in the usage in Proverbs (Prov. 14.8; 22.15 LXX). It is difficult to know which meaning fits here since both are appropriate to the context. Regardless of whether the translation is 'madness' or 'folly', the point is that people who have a good conscience and uncorrupted minds will be able to discern and clearly see the deception, malevolence and malfeasance of the false teachers just as Moses did with respect to Jannes and Jambres.

Paul's Appeal to Timothy for his Commitment to Him and the Gospel (3.10-17)

2 Timothy 3.10-17 comprises the final section dealing with the false teachers that began in 2.14. All the paranaesis Paul has given to Timothy up to this point has been with the false teachers clearly in view. In this section the false teachers recede further into the background as Paul returns to the themes which began this letter (2 Tim. 1.6–2.7): loyalty to Paul and his gospel, coupled with a willingness to suffer for it. Paul knows how difficult and lonely it can feel fighting for the kingdom, preserving the gospel from being tainted and keeping oneself pure and faithful throughout the ministry process. So drawing from his own experience, he enjoins Timothy to remember four things. First, he is to recall and reflect on the lives of those who have remained faithful, like his mother and grandmother mentioned earlier (1.5) but in particular Paul. Second, he must not forget the grim reality that those who want to live a godly life will suffer. Third, he must keep in mind that though sufferings will come, the grace of Christ will be there to walk him through these times. Fourth, he is to rely on Scripture to give him confidence for the tasks ahead of him.

Structurally, 3.10-17 is divided into two major parts: 3.10-13 and 3.14-17. Each part begins with the phrase 'but you' (*su de*). This particular construction is found 17 times in the NT of which three occurrences are in 2 Timothy (3.10, 14; 4.5). The purpose of this literary device is to contrast that which precedes it. In 3.10 Paul contrasts his life, ministry and expectations of ministers (3.10-12) with that of the false teachers and unbelievers in the Last Days (3.1-9). Later, in 2 Tim. 4.5, Paul contrasts the ministry he expects from Timothy with the ministry that people who are self-absorbed desire (4.3-4). Then in 3.14 Paul contrasts the deceptive ministry and nature of the false teachers (though focusing more on their deceptive nature, 3.13) with his expectation of Timothy, namely to hold fast to the paradigms and teaching he received that will keep him on the straight and narrow path.

a. *The Power of Personal Paradigms (3.10-13)*
(i) *Paul's Example (3.10-11)*. Paul begins this segment by reminding Timothy how he has followed Paul's example of ministry, embraced his attitude (particularly perseverance) and accepted persecution in his pursuit of godliness. The word 'follow' can have different nuances. It can be taken to mean that 'Timothy *kept a record of* Paul's journeys and life' since Timothy was not always with Paul, noting he joined Paul in Lystra on his second missionary journey (Acts 16.1). Luke uses this word in the same way when he describes how he followed the events of Jesus in order to write his Gospel (Lk. 1.3). It is possible to take it as a reference to Timothy *observing* Paul since he travelled with him on two of his missionary journeys. But the most likely shade of meaning is that Timothy has been Paul's *disciple* over an extended period of time. This same verb is used among Stoic philosophers to describe the relationship between a student and master (Epictetus, *Diss.* 1.9). It is used similarly in the *Fragments of Papias* 3.4, 7, 15 and by Paul himself in his previous letter concerning the faith and teaching to which Timothy submitted his life (1 Tim. 4.6). The point is that Timothy has been in a student–master relationship with Paul, in much the same way the disciples were with Jesus, for an extended period of time (cf. 1 Cor. 4.16-17) and Paul does not want Timothy to forget his paradigm but rather to keep it at the forefront of his mind.

Although no imperative is used, there is a subtle exhortation in this reminder, to continue to choose the hard life of godliness and suffering instead of the deceitful, even lucrative, life of ungodliness characteristic of the false teachers. In doing so, Timothy will become a model to emulate and hopefully a mentor for others (1 Tim. 4.6, 11, 16; 2 Tim. 2.2).

Those, who hold to a late date and pseudonymous authorship, see in 3.10-13 an incongruity with the rest of 2 Timothy and therefore propose that this material is a later addition to the text. In 3.10-13 Timothy is presented as the ideal leader, who possesses qualities that he lacks elsewhere in the letter (e.g. cowardliness in 2 Tim. 1.7). Their conclusion is unnecessary and doubtful. As I have shown elsewhere, Paul considers Timothy to be a faithful servant and these exhortations are given not because he is not doing these things (e.g. suffering for the gospel) but rather so that he will continue to do these things. It is basic paraenesis.

Paul catalogues eight areas in which Timothy has followed his example (3.10-11). They function as Paul's 'virtue list' which is in direct contrast to the false teachers's 'vice list' (3.3-5) and thereby it presents the important priorities for a servant of the Lord. So to some degree, this list is written for the sake of the Ephesians in order to show them the shortcomings of the false teachers and simultaneously the way to recognize and become a true servant of the Lord.

The importance of sound orthodox teaching runs through both letters to Timothy (eleven times) because of the aberrant teaching of the false teachers which is described as 'unhealthy' (1 Tim. 1.10), 'from demons' (1 Tim. 4.1) and 'contrary to the teaching of godliness' (1 Tim. 6.3). It may be for this reason that 'teaching' is first on the list.

The next word on the list, 'way of life' (*agōgē*), may function as a *head term* of which the following words are a subset. With this term, Paul is making a direct correlation between how he lives and what he believes (cf. 1 Clem. 47.6; 48.1). They must not be mutually exclusive. People should be able to know what Paul believes and teaches by how he lives. Paul knows that Timothy has clearly embraced this idea and this is why he sent him as his apostolic delegate to Corinth (1 Cor. 4.17) and now to Ephesus. The tacit contrast is between the false teachers and the servants of the Lord; both will be easily recognizable by their way of life.

Paul's 'purpose' has been evident to Timothy. The same word is used to refer to God's purposes. Some examples include God's purpose of salvation (Rom. 8.28) and election (Rom. 9.11), his eternal purpose to express his wisdom through the church (Eph. 3.11) and to offer salvation on the basis of grace not works (2 Tim. 1.9). The meaning of 'purpose' in this context is probably consistent with the meaning in Acts 11.23: 'the purpose of the heart [is] to abide in the Lord'. Paul's resolve has been to be devoted to God and to align himself with God's purposes in undivided commitment to Christ.

'Faith' could signify the body of beliefs Paul held (1 Tim. 3.9; 4.1). The strength of this position is that Timothy might need this orthodox standard in the face of the unorthodox teaching of the false teachers. Equally possible is that it denotes the faithfulness and trust Paul has in God (2 Tim. 1.13). Paul may have both in mind but since the latter is the more common meaning, then the emphasis needs to rest there.

The triad of 'patience, love and endurance' introduces the three primary requirements needed in order to persevere through the trials and sufferings Paul mentions in 3.11 so that one can reach the goal of godliness (3.12). 'Patience' is principally a Pauline word (11 of 14 occurrences) expressed by the Father's patient kindness to humankind (Rom. 2.4; 9.22) and experienced personally by Paul through Christ (1 Tim. 1.16). This same patience is expected of all believers (Gal. 5.22) and particularly it is to be expressed toward other believers (Eph. 4.2). But here Paul has in mind the character that is needed to put up with the false teachers (2 Tim. 2.24-25) and to admonish them with sound teaching (2 Tim. 4.2).

'Love' is foundational to Paul's thinking. God's love was expressed through Christ's sacrificial death (Rom. 5.8). It is mediated to believers through the Holy Spirit (Rom. 5.5; 1 Tim. 1.7). Love is expected of all believers (1 Cor. 13.13) both in terms of love of God and love of humankind. If Timothy appropriates a lifestyle of love then the gospel will not be maligned, his opponents will be disarmed and people will be attracted to believe.

'Endurance' is fundamental for spiritual growth. It is an attribute of God (Rom. 15.5) and to be pursued as a characteristic of his servants (2 Cor. 6.4; 1 Tim. 6.11). Perseverance works hand in hand with trials in that trials bring about the need for perseverance. When perseverance is exercised it results in the refinement of the believer's character and ultimately the spawning of greater hope (Rom. 5.3-4). It is this virtue which Timothy has seen in Paul and which he will need as he faces the false teachers. The personal result will be godliness (2 Tim. 3.12).

The context in which these virtues are set is 'persecutions' and 'sufferings'. Persecutions and sufferings are a stark reminder of an earlier enjoinder to suffer (1.8; 2.3) and the previous call for patience, love and perseverance. For Paul, persecutions and sufferings should comprise a significant element of the believer's life, which is probably a teaching that runs contrary to the teaching of the false teachers. Lest Timothy thinks Paul is talking in abstract terms, he roots this presupposition with specific examples from his first missionary journey to Antioch, Iconium and Lystra (Acts 13–14).

The expectation to suffer and be persecuted is rooted in the teaching and paradigm of Jesus (Mk 10.30). For three reasons, Paul solidly embraces the desire to suffer joyfully (Col. 1.24). First, he believes he was suffering on behalf of Christ (Phil. 3.10). Second, he knows these sufferings paled in comparison to the glory to be revealed at the parousia of Christ (Rom. 8.18). Third, he is convinced that through suffering he experienced more of the transforming power and grace of Christ (2 Cor. 12.10).

Paul is generic in his description of these sufferings and persecutions, saying only that they were '*such as* those which happened in [Pisidian] Antioch, Iconium and Lystra'. Scholars have mused why Paul chose to refer to this time period as an example of suffering when Paul did not yet know Timothy. Some have thought a later period would provide a better example, when Timothy was his travelling partner (Acts 16.2) and saw Paul be persecuted (Acts 16–17). I believe there are a few reasons why he includes these first missionary persecutions. First, these persecutions and sufferings were for Paul some of the worst he experienced. Second, Timothy was a believer from Lystra at the time Paul passed through this city and therefore it is certainly possible he would have witnessed at least some of Paul's persecutions. In fact, the manner in which Paul suffered for Christ may have been one of the reasons why Timothy desired to accompany Paul when he returned on his second missionary journey (Acts 16.1-2). Third, the experiences Paul had in these three cities exemplify and remind Timothy of what he can continue to expect as a servant of the Lord and particularly in his context in Ephesus. In Antioch, Paul was verbally abused (Acts 13.45; literally 'blasphemed' which is what the false teachers Hymenaeus and Alexander were accused of doing, 1 Tim. 1.20), persecuted and expelled from the city (Acts 13.50). It is interesting to note that the persecution in Antioch was the result of Jews inciting women to have Paul and Barnabas banished (cf. the negative influence of some women in the Ephesian situation). Paul shook the dust off his feet in Antioch as a warning for rejecting God's word and a symbol of cleansing himself from the Gentiles and the Jews who were acting like pagans. In Iconium, Paul's message led to division, those for the gospel and those opposed to it. Those who opposed, poisoned others against Paul (cf. people against Moses at Meribah, Ps. 106.32; Josephus, *Ant.* 16, 10) and they attempted to stone him so that Paul had to flee for his life (Acts 14.5-6). Finally, in Lystra, Paul was stoned and left for dead outside the city walls (Acts 14.19). Paul's point is that Timothy can expect no less in his ministry, in fact as Paul says in the next verse they are necessary for living a life of godliness. Hopefully I have also shown that it is erroneous, as some have concluded, that the inclusion of these persecutions, from the time period before Timothy's accompaniment with Paul, is strong proof that 2 Timothy is a pseudonymous writing.

A poorly attested textual variant (i.e. in the margin of K [9th century], 181, Syriac version Harclean), 'that is, the things which he suffered on account of Thecla, from the Jews, with those who believe in Christ', is placed between 'Antioch' and 'Iconium'. This variant is easily dismissed because it is so late but it does show how subsequent copyists considered the *Acts of Paul and Thecla* as a useful reference for elucidating the historical situation in Iconium.

The second part of v. 11 begins with the exclamation 'what persecutions I endured' thereby repeating 'persecutions' and stressing the intensity of the difficulty he faced. But in this clause Paul juxtaposes persecutions with deliverance. He loosely quotes Ps. 34.19 (LXX 33.18), 'the Lord [Jesus] delivered me from them all', drawing on the OT imagery of the righteous sufferer found in the Psalms (cf. Ps. 44.22; Rom. 8.36). God delivering his people has its NT roots in the Lord's prayer (Mt. 6.13) and is a foundational truth in the Pauline corpus (Rom. 7.24; 11.26; 15.31; 2 Cor. 1.10). But in what sense does Paul understand the Lord delivering him from persecutions? He cannot mean that he will be spared from persecutions since his point is that everyone who lives a godly life will be persecuted. Furthermore to be spared persecutions would eliminate one important way in which God's transforming grace works (Rom. 5.3-4; 2 Cor. 12.8-10). It is more likely he understands deliverance in terms of receiving the grace to endure the persecution with no guarantee about the results. The same verb is found two more times in this letter: in 4.17 Paul expresses his thanks to God for sustaining him through his imprisonment and voices his confidence of being delivered from death and being released from prison, and in 4.18 he communicates his confidence that this sustaining grace in the face of every evil plot will continue until he enters glory.

(ii) *Paul's Principle: Followers Seeking Godliness Can Expect Persecution (3.12-13)*. Paul contrasts godly people with evil people in order to set up his exhortation to Timothy in 3.14, to remain in the orthodox course he has learned and seen modeled. The main premise of his argument is that all believers, not just leaders, can expect persecution. Paul's inclusivity, through the use of 'all', may be highlighting for the church members that they are not exempt from the detrimental effects and personal cost of the false teachers's pseudo-ministry and a life lived within the context of a world hostile to the Kingdom of God. Commitment to a godly lifestyle is an act of the will and a personal choice coming from a deep place within the human heart. For this reason, Paul uses the verb *thelō*, which has as its root meaning 'will', 'wish' or 'desire'. This is a word Paul uses elsewhere to describe the internal human struggle with good and evil (Rom. 7.15). Similarly, choosing the godly life can be a difficult and costly battle. Paul's teaching here is reminiscent of Jesus' fundamental teaching that 'if any want to be my disciples, let them deny themselves, take up their cross and follow me' (Mk 8.34) and accept that 'if they persecuted me [Jesus] then they will persecute you' (Jn 15.20).

The call is to live in a 'godly manner'. This is the only time this adverb, *eusebōs*, occurs in 2 Timothy though the noun, *eusebeia*, often translated 'godliness', is found in 1 Timothy (2.2; 3.16; 4.7, 8; 6.3, 5, 6, 11) and 2 Timothy (3.5). This may be a term used by the false teachers and reinterpreted by Paul or an expression used in the early church (Acts 3.12) that Paul is appropriating. Certainly Paul's desire is that everyone might live a godly life in contradistinction to the false teachers and others who are living ungodly lives (1 Tim. 1.9; Rom. 1.18; 2 Tim. 2.16, *asebeia*). Godliness is rooted in the teaching of the gospel and the theological profundity of the life, death and resurrection of Jesus (1 Tim. 3.16). Therefore it has certain requirements of those who subscribe to living in a godly manner. For those who appropriate this godliness, it is beneficial in the present and in the future leading to eternal life (1 Tim. 4.8). The godly life does not just happen, it is to be pursued with intentionality (1 Tim. 6.11). It requires commitment and submission to one who is the essence of godliness, Jesus. A godly life can be feigned as the false teachers demonstrated, 'having a form of godliness but denying its power' (2 Tim. 3.5).

The grim reality and general rule for believers, says Paul, is that those who live in a godly manner can expect to be persecuted. This is not a new idea for Paul, for he made this claim on his first missionary journey in Lystra, Iconium and Antioch (Acts 14.22) and later on his second missionary journey in Thessalonica (1 Thess. 3.4). This is consistent with Jesus' teaching on persecution (Mt. 10.22-23). Paul does not elaborate on what constitutes persecution. Usually this included physical afflictions although his list in 2 Corinthians 11 suggests other types too. There is a direct correlation between living a godly life for and with Jesus Christ, and creating conflict with those who are not believers. In today's western world where persecution is minimal, this text can suggest that believers should not shrink back from living the godly life before others, particularly for fear of being rejected. Rejection from the world is a sign of acceptance from God (Mt. 5.11-12; Heb. 10.36-39).

Persecution is a sensitive subject for Paul since he formerly obsessively persecuted Jesus and the church (Acts 22.4, 7). Paul learned from this experience the need to bless one's persecutors and in this way overcome them with love (Rom. 12.14). This philosophy coincides with Herodotus, as quoted by Longinus, 'if you choose to endure a little hardship, you will be able at the cost of some present exertion to overcome your enemies' (Longinus, *Sublime* 22.2). Apparently there is great gain with enduring some pain (1 Cor. 4.12).

Paul names the perpetrators of persecution with a general term, 'evil people', and a specific term, 'charlatans'. In the Pauline corpus, the word 'evil' is used broadly to describe Satan (Eph. 6.16; 2 Thess. 3.3), the present evil age (Gal. 1.4; Eph. 5.18), evil deeds (Col. 1.21) and evil people (2 Thess. 3.2). In each instance, evil conveys the idea of being the opposite of what is right and good. Paul has this type of people in mind, who lack the Holy Spirit and are opposed to godliness. One sub-group of these evil people is the 'charlatans', a word only found here in the NT. It can refer to cheaters (Demosthenes, *Zen.* 32.18) though in most religious material it normally refers to sorcerers (*T. Sol.* 19.3) or magicians (Dio Chrysostom, *Or.* 32.11). These are people who rely upon a god for insight or power to perform an action. However they do not rely on the God of Israel and for this reason their sorcery and magic acts are denounced in the Law. By Paul referring to these false teachers with this term, it may suggest these people were involved in sorcery and occultism or they had a magical view towards invoking the name of a god or even God, as did the Jewish exorcists in Acts 19. The earlier reference in chap. 3, in which these people were compared with Jannes and Jambres (3.8), who are called *pharmakoi* in Exod. 7.11, lends credence to this postulation. It is interesting to note in *Ep. Diog.* 8.4, that the sorcerers are rebuked because of their false doctrine in which they incorrectly identify God in terms of some element of nature (e.g. fire, water). Similarly, these false teachers have an unhealthy doctrine and understanding of who God is.

The problem with these false teachers and evil people is that they keep getting worse, literally 'they advance from bad to worse', a common contemporary phrase. Paul, in his pre-Christian days, spent great energy advancing above his peers (Gal. 1.14) to no avail (Phil. 3.8). Paul's opponents in Ephesus were advancing too, though not in godliness, *eusebeia* (2 Tim. 3.9), but rather in 'ungodliness', *asebeia* (2.16). Though these people think they are advancing or are advanced in their understanding of the Law (1 Tim. 1.3-11), piety (4.3) and doctrine (2 Tim. 2.15), they are actually deceived and becoming more deceived as they deceive others with their message and lifestyle.

There is an irony in 3.12-13. To the outsider it may look like godly people have it worse since they are being persecuted as believers for Christ's sake (Phil. 1.12-21; Col. 1.24) when in fact they are destined for glory as Paul points out later (in 2 Tim. 4.8). The evil people's situation may look good but in fact they are destined for destruction (2.12; 1 Tim. 6.9). As one Rabbi writes in the Mishnah, 'according to the suffering so is the reward' (*P. Ab.* 5.21).

b. *Exhortation to Abide in Godly Teaching (3.14-17)*
The previous section (3.10-13) ended with the 'evil men' in 3.13 being portrayed as advancing in the wrong direction, making things continually worse for themselves and others. This demise is due to their invidious character and misuse of Scripture. This next section (3.14-17) begins with the same phrase 'but you' and signals a contrast with what precedes. The first usage of this term in 2 Tim. 3.10 indicated the contrast between the faithful discipleship of Timothy under Paul with the self-absorbed destructive desires and pursuits of the ungodly. The second usage of this term in 3.14 denotes a contrast between the 'evil persons' of 3.13 and Timothy in 3.14-17. In contrast to the evil persons, Paul wants Timothy to abide and stand firm in what he knows is godly teaching because of the character of those who taught him and because of the effectiveness of the proper use of Scripture in their lives and the lives of those they taught, which includes Timothy. Scripture has been an anchor and a fundamental tool in Paul's life and ministry so he reminds Timothy of his experience of the foundational role Scripture has played in his life and will continue to play in his future ministry.

(i) *Because of the Integrity of Those Who Taught Timothy (3.14-15a)*. Paul's first reason for Timothy to hold fast to the godly teaching he has received from the Scriptures is based on the integrity of those who had taught him. Timothy has been taught well by many good people. These people are very different from those Paul has described in 3.7-8. The following chart (Figure 8) lays out the contrast between the false teachers of 3.7-8 and Timothy's experience under godly mentors (3.14-15).

False Teachers (3.7-8)	Timothy (3.14-15)
always learning	learning from childhood
teaching unable to come to truth	teaching able to make wise
teaching that opposed the truth	teaching leading to wisdom
reject the faith	firmly believing
paradigms: Jannes and Jambres	paradigms: Paul, Eunice, others

Figure 8. *Contrast between the False Teachers and Timothy*

The image in 3.7-8 is of 'evil men' advancing into the wrong direction, making things worse and worse. In contrast, Timothy is to abide, standing firm in what he knows is true.

Paul begins in v. 14 by exhorting Timothy to abide in the things that he learned. The generic reference to 'these things' may be referring back to the deposit with which Timothy was entrusted (1.14; 1 Tim. 6.20) though more likely it refers more broadly to the gospel and the practical teachings and personal examples of Paul and others in 3.10-11.

Some think this command sounds more like a Johannine statement, similar to 'if you remain in my word, truly you will be my disciples' (Jn 8.31). Although John uses the verb *menō*, 'to remain' or 'abide', frequently (40 times), Paul is not unacquainted with this verb; he uses it 17 times. More important for this discussion are the two usages in 1 Tim. 2.15 and 2 Tim. 2.13. The former text was addressed to misguided women in order to redirect their attention to abiding in love, faith and holiness instead of disrupting worship. The latter text reminds the reader of the character of God who remains faithful in spite of our unfaithfulness. Paul is calling Timothy to emulate the same character of abiding he has learned from the example of Christ and others. This is to be an ongoing experience, continually building on this foundation (cf. Phil. 3.16).

The verb for 'learn' is not frequent in the NT (only 25 usages). Surprisingly 16 of these usages are found in Paul's Epistles. The term in NT usage means to learn cognitively through the study of Scripture (Mt. 9.13) and nature (Mt. 24.32), through God (Jn 6.45), teachers (1 Cor. 4.6), Spiritual gifts (1 Cor. 14.1) and fellow believers (1 Cor. 14.35). Paul's usage in 3.14 has a tacit understanding of discipleship attached to it as it does in the Gospels; Timothy has learned by being in relationship with others.

As one would expect, learning has special significance in 1 and 2 Timothy because of the adverse influence of the false teachers. The problem with the false teachers and those who followed them is that they were always learning, and liked to look knowledgeable. Paul is clearly in favour of all people learning but when they have learned that which does not lead to the truth (2 Tim. 3.7) then he calls them to account as in the case of some women who needed to learn anew with humility (1 Tim. 2.11) or some elders who required reproof (1 Tim. 5.20). Part of the purpose for learning is to teach others but Paul forbids this if their teaching leads to disunity and destruction (1 Tim. 5.13).

Learning entails more than accumulating information. First, it must be applied. In the former letter Paul rebukes the children of widows for not putting their knowledge in practice by caring for their own household (1 Tim. 5.4). This type of applied knowledge is acceptable before God. Second, this knowledge of faith must be tried, tested and approved. For this reason Paul juxtaposes 'learning' with 'believing'. But the verb he includes in 2 Tim.

3.14 is not the commonly used verb *pisteuō*, which means 'to believe'; rather it is the hapax legomenon *pistoō*, which means 'to believe firmly'. Paul is reminding Timothy that these things he learned are not things to which he has given 'mental ascent' but rather these are things which he has seen, experienced and held firmly so that they have become a solid basis for the way he thinks, lives and ministers. Forty years later, using the same verb, Clement contrasts those who did not firmly believe Christ and his teaching (1 Clem. 15.4) with the apostles who did and were therefore able to have a fruitful ministry (1 Clem. 42.3).

What makes Timothy's learning valuable and reliable is the integrity of the people through whom he learned. There is a textual variant in this clause giving three possible readings: neuter, 'from what [source(s)]'; singular, 'from whom'; and plural, 'from whom'. The first option would be stressing the reliability of the Scriptures from which Timothy learned. The attractiveness of this position is the fact that later in 3.16 Paul elaborates on the effectiveness of Scripture. But it should probably be rejected since it is an awkward reading in light of the emphasis on the people in the immediate and greater context of the letter. Therefore it is more likely this phrase is pointing towards the person or persons from whom Timothy has learned. The second option, 'from whom' (singular), proposes Paul as the person from whom Timothy has learned these things and therefore establishes their reliability. The proximate preceding context presents Paul as the model Timothy has followed (3.10). Earlier in the letter Paul is the source of Timothy's teaching (1.13) and mentorship (2.2). Paul is also the one present when Timothy was set apart as a minister for Christ (1.6). Clearly, there are good reasons in favour of this position. But there are two significant roadblocks. The external evidence is not in favour of this reading: the strongest and earliest manuscript readings support the plural reading (Codex Sinaiticus, fourth century AD; and Alexandrinus, fifth century). Notwithstanding, the corrected reading of MSS C may suggest the copyist has changed the text to a singular reading from a plural reading because of an earlier manuscript. Nevertheless, it is more likely he changed it to make Paul the only source for the reasons stated above. The second roadblock is that the subsequent context of having known these Scriptures from childhood suggests other people like Lois and Eunice, his grandmother and mother respectively, who are quoted earlier in the letter (1.6), should be included among those from whom Timothy learned. So the third option, 'from whom' (plural), is still the most likely one. Paul is reminding Timothy that the things he has learned can be trusted and relied upon because of the integrity of *those* from whom he learned them.

It is not clear when Timothy's grounding in the Scripture began: from infancy or from childhood. Many scholars assume Paul is referring to Timothy's childhood as the starting point and quote from the Mishnaic tractate

Pirke Aboth (5.21) for support because it states that a boy at five years old is fit for the Scripture. Yet the word used in 2 Tim. 3.15a is *brephos*, a word only found once here in the Pauline corpus and seven more times in the NT, and in each instance it refers to an 'infant' (Lk. 2.12, 16; 18.15; 1 Pet. 2:2) and even an unborn child in the womb (Lk. 1.41, 44). Paul is probably not referring to the time when the child could begin to read Scripture but to the earliest time of his life. Paul's point is that at no time was Timothy without the influence of Scripture, especially through his mother Eunice and grandmother Lois (2 Tim. 1.5) which is interesting in terms of women transmitting scriptural knowledge (cf. Tit. 2.4). Even though Timothy had a Gentile father, it is likely he grew up as a Jew since Luke refers to his mother as a 'faithful Jewish woman' which is best understood as one who practised the Jewish religion. It was expected for the woman to follow the husband's religion, which probably accounts for why Timothy was not circumcised (Acts 16.2-3). Timothy's grounding in Scripture may explain in part the affirmation Timothy received through the believers in Lystra and Iconium (Acts 16.2).

Paul says literally, 'from infancy you have known the *holy letters*'. The phrase 'holy letters' is comprised of two words, 'holy' (*hiera*) and 'letters' (*grammata*). *Grammata* has a wide variety of meanings. It can refer to a 'letter' in the alphabet, so Paul claims that he writes the ending of his missive to the Galatians in his own large 'letters' (Gal. 6.11) or in 2 Cor. 3.7 he comments on the OT Law, the letters of which were engraved on stone. The word can denote a 'letter' in the sense of an epistle, so the Roman Jews declare to Paul that they never received any 'letters' from the Judeans (Acts 28.21). Similarly it can describe a 'promissory note' as Luke uses it when he describes the shrewd manager reducing the buyer's debt (Lk. 16.7). It is also used in Jn 7.15 to represent 'a body of knowledge'; in this instance the Jews are shocked that Jesus knows so much without any formal education. Finally Paul uses it to depict the Law (Rom. 2.27, 29; 7.6; 2 Cor. 3.6, 7) and in particular the literal aspect of it.

When the two words 'holy' (*hiera*) and 'letters' (*grammata*) are placed together they refer to OT Scripture. Later this phrase is used of Christian writings (Methodius, *Symp*. 5.1) but it is anachronistic to apply this term to the NT writings. Outside the OT, different authors use it to refer to the Scriptures either with an article (Philo, *Leg. gai.* 195; *Mos*. 2.290; Josephus, *Ant*. 1.13; 10.210) or without (Philo, *Rer. div. her.* 106, 159). Two readings of 3.15 exist: one with the article, '*the* holy Scriptures', and one without the article, 'holy Scriptures'. The manuscript evidence for both readings is strong and there is little difference in meaning. Probably the latter reading should be embraced since *grammata*, when it is found by itself as a reference to the OT Scriptures, is anarthrous.

What is not so clear is why Paul refers to Scriptures in this way since in the very next verse he unambiguously refers to the Scriptures as *graphē*, which is the more usual expression. There are a few possible reasons. In referring to them as 'letters', Paul may be pointing back to the experience of a child who would have learned Scripture by spelling out the letters of the text. Paul could be using the contemporary education jargon for religious training (cf. *T. Levi* 13.2). Equally possible, Paul is laying emphasis on 'holy' in order to contrast the source and teaching Timothy received in contrast to the false teachers. The false teachers's use of Scripture is misinformed and founded on faulty human tradition and spurious ideas (1 Tim. 1.8-11). Also, Ephesus was known for its unhealthy penchant for books on magic (Acts 19.19). Paul's point is to remind Timothy that he has had a much healthier upbringing in terms of content and instructors than those around him.

(ii) *Because of the Effective Helpful Nature of Scripture (3.15b-16)*. The second reason Paul wants Timothy to abide in this godly teaching of Scripture is because it is effective and personally transformative and will be equally so in those to whom Timothy will minister. Too often scholars get caught up in the 'inspiration' of scriptural debate that surfaces from this text and 2 Pet. 1.21. This is an important issue and I will address this. But it is important to keep our eyes on the context since this is what Paul enjoins Timothy to remember, namely Scripture makes one wise and helps one minister effectively to others so that the church may in turn be equipped to fulfill its purpose (Mt. 28.19-20).

1. *Personal Benefit (3.15b)*. The personal benefit of the teaching Timothy has received is that it has the capacity to make him wise and has in fact done so. Paul uses 'make wise' in a positive sense here though Peter uses it in the negative sense of wisdom craftily devising something misleading (2 Pet. 1.16) which has been the outcome of the false teachers's instruction. Paul appears to be drawing from the LXX reading of Ps. 19.7 (18.8 LXX) because of its inclusion of the same verb 'to make wise'. He applies this text to Timothy, directly changing the word from 'children' (as in LXX) or 'the simple' (as in MT) to 'you'.

The idea of Scripture making Timothy wise is reminiscent of the book of Proverbs in which the son is encouraged to learn wisdom from his father and mother since it will lead to life. Likewise, Paul proclaims that the OT Scripture can bring about saving wisdom in matters of faith and life provided they are read through the christological lens of *faith in Christ Jesus*. This was certainly Paul's experience (Rom. 1.2-4; Gal. 1.13-17). Jesus assumed himself to be the one of whom the OT Scriptures spoke (Jn 5.39, 46) and this was the position from which the evangelists wrote (Mt. 26.56; Lk. 24.44-47). Yet just studying Scriptures will not bring about salvation; they must be mixed with faith in order to be effective (Heb. 4.2). When

Scripture is read in this way and as it is saturated with a deep-seated faith in Christ, it will lead the reader to Scripture's appointed goal of salvation.

2. *Authoritative Nature of Scripture (3.16a)*. As we will see, the main purpose for Paul including this clause is to state that God is the originator of Scripture and therefore it is authoritative and useful for the person of God to be prepared (3.17) to do the things listed in 3.16b. Though the main purpose is evident, this sentence is fraught with many problems. Commentators have wrestled over what constitutes 'Scripture', the meaning of 'all/every', the syntax of the sentence and the meaning of the word *theopneustos* often translated 'God-breathed'.

Paul does not use the plural 'Scriptures' but rather the singular 'Scripture' which at first might seem odd since he uses the plural with respect to Scripture in 3.15. The word used here for 'Scripture', *graphē*, simply means, at its basic level, 'writing'. For example, David passes onto Solomon in written form everything he received from the Lord concerning the building of the temple (1 Chron. 28.19). The author of Exodus applies this term to describe the writing on both sides of the tablets containing the Ten Commandments (Exod. 32.16). These writings take on a special significance because the source of the writing is God. The term eventually was used to refer to the OT Scriptures. In the NT, *graphē* is found 50 times. At times it is included to denote a passage of OT Scripture. The Gospel writers (Mk 12.10; Lk. 4.21; Jn 7.42), Luke (Acts 8.35) and Paul (Rom. 10.11) employ it in this way. Occasionally the plural form denotes the OT Scriptures (Mt. 21.42; Mk 12.24; Lk. 24.32), though rarely, and Paul uses it in this way (Rom. 15.4). Finally, the single form of this word, 'Scripture', is utilized when referencing Scripture as a whole. Oddly it is not used this way in the Gospels.

Eight other references of the singular form of *graphē* can be found in Paul's letters. Even though all of the instances use the article, most of them are debatable since Paul could be referring to a specific passage or the Scriptures as a whole. More obvious instances pointing to a specific OT Scripture include Gal. 4.30 ('the Scripture says, "cast out the young woman and her son..."') and 1 Tim. 5.18 ('the Scripture says, "do not muzzle an ox that is threshing..."'). There are a few examples that seem to point to the whole of OT Scriptures like Gal. 3.22 ('Scripture shuts out everyone under sin') and Gal. 3.8 ('Scripture saw ahead of time that God would justify the Gentiles through faith') since they do not point to specific texts. The evidence is inconclusive whether the singular usage of *graphē* in 2 Tim. 3.16 refers to 'the Scriptures' or 'Scripture' singular.

The uniqueness of 2 Tim. 3.16 is that *graphē* has no article but it does include the adjective *pas*, which can be translated 'all' or 'every'. Surveying Paul's letters shows that when *pas* is coupled with a singular noun without an article it means 'every'. Therefore the clause is better translated 'every Scripture is God-breathed' thereby placing the emphasis on each individual passage of Scripture being God-breathed.

Syntactically 2 Tim. 3.16 could be translated 'every God-breathed Scripture is useful...' or 'every Scripture is God-breathed and useful...'. Although both are possible the latter is more likely. First, Paul is likely following the syntactical pattern found in 1 Tim. 4.1.

	adjective		verb	adjective	conjunction	
1 Tim. 4.1	'every	creature of God	is	good	and	useful'
2 Tim. 3.16	'every	Scripture	is	God-breathed	and	useful'

Second, the conjunction *kai* that follows 'God-breathed' is awkward to translate in the sentence (literally 'every God-breathed Scripture is *and* useful'). Similarly it makes little sense to translate *kai* as 'also', i.e. 'every God-breathed Scripture is *also* useful'. It is possible to translate *kai* as 'indeed' thereby stressing Scripture's usefulness because it is God-breathed, i.e. 'every God-breathed Scripture is *indeed* useful'.

It is still best to translate *kai* as 'and' and translate the clause as 'every Scripture is God-breathed *and* is useful'. The point of this statement is to give the origin of the Scripture (and therefore its authority) *and* its usefulness in different aspects of ministry because of its divine origin and authority.

What does Paul mean by 'God-breathed'? The word 'God-breathed' is a NT hapax legomenon. It is not found at all in the LXX and so this is the earliest known usage of the word and therefore it is possibly a word created by Paul. It is found only once in the Church Fathers (Fr. Pap. 10.1) though this verse is found over 100 times in the later patristic works. The greatest number of examples comes from the Pseudepigraphic material and Philo.

Etymologically, this word is a compound word which comprises two words, *theo* and *pneustos*, derived from the noun *theos* ('God') and the verb *pneō* ('to breathe out or in'). Unfortunately, some scholars have let the etymology overly influence their understanding of this word.

There are basically two interpretations of this word. The first interpretation stresses the effect of Scripture on the reader in the sense that 'Scripture inspires the reader'. This option takes *theopneustos* in the active sense in that God inspires or 'breathes into the reader' through Scripture. This interpretation is unlikely for two reasons. First, Greek nouns ending in *tos* typically are not active in their meaning but rather passive. For example, *agapētos* means 'beloved' not 'loving', and *eulogētos* means 'blessed' not 'blessing'. Second, the usage of this noun outside the NT does not support an active meaning but rather a passive meaning of 'God-breathed' or 'divinely inspired'. The fragment of Papias 10.1 (AD 100–25) states that the book of Revelation was divinely inspired. The Sibylline Oracles refer to 'divinely inspired streams' (*Syb. Or.* 308) and 'divinely inspired people' giving holy sacrifices (*Syb. Or.* 406). Plutarch wrote of 'divinely inspired dreams' and natural ones (Plutarch, *De plac. phil.* 5.2). The author of *Sentences* refers to 'the message of divinely inspired wisdom as the best message' (Ps. Phoc., *Sent.* 129).

Paul's interest in this term is to affirm the authoritative and foundational nature of Scripture to authenticate the gospel message and provide a pastoral tool. Elsewhere Paul has affirmed the authoritative nature of Scripture, which is active, helpful and effective. In Gal. 3.9 he declares that Scripture foreknew the inclusion of Gentiles as sons and daughters of Abraham. Similarly in Gal. 3.22 he avows that Scripture 'imprisoned everyone under sin' through its message.

Paul does not mention in 2 Tim. 3.16 how Scripture was divinely inspired but through the use of this term 'God-breathed' Paul is communicating that he adheres to his Jewish tradition that the OT Scriptures are divinely inspired. Jewish tradition recognized that on occasion, in the past, God directly wrote (Deut. 5.22) or dictated his message (Exod. 24.4). Traditionally, though, Judaism understood that people who spoke for God (i.e. prophets) and those who wrote on behalf of God were inspired. So the OT speaks of the inspired utterances of David (2 Sam. 23.1), Agur (Prov. 30.1), King Lemuel (Prov. 31.1) and of the prophets (Num. 24.2; Hos. 9.7). This tradition is found outside the OT too. In Hellenistic Judaism, the author of 4 Ezra uses the metaphor of light for inspiration: 'I [God] will light in your heart the lamp of understanding' (4 Ezra 14.25). Philo's understanding of divine inspiration is significant. Philo describes the process as 'being full of the divine spirit (*katapneō*) and under the influence of that spirit' (Philo, *Mos.* 1.175; cf. 2.291, 'filled with the Holy Spirit') so that 'the power of God breathing (*epipneō*) vigorously, arouse[s] and excite[s] a new kind of miraculous voice' (Philo, *Dec.* 35). The person under divine inspiration utters words 'as if another were prompting him' (Philo, *Spec. leg.* 1.65) because the 'divine spirit has entered in and taken up abode there' (Philo, *Spec. leg.* 4.49). He elaborates on this experience as a moment in which 'I have suddenly become full, ideas being, in an invisible manner, showered upon me and implanted in me from on high' (Philo, *Migr. Abr.* 35).

Philo's understanding of divine inspiration is consistent with that depicted in 2 Tim. 3.16 and 2 Pet. 1.21 in that it allows for human authorship but under the direct influence of the Holy Spirit. Clement, the early Church Father and probable author of 1 Clement, concludes similarly that 'the Scriptures [were] given through the Holy Spirit' (1 Clem. 45.2). Some later Church Fathers, deviated from this position espousing very minimal human participation.

3. *Beneficial Nature of Scripture for the Follower of God (3.16b)*. Not only is Scripture authoritative because of its intimate connection with God, it is also beneficial for ministry. The correct handling of Scripture enables the minister to serve the needs of people in the church though in this context Paul still has the false teachers in mind as those who need the threefold benefit of Scripture in terms of teaching, reproving and correcting. The same word for 'beneficial', *ōphelimos*, is used in two other contexts. First, Paul uses this term to stress for Titus the excellence and beneficial nature of good works since they provide proof of the saving, renewing work of the Holy Spirit. In 1 Tim. 4.8 Paul holds up the merits of physical training though he concludes that they are short-lived in comparison to the eternal benefits of godliness. Paul's hope in 2 Tim. 3.16 is that the false teachers will experience this godliness and turn away from their false teaching. To do so the false teachers will have to accept Timothy's refutation of their false teaching and embrace his sound teaching and instruction in righteousness.

Paul has probably listed the four benefits of Scripture in a certain order. This order has a chiastic arrangement (ABBA) and a sequential one.

The chiasm begins and ends with instruction.

   A Teaching
       B Convicting
       B Correcting
   A Instructing

The former emphasizes the false teachers's need to be taught orthodox teaching whereas the latter term stresses their need to be taught righteous behaviour. Clearly the emphasis in the chiasm is upon convicting and correcting the false teachers. Before these false teachers can embrace a new lifestyle and teaching, they need to recognize the error of their ways.

There is a logical sequence in the list. The false teachers require healthy teaching. This teaching exposes their errors, which in turn leads to correction. Healthy teaching culminates in transformed behaviour. This list is really the outworking of 2.21 in which the dishonourable vessel is cleansed to become a useful honourable vessel.

The importance of teaching runs through 1 and 2 Timothy as this word is found eleven times in these two letters (four more times in Titus) since false teaching is the main problem in Ephesus. The teaching Paul has in mind for Timothy to share is that which Paul passed on to him through the OT Scriptures (1 Tim. 4.6). It is this teaching that elders need to possess which some elders in Ephesus have abandoned and distorted (Acts 20.30). Godly teaching exposes sin (1 Tim. 1.10) and unorthodox teaching is taught by demons (1 Tim. 4.1). This function of teaching leads naturally to the next benefit on the list.

Paul's second term, *elegmos*, is a hapax legomenon that can mean 'convicting' or 'punishment' (Jdt. 2.10; 1 Macc. 2.49) though the former is more likely in this context since the meaning is closer to the cognate verb, *elegchō*, 'to convict' (Eph. 5.11, 13). People, certainly the false teachers, want to avoid exposure of their sin (Jn 3.20) though it is the responsibility of all believers to expose and convict one another of their sin (Mt. 18.15; Eph. 5.11. 13). To be convicted of one's sin through a person or directly by God is an expression of God's love (Rev. 3.19). In the subsequent charge, Paul exhorts Timothy to convict and reprove the false teachers as part of his ministry in Ephesus (2 Tim. 4.2).

The third term in the list, *epanorthōsin*, is also a hapax legomenon and means 'to correct someone'. Timothy is expected not only to show the false teachers their errors but also to correct their thinking. When this word is used in the LXX there is a restorative element in the sense of getting someone back on the straight path (1 Esdr. 8.52; 1 Macc. 14.34). Paul's goal has always been to restore the false teachers (2.25-26) but those who will not submit to sound teaching and righteous behaviour are to be removed (1 Tim. 5.20).

The final term, 'instruction in righteousness', represents the final stage in the hopeful restoration of the false teachers. This word, *paideia*, is used only here in the Pastorals, once in Eph. 6.4 and four times in Hebrews (Heb. 12.5, 7, 8, 11). Scholars often try to separate this word into two distinct meanings, 'discipline' or 'instruction'. More likely the meanings are fused in the sense of 'instruction attained through discipline or correction'. Instruction is necessary for all God's children (Heb. 12.5, 7); although it may not feel pleasant at the time, it will bring about 'the fruit of righteousness and peace' (Heb. 12.11). Paul is hoping this for the false teachers.

(iii) *Resulting in an Equipped Leader (3.17)*. Paul draws this section to a close with a concluding statement with respect to the presence of the false teachers that Timothy, a man of God, will be prepared through Scripture for any good work but specifically for dealing with the false teachers. The intention of v. 17 is blurred and probably functions both as a statement of purpose and result. Paul believes that Scripture serves the purpose of preparing the minister of God and should lead to the result of being prepared if the minister remains faithful and persevering. Syntactically this clause could refer to those who receive the instruction as the ones being prepared. The singular reference to 'man of God' and because the focus is on Timothy makes this option most unlikely.

Paul uses a hapax-legomenon adjective, *artios*, which means 'prepared', coupled with a cognate participle, *exartizomenos*, 'thoroughly prepared', to assure Timothy that Scripture equips and provides a more than sufficient base from which to minister. One could paraphrase 3.17 as 'so that the man of God might be thoroughly equipped and able to meet the demands of any good work'.

'Man of God' is the third of a series of phrases Paul has used to describe believers in general but Timothy in particular. Like the other two phrases, 'worker' (2.15) and 'servant of the Lord' (2.22), which captures a specific aspect of a believer, 'man of God' emphasizes 'belonging to God'. The phrase 'man of God' is also found in 1 Tim. 6.1 and it has its roots in the OT. It is a person of God who brings news of the downfall of the household of Eli the priest (1 Sam. 2.27). When Elijah raises the son of the widow she exclaims that he is a man of God (1 Kgs 17.24).

'Good works' is a phrase found twelve times in the NT: once in Acts 9.36, six times in the Pastorals and the remaining instances in Paul's corpus. Only Phil. 1.6 specifically refers to the good work as the transforming work of God in a believer's life. All eleven instances of works are generic and general and in each case people are the agents performing the good works. The emphasis in this phrase is on 'good' since they reflect the character of God (Mk 10.18). These are the kind of works Paul wants Timothy to perform because they are in direct contrast with the evil, destructive works of the false teachers (2 Tim. 2.17; 3.13; cf. 4.14, 18). More narrowly the good works in this instance probably denote the teaching, convicting, correcting and instructing of v. 16, which are but a sample of the many kinds of good works a believer might perform. In the subsequent charge in 4.2-5 Paul will indicate more explicitly the 'good works' he wants Timothy to continue to perform until they are reunited in Rome.

2 Timothy 4.1-8
Paul's Final Charge to Timothy

This charge comes at the end of the body of the letter in which Paul has addressed three major areas. First, he has requested Timothy to suffer with him for the gospel message, which might sound like foolishness compared to the false teachers's teaching, but in fact it is the wisdom of God (1 Cor. 1.21-25). Second, he has exhorted Timothy to suffer with him for the ministry of proclaiming this message in whatever form this suffering might take, verbal (1 Tim. 4.12) or physical (2 Tim. 3.12). Third, Paul has urged Timothy to remain committed to him and the gospel in spite of the resistance and destructive effect of the false teachers. In 4.1-8 Paul distills these main points and re-emphasizes them through a series of imperatives with the promise of a reward for faithful commitment to the task. One line of exhortation in this charge deals with Timothy discharging the basic responsibilities of ministry (e.g. preaching, evangelism) in a context of intolerance of the true gospel. Another line of encouragement has the false teachers in view: Timothy is to correct, rebuke and be level-headed coupled with patience and good teaching. On top of all this Paul insists on Timothy enduring hardship.

Most scholars have used this text to substantiate their position that Paul is about to die and therefore is asking for Timothy to join him immediately so that he might pass the baton of apostolic ministry to Timothy. This traditional position has been arrived at largely through interpreting 4.6-7 as proof of his imminent death after his trial in Rome. This idea is then read back into the surrounding context and letter thus proposing that Paul is writing his farewell letter or last will and testament. I take a very different approach to 4.1-8 in terms of its literary form and the interpretation of vv. 6-7. Paul is writing a paranetic letter and 4.1-8 is a literary form, called a 'charge form', in which he gives a strong command to Timothy to stay the course amidst a very difficult situation. A fuller explanation of my ideas can be found in my book *Timothy's Task, Paul's Prospect: A New Reading of 2 Timothy* (Sheffield: Sheffield Phoenix Press, 2006).

The 'Charge' as a Distinct Literary Form

Those who take the position that 4.1-8 is Paul's farewell speech or last will and testament are not able to show that it is one since it does not resemble either one of them in content and especially in structure. The best way to identify a literary form is on the basis of its structure and then its content and purpose. 2 Tim. 4.1-8 is a highly structured literary form called a *charge*. Charges are comprised of four basic elements (sometimes a fifth is found).

Charge Verb
Person/s Charged
Authority Phrase
Content of the Charge
Implications of the Charge (optional)

Figure 9. *The Structure of the Charge Form*

The purpose of a charge is to give an authoritative command from one party to another, through a greater authority (note that often the name of God is used), thereby creating a heightened demand for obedience from the person charged.

	2 Timothy 4.1-8	*Acts 16.18*
Charge Verb	'I charge	'I command
Person/s Charged	'you	'you
Authority Phrase	'before God and Jesus Christ... his appearance and kingdom	'in the name of Jesus Christ
Content of Charge	'preach the word...admonish with all patience and teaching... be level headed...fulfill you ministry	'come out of her
Implications of Charge	'furthermore the crown of righteousness awaits me...and to all who await his appearance'	'at that moment the spirit left her'

Figure 10. *Comparison of a Charge and an Exorcism*

As one can see, the exorcism recorded by Luke in Acts 16.18 is actually a particular usage of the charge form. The charge represents the strongest form of command in the Greek language. It is found in magic papyri in which people invoke a spell on someone (often to fall in love with them: Paris Magical Papyrus 3039–44). Examples of charges are found in a wide and diverse body of literature including Latin texts. Many examples are found in the LXX (Gen. 24.3; Deut. 30.19-20), Pseudepigrapha (*Testament of Reuben* 6.9), Church Fathers (Ignatius, *Pol.* 1.2) and secular writers (Virgil, *Aen.* 2.141-44; Curtius Rufus, *Hist. Alex. Mag.* 9.2.28).

Paul adapts the charge by including the 'reason for the charge', which he places in a chiasm with the content of the charge, and by including some 'autobiographical comments'.

Charge Verb and Authority Phrase 4.1
    Content of the Charge 4.2   A
        Reason for the Charge 4.3-4   B *chiasm*
    Content of the Charge 4.5   A
Paul's Autobiographical Comments 4.6-7
Implications of the Charge 4.8

Figure 11. *Chiastic Structure of 2 Tim. 4.1-8*

There is logic in this charge. Paul commands Timothy to fulfill his ministry. This command comes from Paul but is rooted in the authority of God the Father and Jesus the Son. The situation is grim and Paul is aware that the people want a different message taught by dilettantish teachers even though it is not good for them. Paul does not want Timothy to get drawn into the false teachers's teaching or methods but rather by following his example he can be assured of a future reward.

Paul's Charge to Timothy before God (4.1)

This is the third charge Paul has used in the Pastorals (1 Tim. 5.21; 6.13), twice with the same verb *diamarturomai* (5.21). Paul explicitly draws upon the authority of God the Father and Jesus the Son. The imagery developed here is that of Timothy being brought before the heavenly council where Paul solemnly speaks on behalf of the Father and the Son. These are the ones before whom Timothy has received his charge and those to whom he will have to give an account. Paul is stressing Timothy's accountability as this charge has been made before God and humankind. For this reason Paul adds the phrase 'who is about to judge the living and the dead' to the appellation 'Christ Jesus'.

The phrase 'judge the living and the dead' is a reference to the judgment at the Second Coming of Christ in which those alive at the parousia will be judged along with the dead (1 Thess. 4.16-18). The early church embraced it as a semi-creedal formula (*Barn.* 7.2; Polycarp, *Phil.* 2.1; *Ep. apost.* 16) based on the belief that God appointed Jesus as the judge of the living and the dead (Acts 10.42). Jesus has this right to judge because he died and rose to life and thereby became 'the Lord of both the living and the dead' (Rom. 14.9-10). Jesus came in the first parousia to bring salvation and in the second parousia to complete this salvation and bring judgment (1 Pet. 4.5).

The theme of judgment and parousia begins and ends the charge, thereby forming an *inclusio* (i.e. when the same word begins and ends a section) through the repetition of 'judge' and 'appearing' (4.1, 8).

144   *2 Timothy 4.1-8*

   Paul's Charge to Timothy before God for Loyalty to the Ministry (4.1)
   Paul's Expectation of a Reward for his Loyalty to the Ministry (4.8)

Figure 12. Inclusio *in 2 Tim. 4.1-8*

The judgment in 4.1 refers to the 'judgment of salvation' at the throne of judgment before which everyone will stand (Phil. 2.9-11). The judgment in 4.8 refers to the 'judgment of rewards for faithful ministry' (2 Cor. 5.9-10).

The purpose of 4.1 is to show that Christ's judgment is all-inclusive (i.e. Timothy, Paul, false teachers etc.) and no one will be able to escape it. There is a subtle reminder to Timothy in this clause dealing with eternal judgment that Timothy not 'turn away' from the gospel as the false teachers and others have (cf. Phygelus and Hermogenes in 1.15; Demas in 4.10; Alexander in 4.14). Paul is confident that Timothy will finish the race well and attain the prize of eternal life (2.5). Certainty of his future eternal reward should motivate him, as it did Paul, to serve God faithfully.

The charge is given in the first person and although Paul is absent, it expresses what scholars often refer to as 'Paul's apostolic parousia'.

This charge is also given in light of Christ's Second Coming (literally 'the appearing of him') and the Future Eternal Kingdom. Both terms can be used to refer to the present, that is the first appearance of Christ (1.10) and the present kingdom (Col. 1.13). Paul's usage here refers to the future 'appearing' of Christ (4.8; 1 Tim. 6.14; Tit. 2.13) and the future kingdom (4.18). Paul uses these terms to emphasize the certainty of future blessing and Christ's sovereign protection (4.18) in order to motivate Timothy into ongoing faithful service just as it has done for Paul.

Content of the Charge (4.2)

The content of Paul's charge to Timothy is divided into two parts (4.2 and 4.5) with a section on the reason for the charge in the middle (4.3-4), which is people's intolerance for the truth. This chiastic structure means that the commands given by Paul to Timothy are to be read with respect to the problem of the people who are being duped into believing the false teachers. There are five imperatives in 4.2 with very little or no explanation.

Preach the Word (4.2a)

The first imperative 'preach the word' probably serves as the head term since the subsequent commands are related in some way to preaching the word. Paul has spent a great part of this letter encouraging Timothy to bring an orthodox message to the Ephesians because of the existence of false teachers. He reiterates this now, stating simply the need for Timothy to continue preaching the Word. 'Word', *logos*, does not carry the narrow meaning to expound the Scriptures from the pulpit, which would be to import a present idea into the past. It seems somewhat odd that Paul does not qualify 'Word' with 'of God' as he does in 2.9 where it means 'message of God' as it does here. There are two messages circulating in Ephesus. One is the message of the false teachers that is based on myth and falsehood resulting in gangrene (2.19). The other message is the message of truth (2.15), which is God-breathed (3.16) and brings health and wholeness (1.13; 1 Tim. 6.3).

Earlier in the letter Paul referred to himself as a herald (1.11), who is someone who proclaims the message of a king. Paul is asking the same of Timothy. Timothy's message consists of preaching the gospel to unbelievers, since he is to do the work of an evangelist (4.5), and teaching, which is instructional for the converted and correctional for those embracing false teaching. In doing this, Timothy will in effect be guarding the good deposit (1 Tim. 6.20).

Keep at It When It Is Convenient and Inconvenient (4.2b)

This imperative can be translated in a couple of different ways. First, it can mean 'stay at one's post', drawing on the military metaphor and suggesting that Timothy should not move about. Jesus gives a similar command when he sends out his disciples (Mt. 10.11-15). This is an unlikely interpretation since Paul asks Timothy to leave Ephesus quickly for Rome (4.9, 21) and because this imperative, like the others, is related to preaching the Word. Second, it can mean 'stand by it' or 'keep at it'. In this context, Timothy is to keep at preaching the gospel and persevering in this task (note that perseverance is highlighted at the end of 4.2).

Paul qualifies the need to keep at preaching with two interesting adverbs which have been translated 'in season and out of season' or 'when convenient or inconvenient'. The latter translation is to be favoured. The first of these words is used in Mk 14.11 to describe Judas's attempt to find a convenient or suitable time when he could hand over Jesus to the High Priest (i.e. when he might not be caught or draw attention). The noun is used in Mk 6.21 to describe how Herodias looked for a suitable time to have John the Baptist killed, when the right circumstances presented themselves. In Heb. 4.16 God helps his people at just the right time.

The question becomes 'suitable or convenient for whom?' Paul's intention could be that Timothy is to stick with preaching the Word when it is convenient or inconvenient for him, in other words when he feels like preaching or not. Those who espouse this position suppose that Timothy's tendency towards reticence requires this exhortation of encouragement (1.6-7). I have already shown that this is false. Paul's more likely intention is for Timothy to stick at his preaching whether it is convenient for his audience to listen or not. This makes better sense of the context (4.3) since it is the hearers of the preaching who do not want to hear the message even though this is what they need. It is like feeding children what they need versus what they want.

Threefold Command Needed to Confront False Teaching and Teachers (4.2c)

All three commands in 4.2c deal with the method a herald needs to employ in order to combat false teachers and those who embrace their teaching. The combination of these three commands addresses the internal world of an individual in terms of his or her cognitive reasoning, ethical consciousness and internal will. The verse constitutes a summary of Paul's strategy for dealing with false teaching.

a. *Reprove*

To correct false teachers requires engaging them and appealing to logic in order to show the shortcomings of their teaching. There are two aspects to reproof. It requires exposing the sin (Eph. 5.11, 13; Hermas, *Vis.* 1.5) and then convicting someone of this sin (1 Cor. 14.24). This reproof can occur privately through reading Scripture (3.16) or publicly in a congregational setting (1 Tim. 5.20). Reproof assumes a certain amount of intentionality to confront and not avoid. Whatever way Timothy confronts the false teachers, he cannot ignore them hoping the problem will go away on its own. He will have to change them or remove them.

b. *Warn*

This word is found most often in the Gospels (27 of 29 occurrences). It is used infrequently in the sense of 'warn', as in the time Jesus warned the disciples not to tell anyone about his identity (Lk. 9.21). It is employed many times in the sense of 'rebuke'. Most of these occurrences are when Jesus rebukes a hostile force either in nature (Mt. 8.26), the demonic realm (Mk 1.25), the realm of sickness (Lk. 4.39) or that of sin (Mk 8.33). Several times people (especially the disciples) are rebuking others when they should not be, as in the case of Jesus (Mt. 16.22), children (Mt. 19.13) and a sick man (Mk 10.48) but only once appropriately by the thief on the cross (Lk. 23.40). Believers are told not to rebuke spiritual beings (Jude 9). Although people tend to rebuke inappropriately, Jesus requires believers to rebuke a brother or sister who is sinning and he expects believers to be alert to confront sin among members (Lk. 17.3; Heb. 3.12).

'To warn' includes both the idea of stopping an existing action and not beginning a new one. The degree to which one is warned is to be congruent with the magnitude and extent of the sin and the respective authority of the individual. Though not stated, Paul expects due process. Paul's objective is to establish boundaries beyond which there will be discipline. So in the case of the false teachers who are elders Paul hopes that Timothy can win them over through warning and gentle correction (2.24-26). Should this fail then Timothy may have to rebuke them publicly because of their public position of authority (1 Tim. 5.20). Specific things Paul wants Timothy to confront the false teachers about are their penchant for foolish arguments, inappropriate relations with single women, greed etc.

c. *Exhort or Implore*
Paul wants Timothy, in his fight against false teaching, to appeal to the wills of the false teachers so that they might change their position. He utilizes a common verb, *parakaleō*, which can mean either 'exhort' or 'implore'. Some scholars see the emphasis on confrontation and the need to implore the false teachers and their adherents because the immediate context deals with opposition to the orthodox gospel message (4.3-4). Others see the emphasis on encouragement and therefore the need for exhortation because of the earlier and immediate stress on patient teaching (2.24; 4.2c). Most likely Paul has both ideas in mind and wants Timothy to use discretion that would be appropriate in any given situation.

d. *With All Patience and Every Kind of Teaching*
This phrase is found at the end of 4.2. It is not clear whether it applies only to the last command to exhort or to all three commands. Given the gravity and difficulty of the situation Timothy is facing it is very likely that this phrase applies to all three commands, thereby underscoring the disposition Timothy will need. From this we can gather that the goal is restoration over the long haul and Paul does not foresee a short-term fix, which is the reason he sends Tychicus to continue Timothy's work.

Patience is highlighted because this is what Paul experienced at his conversion and concluded to be necessary for anyone who is about to believe in Christ for eternal life and transformation (1 Tim. 1.16; Eph. 4.2). It is a fruit of the Spirit and necessary for leadership (Gal. 5.22; 2 Tim. 3.10).

The word 'all' modifying 'teaching' may be best translated as 'every kind of teaching' (cf. 1 Tim. 6.10 for a similar translation of 'all'). There is a subtle hint to be creative and varied in one's use of teaching styles, methods, venues etc.

Reason for the Charge: It is a Time of Intolerance of Truth (4.3-4)

This section, which is not in the typical charge form, gives us great insight into the problems in Ephesus. Through most of the letter Paul has been addressing his comments to the problem of the false teachers and their insidious effects on the church community. However in this section Paul puts the focus of the problem on the people who listen to the false teachers and not the false teachers themselves. The future time of intolerance of the truth has is in effect already come in Ephesus (cf. 3.1 where the future verb 'will be' does not convey the temporal idea of something yet to come but the logical sense of expectation which is already being realized). Timothy is living in the time in which wholesome teaching of the gospel is not considered by the hearers as convenient or suitable. There are three parts to Paul's evaluation of the problem.

They Reject Healthy Teaching for Unhealthy Teaching (4.3a)
'Healthy' is a word found almost exclusively in Luke and the Pastorals (one exception is 3 John 2). The teaching Paul passed onto Timothy he claims is 'healthy doctrine' (1.13) and is founded on the 'healthy words' of the Lord Jesus Christ's teaching (1 Tim. 6.3). For Paul, healthy teaching is the gospel and anything contrary to it is 'unhealthy teaching' (1 Tim. 1.10). By definition healthy teaching is truth and will bring life and sustenance. The fact is that certain people find the content, with its focus on God and not religiosity (1 Tim. 3.16–4.5), and the demands of this teaching for godliness to be unpalatable. The proof of this is found in that they choose the teaching of demons taught by hypocritical liars over the gospel (1 Tim. 4.1). The irony of the matter is that they will not 'endure' that which is good for them because of the costly nature of the gospel and the kingdom of God, yet they will put up with destructive false teaching (cf. 2 Cor. 11.20).

They Pile Up Teachers (4.3b)
The Ephesians want a plethora of teachers, certainly not just Timothy, thinking wisdom is found in numbers not quality, much like the Corinthians (1 Cor. 1.18–2.5). This idea may be influenced by the contemporary culture in which there would be many rhetoricians each of whom had their own brand of wisdom and philosophy. The readers of *Barn.* 4.6 were piling their sins one on top of another and not seeing the destructive effect. Similarly, the image created by the verb *episōreuō* in 2 Tim. 4.3 is that of 'piling up one teacher on top of another' but with no positive effect.

There are two possible ways to interpret the metaphor 'scratching' or 'tickling'. It could mean that some Ephesians have an 'itch' to hear some intriguing knowledge which they believe can only be satisfied through the readily available false teaching. The other interpretation, and the more likely one, is that the listeners want a teaching that entertains and elicits a pleasurable experience just as a baby laughs and smiles when it is gently tickled. They long for teachers who titillate their curiosity for 'knowledge' but do not challenge their lifestyle. According to Paul, their teaching is 'godless chatter' and not real 'knowledge' (1 Tim. 6.20). Clement of Alexandria, though writing in the second century AD, is probably describing the same kind of teachers as Timothy is facing. They are those who 'show themselves as greater chatterers than turtle-doves; scratching and tickling, not in a manly way, in my opinion, the ears of those who wish to be tickled' (*Strom.* 1.2.21.2–3.24.4).

They Substitute the Truth of the Gospel for Myths (4.4)

Verse 4 explains what the Ephesians are actually doing by not enduring healthy teaching. They are turning away from hearing (note that this is the same word as used in 4.3, *akoen*, to make the contrast clear) the truth and at the same time turning to myths. Paul uses a strong term, *apostrephō*, to describe the manner in which these people are turning from the truth. The same word is found in 1.15 (see my discussion there) where it refers to apostasy. Through this verb Paul shows the effect of the substitution of truth for myths as moving from a position of belief to rejection of God.

The second clause, 'turning aside to myths', also suggests the danger of apostasy through avoiding a diet of healthy teaching. 'Turning aside' is found three times in 1 Timothy to describe those who have lost their way and turned aside to empty talk (1.6), to describe those who have turned to Satan (5.15), and finally to give a warning to Timothy not to turn to godless foolish talk (6.20). Elsewhere Paul describes these myths as material circulating among Jews, possibly based on Jewish stories, and as 'human commandments' and therefore inferior to his apostolic teaching (Tit. 1.14). Such material was comprised of endless genealogies and fallacious stories (1 Tim. 1.14) that Paul deems as godless and foolish (1 Tim. 4.7) in the sense of the Proverbs 'fool' (Prov. 10.14). The deception of embracing these myths is that they feel they have the truth but instead they have chosen the wide road to destruction instead of the narrow path to life.

Although these people have chosen this gangrenous teaching, Paul still holds out the hope that they can be won back to orthodox teaching and change just as he changed from being a blasphemer and persecutor of the church (1 Tim. 1.13).

Content of the Charge Continued (4.5)

Verse 5 constitutes the second half of the content of the charge section in the chiasm of 4.2-5 (see Figure 11). Through the use of 'but you', Paul sets up the contrast between Timothy and the straying Ephesians but with the false teachers in view too since this list of commands deals with how Timothy is to minister in a context of intolerance of healthy teaching (cf. *Apoc. Elij.* 1.13). The fourfold command combines personal exhortations of character with specific ministerial actions.

Be Sober-minded (4.5a)

Literally the verb used, *nephō*, means 'to be sober'. It is only used in the NT in the metaphorical sense of abstaining from any form of spiritual drunkenness and imbibing some spiritual grace. It is sometimes found with the verb *gregoreō*, 'to watch' (1 Pet. 5.8), which is the word Jesus gave to his disciples (Mk 13.37). Paul says being sober-minded is worked out by holding fast to faith, hope and love (1 Thess. 5.6, 8). Peter uses the term three times: first, to express the need for moral preparedness amidst the temptation of sin while keeping the hope of grace at Christ's return fixed firmly in one's mind (1 Pet. 1.13); second, to be sober-minded in order to be able to pray (1 Pet. 4.7); and third, to be alert for one's adversary, the Devil (1 Pet. 5.8).

In a context of enticing false teaching and false teachers, it is important for Timothy to hold fast to orthodoxy in his behaviour and belief in every situation, especially in compromising situations when he has to confront false teachers (2 Tim. 2.25) or young women influenced by these false teachers (1 Tim. 5.2).

This term suggests the need for Timothy to be composed but more importantly it stresses the importance of him discerning false teaching and not becoming enamoured with it.

Endure Suffering (4.5b)
Fidelity to the gospel will mean persecution (cf. *2 En.* 50.3-4 for the same exhortation). This is a very important theme that runs throughout the letter (1.8; 2.3; 3.12) and sets up Paul's example in 4.6-8 as one who suffered but will one day receive a crown for his faithful work. Personal harm will come to Timothy in part because of his belief in the gospel and in part through ministering to people hostile to the gospel. Suffering in these ways may be a temptation for Timothy to move from his firm position but to do so would be foolishness.

There is a textual variant in this text. Codex Alexandrinus (fifth century) has 'endure suffering *as a good soldier of Christ Jesus*'. The manuscript support for the omission of the phrase '*as a good soldier of Christ Jesus*' is slightly stronger (Codex Sinaticus, fourth century). Therefore it is doubtful that the phrase is original but rather an intentional insertion of the phrase in order to coincide with 2 Tim. 2.3 in which the same cognate verb is used, 'to endure suffering together' (*sunkakopatheō*).

Do the Work of an Evangelist (4.5c)
'Work' or *ergon* is a very common word in the NT (169 times) and most occurrences refer to an 'action' or 'deed' but as in this case it can take on the more narrow meaning of 'task' or even 'occupation'. The 'work of the Lord' (1 Cor. 15.58; 16.10) is varied (Mk 13.34) and can include serving a person's needs (Phil. 2.30) and performing the different aspects of an overseer (1 Tim. 3.1) or apostle (Acts 13.2; 15.38). One of Timothy's tasks is that of an evangelist.

There is some debate whether 'evangelist' is *titular* designating a specific office in the church or *functional* alluding to a particular task that church leaders should be doing. Early commentators believed that evangelists held a temporary position in a church between the time of the apostles and the establishment of church leaders. Certainly in this instance Paul is asking Timothy to make sure that he continues to incorporate evangelism among his other leadership duties. It would be easy for Timothy to overlook evangelism as he is preoccupied with the problem of the false teachers. A view to outward growth is vital and cannot be compromised even during a time of internal introspection and transformation.

This imperative is really a reiteration in summary form of the commands in 4.2, centering on preaching the Word, but directed towards those outside the church.

Fulfill Your Ministry (4.5d)

This final imperative condenses the content of the charge and letter, encompassing all aspects of Timothy's ministry that he is to accomplish. Paul reminds Timothy that just as he (Paul) was appointed to the Lord's ministry (1 Tim. 1.12), Timothy has been appointed too. This ministry is based upon the model of Jesus the humble servant and therefore can include acts of service as mundane as preparing a meal (Lk. 10.40), collecting offerings (2 Cor. 8.4), preaching (Acts 20.24) or preparing the body of Christ for ministry (1 Cor. 16.15; Eph. 4.12). There is no act of service too low for a servant of Christ and all must be done in humility and purity so that the ministry in Christ's name is not discredited (2 Cor. 6.3).

Timothy belongs to a long line of servants to the Lord like the Levites (1 Clem. 40.5) and apostles (Acts 1.17, 25). The verb used here, *plērophoreō* (Lk. 1.1), like its cognate, *plēroō*, means 'to fulfill' (Col. 4.17). Most of the occurrences of this verb in the NT carry the meaning of 'to convince fully'. Here, Paul may be drawing on the meaning found in some of the ancient papyri, 'to pay back a debt in full'. Paul is telling Timothy to fulfill his ministry in the sense of discharging all the duties of his ministry under his obligation to God and in doing so he is fulfilling the prophecy pronounced over him (1 Tim. 1.18; 2 Tim. 1.6).

Paul's Autobiographical Comments (4.6-7)

Scholars have attempted to determine the relationship between vv. 6-7 and the preceding verses. Some believe that Paul is contrasting his life in 4.6-7 with the false teachers in 4.3-4 or Timothy in 4.5. This is very unlikely since the conjunction *gar*, 'for I', is never used as a contrasting conjunction. There is a contrast in 4.1-8 but it is between the false teachers in 4.3-4 and Timothy in 4.5 who ministers in a different manner than they. Each time 'but you' (4.5) is found in 2 Timothy the contrast is with the preceding verse (cf. 3.10, 14).

Some propose that there is a causal relationship between vv. 6-7 and v. 5. Verses 6-7 state the reason for the urgency of the commands given in v. 5. It is suggested that Paul will soon die as stated in 4.6-7 so Timothy must take over Paul's ministry, fulfilling the commands in 4.5.

More likely *gar egō*, 'for I', should be understood as an *explanatory conjunction* as it is commonly used in Paul's letters (1 Cor. 11.23; 15.9; 2 Cor. 2.11; Gal. 2.11; 6.17; Phil. 4.11). This means that vv. 6-7 are used to explain the imperatives given in v. 5 through the example of Paul's experiences in Rome. While in prison, Paul has fully discharged the duties of his ministry.

The main purpose of these autobiographical comments is to present Paul as an example of one who has faithfully fulfilled the content of the charge and thereby provides a paradigm for Timothy and others to follow. For those who are faithful to their calling, the heavenly reward awaits them (4.8). Although Paul is in prison, there is a steadfast certainty in his words with respect to his future reward and Christ's sovereign protection (4.18) as he reflects on his situation. Since the eternal kingdom is certain and secure, he is sure that Christ will award him this either immediately should he be executed or later should he be spared.

Many scholars believe that these verses point to Paul's imminent death but I will show that they indicate quite the contrary. Through these verses Paul expresses his hopeful expectation of being released from prison in Rome under the tyrannical rule of Nero.

Paul includes five statements and although most of them could describe his lifelong experience of ministry, it is quite certain that they express his reflection subsequent to his first trial. Each statement conveys its own unique image. His preaching in particular and his trial and incarceration in general are like a drink offering. Like a ship released from its moorings, he hopes to be released from prison. His trial he compares to a fight and a race through which he has kept the faith and is confident he will be released by the time Timothy arrives in order to continue their ministry together.

Cultic Metaphor: Being Poured Out as a Drink Offering (4.6a)

There are five possible ways to interpret this text. First, Paul could be drawing on the pagan background in which a libation was given to mark the end of a person's life based on the libation given to *Zeus saviour* to mark the end of a festival. Tacitus records the suicides of Seneca, who was Nero's guardian for several years, and Thrasea, a dissenting Roman nobleman during Nero's reign, who considered their blood falling to the ground a libation to Zeus. It is very doubtful that Paul would draw on a pagan background when the Jewish background for 'pouring out' exists. Also that text is in Latin and therefore does not provide a clear link to the Greek word *spendomai*, which is used in 2 Tim. 4.6.

A second position is that the verb *spendomai* should be translated in the middle voice, meaning 'I am pouring myself out' in the sense of 'expending oneself'. This position eliminates the idea of any cultic imagery of blood or wine being poured out. Though there is some merit that Paul does expend himself on behalf of the Romans it is more likely, as we will see, that the Jewish cultic imagery is fundamental in this text.

A possible third position, which I originated and formerly held, is that the 'pouring out' could refer to the pouring out of the drink offering associated with the Nazirite vow. Nazirite vows are explained in Num. 6.1-23 and the Mishnaic tractate *m. Naz*. Samson (Judg. 13.4-7), Samuel (1 Sam. 1.11) and John the Baptist (Lk. 1.15) were lifelong Nazirites. These vows were taken to signify that a person was separating himself or herself to the Lord and occasionally as an act of thanksgiving. Paul was familiar with Nazirite vows and had fulfilled some in his lifetime (Acts 18.18; 21.23). In light of this background, the metaphor of being poured out could signify that the time of Paul's separation to the Lord as his minister is about to end since he is about to die. It is also possible to interpret this metaphor as Paul being poured out as a thanksgiving to God for the privilege of suffering and witnessing for him (Acts 9.15; 20.24; 21.13; Rom. 8.18. Phil. 3.10; Col. 1.24). Though both of these are attractive and make sense of the context, there are two problems. First, the contrast is between what Paul is doing in his present circumstances (i.e. preaching in the Roman court) and how these actions coincide with the purpose and effect of drink offerings being poured out on a sacrifice. This connection is not clear. Second, it is unlikely that the Ephesians would readily identify this word with the fairly obscure usage of drink offerings in Nazirite vows. It is more likely that they would identify *spendomai* with the drink offerings offered in the temple.

The fourth position is what I call the 'traditional position'. Most scholars agree that the imagery in this clause is the OT drink offering or libation offered in conjunction with the daily burnt and fellowship offerings in the temple and tabernacle (Exod. 29.40; Num. 15.1-10). The drink offering consisted of pouring out wine, not blood, which distinguished it from pagan sacrifices (Ps. 16.4), on the altar.

The traditional understanding of this clause is that it is a metaphor for Paul's impending death in which he is like a sacrifice being poured out on the altar. Paul's trial marks the beginning of this effusion that culminates in his martyrdom at which time his blood is actually spilt. These scholars understand the verb *spendomai*, which means to pour out wine, as the pouring out of blood and thus a metaphor for death.

The main problem with this position is that this verb is never used in the NT or OT as the pouring out of blood. It is used once to refer to pouring out 'water' that David's soldiers have brought back to him to drink when he complained of thirst (2 Sam. 23.16). Risking their lives, they go behind enemy lines and bring water back to David. He does not drink it but instead pours it out on the ground as a libation to the Lord since David is not worthy of such honour, only God is. Thus the image of the libation is not of 'death' but rather of 'devotion and commitment for another'.

There are three noteworthy usages of *spendomai* in Philo. *Ebr.* 152 is an allegorical interpretation of 1 Sam. 1.14 in which Philo understands Hannah pouring out her soul before God as a pleasing aroma to God because she followed reason and not the inebriating passions of the world. In *Leg. all* 2.56 Philo takes the term 'nakedness' from Gen. 2.25 and interprets it in light of Leviticus 16 and Exod. 33.7. The priest enters the holy of holies naked (actually clothed in sacred vestments instead of his ordinary priestly garments) in order to pour out 'soul-blood'. Soul-blood does not represent a person's death but rather the life of a person who is being dedicated or consecrated to God. Philo probably used *spendomai* instead of *ekcheō*, which typically means 'to pour out blood on the seat of atonement', to avoid any idea that there was an efficacious element to this action (cf. 4 Macc. 6.28-7.9; 17.21-24). The final example is in *Rer. div. her.* 182–84, in which Philo gives an allegorical interpretation of Exod. 24.6. The two bowls of blood (note that one was sprinkled on the altar and the other on the people) represent human and divine wisdom. Divine wisdom, which Philo calls a *spondē*, a cognate of the verb *spendomai*, maintains the image of the wine offerings: divine wisdom, like a wine offering, brings a pleasurable aroma to God. There is no hint of sacrificial death in any of these occurrences.

There are two possible reasons why the traditionalists may have quickly and imperceptibly switched from a wine offering to a blood offering with reference to death. First, there exists a rich Christian tradition of the wine and blood in the Eucharist and the relationship to Jesus' death. Second, some scholars have read back 'blood' imagery into the wine offerings in order to make this verse coincide with church history since Paul was martyred in Rome sometime during this imprisonment.

The verb *spendomai* is better translated in the passive voice, 'I am being poured out'. It may be that God is the agent pouring Paul out though this is not necessary. The image is of Paul willingly being poured out before God since he serves in the ministry as a slave of God and Christ (Tit. 1.1; Rom. 1.1). Paul is 'already' being poured out in that his trial has been an ongoing struggle and will probably continue but in the end he believes that he will be released. So in some sense there is an element of Paul expending himself in this situation but it is in the context of a sovereign God to whom he is fully submitted.

Now I present my position. The main function and purpose of a wine offering was to enhance the aroma of a sacrifice and thereby to make it pleasing to God. For this reason the accompanying Hebrew phrase 'a delightful smell to the Lord' is found (21 times; see Lev. 1.9, 13, 17). It is this cultic imagery that is important to Paul in this context since it corresponds metaphorically with what Paul is doing in Rome. I suggest that the drink offering represents Paul's defence trial where he stood alone with only the Lord beside him as he fully proclaimed the gospel message to the Gentiles (4.17). This action of Paul was like an aromatic drink offering to God. Blood and death play no part in this image.

Paul elsewhere has understood his role as an apostle to carry the Lord's name to the Gentiles and their kings (Acts 9.15) as he did before Agrippa, Felix and Festus (25.11-12; 26.1). This ministry Paul understood in cultic terms. He considered himself a 'servant of Jesus Christ' (Rom. 15.16) using the term *leitourgos* to describe himself which is frequently used to describe a priest serving in the cultic activity of the temple (Num. 4.37, 41; 1 Sam. 2.11, 18; 3.1; Ezra 7.24; Heb. 8.2). Paul expands on this role in Rom. 15.16 through the use of the participle *hierourgounta*, which means 'to serve as a priest'. A translation of Rom. 15.16-17 is 'because of the grace God gave me to be a priest of Jesus Christ to the Gentiles, who serves as a priest with respect to preaching the gospel of God in order that the offering of the Gentiles might be acceptable [to God] sanctified by the Holy Spirit'. Paul understands his preaching of the gospel to the Gentiles as a priestly service. his preaching is like a drink offering that is poured over the Gentiles, who are likened to an oblation. When Paul preaches the gospel to the Gentiles and they believe, they become an acceptable sweet-smelling offering to God. Similarly, when Paul preached the gospel to the Gentiles at his trial, he was being poured out over them in the hope that they might come to faith and he be released.

The same imagery is found in Phil. 2.17. Paul is incarcerated in Rome (AD 60–62) and is awaiting news of the outcome of his trial. He is quite confident that he will be released and will join Timothy again in Philippi (Phil. 2.24). Paul is being poured out in the sense that his personally costly preaching from prison (Phil. 1.12-20) is like a drink offering being poured over the Philippians's costly sacrifice of ministering in a comparable difficult situation. In both contexts Paul considers his preaching ministry in terms of cultic imagery and in neither context does he expect to die imminently.

The Time of My Release is at Hand (4.6b)

The traditional understanding of this clause is that Paul's death is imminent. They translate this sentence as 'the time of departure is at hand' and take the phrase 'time of departure' as a common euphemism for 'death'. There are several problems with this position.

The noun *analusis* used in this context has an active meaning of 'loosing' in the sense of resolving a problem or dissolving something into its elements (Alexander the Philosopher, *De mixtione* 215.7; Philo, *Aet. mundi* 94.4) or dissolving a party (Josephus, *Ant.* 19.239). It also can take a passive meaning, in the sense of 'being loosed from something' or 'release' which is the usage in 2 Tim. 4.6. The meaning always includes a modifier stating that from which something is released or loosed. Philo speaks of the 'release of water' (*Quaest. in Gen.* 2.29.4); Sophocles the 'release of a person from evil' (*Elec.* 142) and Timaeus the 'release of a person from an oath' (*Historicus* 23).

When *analusis* is used to refer to death it always includes a modifier like 'release of the body' (Secundus, *Senten.* 20.1; Ps.-Clem., *Homil.* 3.28.3). The literal translation of 4.6b is 'the release of me is at hand' or 'my release is at hand'. If Paul had meant 'death' he might have written that the 'release of my body' is at hand but more likely he would have used a different verb that means 'to die'.

There are several other reasons why this clause is probably not referring to his imminent death. First, there are no other texts that support the meaning of *analusis* to mean death. Scholars frequently cite three texts (Philo, *Flacc.* 187, 115; 1 Clem. 44.5) as examples of *analusis* referring to death ('final release from life', 'this final release from the festive party' and 'who had a fruitful and mature release [from the body/life/ministry]' respectively). But in each instance it is always *analusis* plus the modifiers that creates the meaning of death. Sometimes scholars look to Phil. 1.23 to attempt to transport the meaning of the cognate verb *analuō* ('to depart') into the noun. But again it is only the surrounding context ('to be with Christ') that conveys the idea of departure in terms of death. Second, *analusis* does have a modifier, 'me' (*mou*), and is translated literally 'release of me' or 'my release' which is the typical meaning of *analusis*. So it is more likely that Paul is referring to his release from prison though he does not explicitly say 'prison' but this can be easily assumed from the letter as a whole. Third, the use of 'and' (*kai*) shows that the clause 'I am already being poured out' and 'and my time of release' are somehow related. The previous clause, I showed, refers to Paul's successful preaching before the Roman legal court as a drink offering and therefore the latter clause expresses his confidence that he will be released soon as a result of this. Fourth, there is a lack of logic if 4.6 refers to Paul's death in light of the context of the whole letter. If 4.6 refers to his death then why does Paul say later in 4.17 that he has been rescued from the lion's mouth (i.e. from death)? If Paul believes his death is imminent then why does he not ask Timothy to come immediately but instead allows him to delay his journey to pick up Mark to help them in their ministry, stop along the way for his scrolls and cloak, wait for Tychicus to arrive in Ephesus and even allow Timothy time to postpone his trip provided he arrives in Rome before winter (2 Tim. 4.11-13, 21). Finally, if Paul is writing a last will and testament and is expecting to die then why would he ask Timothy to come to Rome? People wrote a last will and testament precisely because they did not think the recipients would be around at their death, so clearly Paul is expecting to be alive and so is not writing his last will and testament.

Threefold Description of His Ministry in Rome (4.7a)
Traditionally these three statements are taken to be a summary of Paul's apostolic ministry. Paul sets forth his ministry in metaphorical terms of a fight and a race that he believes is now coming to an end. The third term depicts the steadfast faithfulness he has maintained throughout his ministry. For these scholars these clauses represent the final words of a person giving a farewell speech or final testament. The fact that each of these verbs is in the perfect tense is further proof.

Though it is possible to read these clauses through the lens of his entire ministry, it is just as possible, and I believe even more probable, that these statements refer to the struggle at Rome he has encountered and which, from his perspective, is about to end with his release. The perfect tense of these verbs can just as easily apply to his trial and incarceration at Rome.

There is some debate whether there are three different images or whether the athletic image is maintained throughout these statements. Elsewhere Paul uses military images (Eph. 6.10-18; 1 Thess. 5.8) and athletic images (1 Cor. 9.24-27) for ministry so both are possible in this context. The first image of a fight is most contested since it could refer to a battlefield or an athletic contest. It is more likely in this context that Paul is keeping the athletic imagery throughout since he includes the same image in 1 Tim. 4.10; 6.12 and he conjoins this image with winning a prize (2 Tim. 4.8) as he does elsewhere. Regardless of what image is in Paul's mind, military or athletic, the difference is negligible since the same fighting spirit is needed whether on the battlefield or in the wrestling pit.

a. *I Have Fought the Good Fight*
The verb *agōnizomai*, 'to fight', means to engage in a contest but figuratively to struggle in a various number of ways in the Christian life or ministry. This idea may be derived from Jesus' teaching (Lk. 13.24). Two questions arise: what is Paul's struggle and is this struggle a particular one or a reference to his whole life and ministry?

Paul draws on the image of fighting as a metaphor for the struggles involved in the entirety of the Christian life and ministry (1 Cor. 9.25; Col. 1.29; 1 Tim. 4.10; cf. Heb. 12.3). But he also utilizes this metaphor to describe particular 'fights' or 'struggles' the believer and minister may experience along the way. So Epaphroditus has battles of prayer for the Colossians (Col. 4.12). Paul reflects on a past struggle that is recurring in Philippi (Phil. 1.30). In 1 Thess. 2.2, Paul gives the Thessalonians a reminder about the struggle he and his friends experienced when they first came to Thessalonica. See also Col. 1.29 and 2.1 for the cognate *agōnia*, referring to Jesus' struggle in Gethsemane.

Scholars frequently turn to 1 Tim. 6.12a, 'fight the good fight of faith', as a parallel for this text, suggesting Paul is saying in 2 Tim. 4.7 that he has fought the good fight for the faith all his life. This is unlikely. The good fight of faith in 1 Tim. 6.12a that Paul asks Timothy to engage in, is a particular situation and refers most likely to defending the gospel from the corruption of the false teachers's teaching and distinguishing himself from the flawed character of the false teachers. The phrase 'of faith' is omitted in 2 Tim. 4.7 so the 'fight' probably refers to something else. The mostly likely referent for the 'good fight' is Paul's Roman trial and incarceration.

Paul is not boasting about how he fought this fight, when he calls it a *good* fight, rather he is alluding to the quality of the fight. He is voicing his perspective that his trial and incarceration constitute a noble battle since he was afforded the opportunity to share the gospel fully before many Roman authorities (2 Tim. 4.17). It is good in the same sense that the calling to be an overseer is a 'good [note the same word] work' (1 Tim. 3.1). Paul is committed to the greatest fight, namely the ministry of the gospel, of which one tough fight took place in Rome where he willingly entered into the fray, not avoiding suffering or the difficulty of ministering in this context.

b. *I Have Completed the Race*

Literally, the word *dromos* can mean 'course' of the sun (1 Esdr. 4.34) or heavenly bodies (1 Clem. 20.2) or a 'foot race' (Eccl. 9.11). *Dromos* can be taken metaphorically in which one's entire life is considered a race (Jer. 8.6; 23.10) or some part of this life is a particular race (Hdt., *Hist.* 8.74.1; Philo, *Leg. all.* 3.48; *Vit. Mos.* 2.291). 'Race' is used here in the metaphorical sense. The question is whether it refers to Paul's entire ministry (Ignatius, *Pol.* 1.2) or his trial and imprisonment in Rome. Those that prefer the former position look to Acts 20.24 for support because of the linguistic parallel.

Acts 20.24a	*2 Tim. 4.7*
'I consider my life of no account if only I have completed the race'	'I may complete my race'

Acts 20.24b	*2 Tim. 4.17*
'and the ministry I received from the Lord, testifying to gospel of God's Grace'	'so that through me the message might be fully proclaimed'

For these scholars the race in Acts 20.24 refers to Paul's lifelong ministry of preaching the gospel, which they believe was brought to completion in Rome. There are a couple of problems with this position. First, it is unlikely that Paul thinks that his ministry of preaching the gospel is completed since he asks Timothy to bring Mark with him to Rome because he is useful for the ministry of proclaiming the gospel, which most certainly he expects to continue (2 Tim. 4.11). Second, in light of the previous reason, it is much more likely that 2 Tim. 4.17 means that 'the gospel was fully proclaimed through me [Paul at my trial]' and not that 'his [Paul's] ministry was brought to its completion [at my trial]'.

Paul has finished the race, which in this context refers to his first trial, where he fully proclaimed the gospel. 'Race' therefore is equivalent to 'fight' in the previous clause. It is not uncommon to find the juxtaposition of these two metaphors (1 Cor. 9.24-26; Heb. 12.1). The perfect tense of the verb 'to complete' emphasizes the decisive climactic moment for Paul of preaching before the Roman officials (possibly Nero) and does not signify the end of his ministry. Paul understands his Christian life and ministry as a marathon that God has set before him; Paul refers to this as '*my* race' (Acts 20.24; note the qualifier 'my' which means 'the race for me from the Lord'). But within this metaphorical race there are many 'smaller races' or events. '*The* race' (note the lack of qualifier) in 2 Tim. 4.7 is one such difficult event and after his release he hopes to continue preaching the gospel with Timothy, Luke and Mark.

c. *I Have Kept the Faith*
The two metaphors of fighting the fight and finishing the race naturally lead to the final clause of keeping the faith. There are two ways of understanding 'faith' in this context, *subjectively* or *objectively*.

The first interpretive option takes 'faith' as 'loyalty or faithfulness' meaning 'I have kept myself faithful to God during this time in Rome'. This subjective understanding of 'faith' is the most common usage in 2 Timothy (1.5, 13; 2.18, 22; 3.10, 15). If the athletic metaphor were being maintained in this text then it is reminiscent of the oaths athletes would take before the games, pledging to be loyal to the rules of the games (cf. 2 Tim. 2.5, 'the athlete receives the crown if he competes according to the rules'; cf. Epictetus, *Diss.* 3.10.8). Paul is affirming that he has competed in this fight and race with integrity, endurance and faithfulness and therefore the crown of righteousness will one day await him.

The second interpretive option requires taking 'faith' objectively as 'doctrine' (i.e. content of belief). Paul would be saying that he has preserved the gospel from corruption. This position has merit. First, this meaning is consistent with the many commands for Timothy to protect the purity of the gospel from the corrupting influences of the false teachers, who espoused veneration of myths and genealogies (1 Tim. 1.3-4; 4.7), misuse of the Law (1.8-11), false asceticism (4.3-5), following things taught by demons (4.1-2) and denial of the resurrection (2 Tim. 2.18). Second, this meaning coheres with the many statements in 2 Timothy underscoring the efficacious effect of sound teaching (2 Tim. 2.25-26; 3.15, 17) versus unhealthy teaching (2 Tim. 2.14-23; 4.3-4). Third, this option is harmonious with the abundant instances when Paul contrasts himself or the godly teacher with the ungodly false teachers (1 Tim. 4.1-6; 2 Tim. 2.15-18, 20-24) including the immediate context.

The resolution to this conundrum may be that Paul has both meanings of 'faith' in mind because of the strengths of each position. Though possible, it is still more likely that Paul is emphasizing the subjective aspect of being loyal and faithful throughout the entire Roman imprisonment and trial.

Implications of the Charge (4.8)

The implications of the charge section (4.8) is optional in the charge form but Paul includes it here because it is important for Timothy to know what he can expect for obeying the charge. For Paul, the present Christian life is only a foretaste of what awaits the believer in heaven (Rom. 8.18-25; 2 Cor. 4.16–5.5); this is an expression of Paul's 'now and not yet' theology. It is with this forward-looking attitude that Timothy is being asked to live in the present (cf. Phil. 3.12-14; Heb. 12.1-3).

The imagery is blended. It is a continuation of the athletic imagery in 4.7 but this time the perspective is that of an athlete who is waiting to receive the wreath for winning the race or fight. There is also a judicial image of a righteous judge awarding the one who lovingly longs for the return and judgment of Christ.

Verse 4.8 is connected to 4.6-7 by means of the adverb *loipon*. Most scholars understand this word as a temporal adverb, translating 4.8 as 'from now on...', suggesting that since Paul is about to die all that remains for him is to receive the crown of righteousness. This is an odd interpretation and is partly due to confusing the intention of the clause by conflating the ideas of the verbs of 'awaiting' and 'rewarding' due to Paul's circumstances. For such interpreters the crown of righteousness now awaits Paul and others. But certainly this reward has always been stored away for all believers and in no way can Paul's experience in Rome be the decisive moment for other believers receiving this reward too. This reward was established through the death and resurrection of Jesus, not Paul's experiences. By far the most common usage of *loipon* is logical (i.e. to make a transition to a new thought; BAGD, p. 480) thus translating this clause as 'furthermore the crown of righteousness is stored away...' Therefore Paul is saying that he has persevered through his trial in Rome (4.6-7) and in addition he knows that there is a reward for himself (and all believers) at the return of Christ. Both Paul's actions (4.6-7) and his belief (4.8) serve as a paradigm for Timothy and others to follow.

Paul states that the crown of righteousness is stored away for him. It is assumed from the context that this reward is in heaven (Col. 1.5) and is received after judgment (Heb. 9.27). References to heavenly rewards are found outside the NT (2 Macc. 12.45). There are several references to believers receiving a crown of life (Js 1.12; Rev. 2.10) and a crown of glory (1 Pet. 5.4). Jesus has a golden crown (Rev. 14.14) but only after wearing the crown of thorns (Mk 15.17). There is no other reference to a crown of righteousness in the NT though there are a few references outside the NT (*T. Levi* 8.2; *Ep. Arist.* 281). This phrase in 2 Tim. 4.8 could be interpreted in two ways. First, the crown is righteousness and constitutes the culmination of the process of justification at which point the believer will become truly righteous. Second, the crown is for the righteousness demonstrated by the believer in his or her life. Some scholars have rejected this second option since for them it smells of 'works righteousness'.

The text states that 'the Lord will reward' Paul and others with this crown of righteousness. Elsewhere Paul has made it abundantly clear that this reward is not based on works (Gal. 2.17-21) and it is something he experienced personally (Phil. 3.7-11). A few parables stress the impossibility of someone paying back the debt to God (Mt. 18.21-35; note the same verb) and the need for Jesus to pay the debt on someone's behalf (Mk 10.45; Lk. 7.42). But at the same time there is a swathe of teaching about God rewarding his people for their righteous acts (Mt. 6.4-6, 18; 16.27) and rewarding those who are not his people for their unrighteous acts (Rom. 2.5-8).

Jesus is the righteous judge, who rewards his people justly. The noun *krites* ('judge'; 4.8) coupled with the verb *krinō* ('to judge'; 4.1) creates an *inclusio*, thereby emphasizing the importance of Timothy obeying the charge in light of the charge being given in the name of Jesus who is the judge of the living and the dead. Christ and God are recognized as judge in other texts (Heb. 12.23 and Acts 10.42 respectively). There may be a slight allusion to fallible human judges like Nero, who blatantly was not a righteous judge, as a point of contrast. The reward is not exclusive for Paul but for all who love the Lord's 'appearance'. Paul does not have Christ's incarnation in mind although he does use this word in this way earlier in the letter (2 Tim. 1.10). The parousia refers to the return of Christ (2 Thess. 2.8; 1 Tim. 6.14; 2 Tim. 4.1; Tit. 2.13) which is equivalent to the Day of Judgment or 'that day' in 4.8. The reference to the future judgment is given particularly to motivate Timothy to continue to serve well in the present.

2 Timothy 4.9-22
Closing

Scholars have differed greatly in their estimation of the authenticity of this material. Some believe it genuine material though possibly written by an amanuensis. Others believe this material is made up of fragments of authentic Pauline writing. Finally, there are those who consider the material to be pseudonymous and thus included to give the letters the scent of authenticity for the purpose of depicting Paul as the lone martyr leaving a deposit of edificatory material to be passed on to those succeeding him. It seems to me to be unnecessary to consider this material as an invention of a pseudonymous writer. It is standard material, written in the same manner as any contemporary letter of its kind. It is full of private concerns and personal details, spelling out Paul's closing remarks before sending Tychicus off with the letter to Timothy. Paul's character comes out in the way he handles his situation and thereby serves as a model for others to follow. His closing remarks are consistent with and illustrative of what he has stated previously in the body of the letter. There is a unity here and a private personal content that would be difficult for a pseudepigrapher to create. Therefore I take the position that this material is genuine, reflecting Paul's thinking, but because of his incarceration he has entrusted Luke, his very close confidant, with creating the final product.

The *closing* marks the final section of a typical Graeco-Roman letter. Paul follows contemporary conventions, including *typical* material, like personal greetings and travel plans, and *additional* material, like personal details and requests for clothing and books etc. This particular closing has two parts: *final remarks* (including his present circumstances and future travel plans) and *final greetings* which is consistent with the structure and content of other Pauline letters, notably undisputed ones like Romans and 1 Corinthians. What is unusual is the length of this closing in such a short letter. Proportionately the closing of 2 Timothy is almost four times longer than 1 Corinthians. Only Colossians has a closing that is proportionally similar in length.

Pauline closings frequently reiterate the main purposes for writing the letter. This letter is no exception. First, Paul encourages Timothy to come to him as quickly as possible. No fewer than four times does Paul ask Timothy to come to Rome (4.9, 11, 13, 21). Each request is followed or prefaced with someone who has abandoned Paul (4.10a) or someone Paul has had to send on (4.12) or leave in the course of ministry (4.20). These have the cumulative effect of portraying Paul's sense of isolation and loneliness, even abandonment, which he hopes Timothy's arrival will alleviate. Second, he continues to warn Timothy of false teachers and their destructive nature (4.14-15). Third, he takes this opportunity to share his personal circumstances for the purpose of encouraging Timothy to share in suffering for the gospel and Kingdom ministry.

Finally, Paul uses the closing to pass on his greetings to those in Ephesus and pass along the greetings of those in Rome to Timothy. These final words are for Timothy from a concerned father in the faith to assure him of the Lord's presence in the struggle and the blessing of God's grace for all who read this missive.

Final Remarks (4.9-18)

There is no identifiable formal structure of Graeco-Roman letter closings. As mentioned above, they are characterized by particular content and some literary formulae (e.g. *Grace Benediction*). The uniqueness of this closing is how Psalm 22 (Ps. 21 LXX) is woven through this section. The following chart shows the clear similarities of the two texts.

Psalm 21 LXX		*2 Tim. 4.9-18*	
Verse	Translation	Verse	Translation
21.1	'why have you *abandoned* me	4.10	'for Demas *abandoned* me
		4.16b	'all have *abandoned* me
21.5	'you *rescued* them	4.17	'I was *rescued*
		4.18a	'the Lord will *rescue* me
21.6	'they cried out to you and were *saved*	4.18b	'he will *save* me into his heavenly kingdom
21.12	'there is no one who helps	4.16a	'at my first defence no one appeared with me
21.22	'save me from the *lion's mouth*	4.17	'I was delivered from the *lion's mouth*
21.14	'they opened their *mouth's* against me as a *lion*		
21.17	'many dogs surrounded me, a gathering of *evil doers* seized me'	4.18a	'from every *evil doer*'

Figure 13. *Comparison of Psalm 21 LXX and 2 Tim. 4.9-18*

Paul endeavours to express his concerns for Timothy through the lens of Psalm 22, which includes suffering for the gospel and the need to hope and persevere. Just as the passion of Christ was viewed through Psalm 22, Paul sees his life through the psalmist's experience and he wants Timothy to do the same. Like the author of Psalm 22, who experienced some form of deliverance between Ps. 22.21 and 22.22, Paul believes that he too has experienced his deliverance from death at his trial (4.17-18a) and therefore praises God (4.18b). History suggests otherwise. He died shortly after in Rome.

Keeping in mind the influence of Psalm 22, the content of the closing is structured in the following manner:

Personal comments and exhortations (4.9-15)
    Exhortation for Timothy to Come Quickly (4.9)
    Reason for Exhortation (4.10-11a)
    Preparation for New Ministry (4.11b-13)
    Warning about Alexander (4.14-15)
Trial at Rome (4.16-18a)
Doxology (4.18b)
Final Greetings (4.19-22)

Figure 14. *Structure of 2 Tim. 4.9-22*

Personal Comments and Exhortations (4.9-15)

a. *Exhortation for Timothy to Come Quickly (4.9)*

Paul piles together the imperative *spoudazō*, 'make haste', with the adverb *tacheōs*, 'quickly', in order to emphasize his desire for Timothy to come to him quickly (cf. Tit. 3.12 for the same sentence structure without the adverb). This urgency is similar to Jesus' cry at Gethsemane to have his closest companions be with him in his time of trial. The same imperative is used earlier in the letter (2 Tim. 2.15) but with a slightly different nuance, 'to make every effort' with respect to Timothy presenting himself as one approved by God. In this context the imperative focuses on Timothy making haste to get to Paul in Rome. It is doubtful that the usage of this term here is an epistolary cliché as it is sometimes found in some Graeco-Roman letters. Paul's point is straightforward: he wants to see Timothy as soon as possible. He reiterates his urgent appeal in 4.21, using the same imperative, except he adds that he would like Timothy to arrive before winter. The purpose for this command is consistent with Paul's purpose for writing, namely that he might see Timothy as soon as possible to quell his loneliness (2 Tim. 1.4) and so that they might reunite in order to continue their ministry together (4.11). Death is always possible for Paul so his insistence to see Timothy could be due to his concern of an adverse decision in his court case. At this point, though, his attitude is hopeful for an acquittal (4.17).

Before Timothy can make haste, he must wait for his replacement, Tychicus, to arrive (4.12) and the situation in Ephesus to settle down. Once this has happened then Timothy must not delay coming to Rome before the winter storms settle in, making traveling on the seas treacherous.

b. *Reason for Exhortation (4.10-11a)*
In this section Paul gives one major reason for asking Timothy to come quickly: he feels isolated and alone. He is looking for comradeship from his closest companions in the same way Jesus did on occasion (Mk 5.37; 14.33). Unfortunately three of these have left Paul. The effect on Paul's psyche is that he feels abandoned although the fact is Luke is with him. There are others around too, probably from the local church (4.21; Eubulus, Pudens, Linus, Claudia and all the brothers), though they are not the same for him as having his closest friends, like Timothy, beside him.

Of the three who have left Paul, probably the departure of Demas, who is listed first, has been the hardest on Paul. The reader can be quite certain that the Demas mentioned here is the same Demas mentioned elsewhere in the NT. Demas, not a Jew (Col. 4.11, 13), was likely Paul's fellow prisoner in an earlier Roman imprisonment (Col. 4.14) and is considered by Paul as one of his 'fellow workers' (Philemon 24). Because of this intimate bond, Paul uses a strong word, *egkataleipō*, 'to abandon', to describe the effect of Demas's actions. The same word is used to express the abandonment at death one can feel (Acts 2.27, 31) and the abandonment Jesus felt when the Father turned away from him at the cross (Mt. 27.46). Paul uses the same word later to describe his feeling of abandonment at his trial (2 Tim. 4.16). He knows rejection is part of the persecution of being a follower of Christ (2 Cor. 4.9a) and that Christ will never abandon him (2 Cor. 4.9b; cf. Deut. 31.6), and in fact he can confidently say 'he has not' (2 Tim. 4.17). For Paul there is a difference between knowledge and experience and presently he is experiencing this truth first-hand through the rejection of a dear friend. The reader catches a glimpse of Paul's humanity.

It is 'love of the world' that has led Demas away to Thessalonica. There is a clear contrast between those in 4.8, who love Christ's appearing, and Demas, who loves the present world. This contrast may reflect Paul's apocalyptic worldview in which the present world is evil in comparison to the surpassing glory of the world to come. Though it is possible to understand this as a reference to Demas's apostasy (cf. Polycarp appearing to use this clause in this way in his *Phil.* 9.1-2), it is more likely to mean that a Christianity lived in the safety and comfort of the world is more desirable for Demas than facing persecution and suffering (martyrdom?) along with Paul in Rome. His earlier experience of a Roman prison with Paul is probably still too fresh in his mind (Col. 4.14). According to Chrysostom (*Hom.*, 2 Tim. 4.11), Demas heads to his home in Thessalonica. *The Acts of Paul and Thecla* (second century AD), an apocryphal book, provides a very negative portrayal of Demas who works against Paul out of jealousy of

Onesiphorus and betrays him (2.4, 12-16). This book is spurious in nature and not particularly helpful in creating a profile on Demas. Similarly some scholars try to identify Demas (shortened form of Demetrius) with Demetrius in 3 John to no avail.

The next two colleagues, Crescens and Titus, have not abandoned Paul in the way that Demas has but rather they have gone away on missionary service. Crescens has a Latin name and though Paul's colleague he is only mentioned here in the NT. It can be assumed he was a dear friend of Paul's since he is found together in the list with Demas and Titus. There is a textual variant concerning the location to which Crescens is going. There is good early (Codex Alexandrinus) and abundant manuscript evidence for the reading of *Galatia*. The *Gallian* (i.e. Gaul) reading has less manuscript support though it has the early excellent backing of Codex Sinaiticus. Both words can refer to Gaul, present-day France. Often 'of Asia' is added to 'Galatia' to avoid confusion with the area in Europe. There are a few reasons to support the idea that Crescens went to Gaul. First, if Paul did travel to Spain then he likely traveled through Gaul evangelizing and Crescens could be doing follow-up ministry. Second, several Church Fathers support the Gaul reading (Eusebius, *HE* 3.4, 9). Third, tradition states that Crescens founded the church in Vienne, outside Lyons, and became the bishop of Gaul. Fourth, Crescens, a Latin name, is more likely to be found in a Roman province like Gaul than a Greek-speaking province like Galatia. It is impossible to be conclusive but Galatia should be preferred since the textual evidence slightly favours the 'Galatia [in Asia]' reading, all the geographical regions mentioned are east of Rome and Galatia is the area in which we know Paul had a significant ministry.

Titus, a Gentile, is referred to as Paul's 'genuine child' which is the exact phrase used of Timothy elsewhere (1 Tim. 1.2). They have been partners in ministry from at least the time of the Jerusalem council in AD 49 (Gal. 2.1-3). This intimate relationship accounts for part of the sadness Paul feels with Titus's departure. Paul also feels a loss because Titus has proved himself over and over again as a competent minister. Titus was sent as his apostolic delegate to Crete (Tit. 1.5). Eusebius refers to him later as the 'first bishop of Crete' though it is not clear if he means this in the informal (overseer) or formal sense (*Church History* 3.4). On another occasion, Paul gave him further praise as an 'apostle of the church' and 'glory of Christ' (2 Cor. 8.23) and for this reason entrusted Titus with administering the collection in Corinth for the Jerusalem church (2 Cor. 8.6, 16-21).

Now years later, Titus has left for Dalmatia, the Roman province along the eastern shore of the Adriatic Sea, north of Macedonia, that was separated off from Illyricum after the Illyrian-Pannonian revolt of AD 6–9. Dalmatia is a mountainous region with rugged people and it took Octavian some effort to vanquish them in 33 BC. Paul declares in Rom. 15.19 that he had ministered in this area. When Titus completed his work in Crete, he probably departed for Nicopolis to stay with Paul for the winter (Tit. 3.12). When it was time to leave Nicopolis, Paul headed south towards Corinth and Titus was probably sent north to Dalmatia to start a new work or continue a work started by Paul, assuming that he had been that far north on an earlier mission.

Then Paul makes a hyperbolic statement, 'only Luke is with me', which should be read in the same way Paul says earlier that 'everybody in Asia abandoned me' with the exception of faithful Onesiphorus (2 Tim. 1.15-18). Paul likely has some people around him, though they are from the local church (4.21). What he is missing is his closest co-workers and friends in the ministry who have left for mission work or in Demas's case to avoid suffering with Paul.

Luke was a fellow-worker of Paul (Phlm. 24), a former physician (Col. 4.14) and an inhabitant of Antioch (according to Eusebius, *Church History* 3.4) before he joined Paul in Troas during his second missionary journey, if the 'we' statements in Acts can be trusted as the start of Luke's ministry with Paul (Acts 16.8-11). It was Luke who stood by Paul at his last Roman imprisonment (Philemon 23) and several years later he is doing the same. If the original translation of the Latin of the *Muratorian Canon* is correct, which says Luke was 'a student of the law' (*Mur*. 5), and 'law' refers to secular law not Jewish Law, then having Luke around may be an added bonus as he faces his court case. There are no other references that suggest that he had expertise in secular law (or in Jewish Law as a Gentile) so one should be hesitant to build a case on this. Nevertheless it is possible that Paul feels alone because there is no one around with legal expertise to help him since he had to face his first trial alone (2 Tim. 4.16).

c. *Preparation for New Ministry (4.11b-13)*
Paul shifts his focus from the abandonment he has experienced in his present circumstances to the new ministry opportunities that lie ahead though he gives no indication where this might be. With renewed optimism that comes out later in the chapter, he begins to strategize and prepare for the future. He begins his strategy in a somewhat surprising way when he asks Timothy to bring Mark with him. Two verses earlier in the letter, Paul tells Timothy *how* to come (i.e. 'quickly'). Now he assumes Timothy will come. Later in this letter he will tell Timothy *when* to come (i.e. 'before winter'). Mark, whom we can quite safely assume to be the Gospel writer and former travelling companion of Barnabas (his cousin) and Paul, abandoned them in Perga, part-way through their first missionary journey (Acts 13.13). This angered Paul so much that he refused to take him along on their second missionary journey (Acts 15.36-41). During the next twelve years, he and Mark must have reconciled because Paul commends him to the congregation in

Colossae (Col. 4.10). Now Paul requests his help because he is 'useful' in the ministry. Paul may have in mind his earlier thoughts in the letter in which he claims that servants of the Lord are useful to the master and prepared for every good work if they have been cleansed from the compromising and contaminating effects of sin (2 Tim. 2.19-21). Just as Onesimus changed and became useful to Paul (Phlm. 11), in the same way Mark has changed (at least in Paul's mind) and Paul believes he will be useful in their subsequent ministry together.

The ministry Paul has in mind for Mark could be to get to Rome in order to meet the personal needs of Paul. Though the practical meaning of *diakonia* is possible here, it is more likely Paul has his typical understanding of *diakonia* in mind, 'ministry of the gospel' (1 Tim. 1.12; 2 Tim. 4.5). Paul's passion is the same as always—preach the gospel of Christ and establish churches in new regions (Rom. 15.20)—and he wants to take Mark along to achieve this end.

At first glance v. 12 seems out of place, an afterthought or lapse of memory that should be placed alongside the coming and goings of Paul's other co-workers in v. 10. More likely the recruitment of Mark and the dispatch of Tychicus are related (at least syntactically) in that the former is the replacement of the latter and is part of Paul's ongoing strategizing for the future. Tychicus, an Asian, accompanied Paul on his third missionary journey through Macedonia to Jerusalem (Acts 20.4-5). He was used as the messenger to bring Paul's letters to the Ephesians and Colossians (Eph. 6.21; Col. 4.7). Paul has intentionally chosen Tychicus because of his character ('beloved brother and faithful servant in the Lord') and experience in the area and with the people of Ephesus (Eph. 6.21-22). The tense of this Greek verb (aorist) usually denotes *past* time, suggesting that Tychicus has already left for Ephesus and someone else would be the letter bearer. More likely it is an epistolary aorist, which reflects the perspective of the author. Thus in Paul's mind he has decided that he is sending Tychicus as Timothy's replacement and bearer of the letter.

As part of Paul's continuing preparation for future ministry, he makes a request of Timothy to stop by Carpus's house in Troas on his way to Rome and bring along certain personal effects. The first request for a 'cloak', *phailonē*, is a very practical one. Due to the approaching Roman winter, Paul needs his substantial outer garment, which was shaped liked a Mexican poncho. Some have postulated that this cloak is his Roman toga that he would need for court but this is doubtful since he would have used a different word for this. One wonders why Paul requests that Timothy bring his garment over 1,500 kilometres and not get one locally. It is possible that this action exemplifies his teaching on contentment with the basics and thereby not needing to trouble others for more than what he has (1 Tim. 6.6-8). Others see a symbolic gesture in that Paul is passing the mantle (like Elijah to Elisha in 2 Kgs 2.9-14) or 'baton' of ministry to Timothy, which is doubtful since Paul thinks he will be released for further ministry. The only baton being passed in 2 Timothy is from Timothy to Tychicus. Chrysostom takes an entirely different position and says the garment is a bag to hold the books (*Hom. on 2 Timothy* 10).

Identifying the content of the books and parchments has proven difficult. In part this is due to the fact that it is not clear if Paul is referring to one or two sets of material because of the word *malista*, which can be translated 'especially' (1 Tim. 5.8, 17) or 'I mean' (1 Tim. 4.10). The text could be translated as 'bring my scrolls, *I mean* the parchments' or 'bring my scrolls, *especially* the parchments'. The more likely meaning of *malista* is 'especially' and therefore Paul is most likely referring to two materials. The first materials are books, *biblia*, made of papyrus and found in the form of scrolls or codices. The singular of this noun, *biblion*, refers frequently to a book of the OT (Lk. 4.17; Gal. 3.10). Therefore it is probable that these *biblia* were books of the Jewish Scriptures or accounts of Jesus compiled by Mark, Luke or others (see Lk. 1.1-4) or *testimonia*, excerpts from the Scriptures focusing on a certain theme or idea (e.g. Christ as the Servant of the Lord). Scripture was, of course, fundamental to Paul's ministry (1 Tim. 1.8; 2 Tim. 3.14-17). Paul, as a leather-worker, would be very familiar with the second type of material, *membranas* or 'parchments', since they were made of animal skins. The identification of these parchments is difficult to determine. It is feasible that they were copies of Paul's letters or important papers like his Roman citizenship or official documents from his previous trials or his notes and ideas from studying.

One possible scenario is that Paul left his outer coat and books with Carpus on his way to Nicopolis with the view to retrieving them upon his return to Asia. It is hard to imagine that Paul would do this since he would need the outer coat for the winter weather in Nicopolis and certainly he would want his books (especially if they are a collection of the Scriptures). A more likely reconstruction of events is that on Paul's return to Ephesus from Nicopolis, through Corinth, he is arrested in Troas at the instigation of Alexander the metal-worker (see the section on 'Historical Situation' in the Introduction for more details) without a chance to collect his books and garment.

d. *Warning about Alexander (4.14-15)*
Paul's remembrance of Carpus's house and his belongings in Troas reminds him of the harm of Alexander the metal-worker who most likely resided in Troas. Alexander is a common name in the Graeco-Roman world even among Jews (Acts 4.6; 19.33; a name found in the high priest's family, Mk 15.21) who might take this as their *praenomen* (i.e. forename) or *nomen gentile* (i.e. family name) especially if they became Roman citizens.

Alexander is qualified as a 'metal worker' and is therefore to be differentiated from the Alexander in Acts 19.33 but likely the same one excommunicated in 1 Tim. 1.20. Literally, Alexander 'showed (*endeiknumi*) against me [Paul] bad things many times'. This clause is very close in content with the statements in Gen. 50.15, 17 in which the author rehearses the evil shown against Joseph by his brothers (i.e. selling him into slavery and giving false testimony to Jacob about his death). The verb can be used in the legal sense of 'present' (Rom. 2.15; 9.22) and thus suggest that Alexander may have testified against Paul, which led to his arrest in Troas. Paul is not too concerned about Alexander and does not seek revenge; instead he draws on the wisdom of Ps. 62.12 knowing that the Lord rewards people according to their works (cf. 2 Sam. 3.39; Prov. 24.12; Rom. 2.6). On the one hand there will be a reward for faithful service (2 Tim. 4.8) at the judgment but on the other hand there will also be punishment for the opposite, as in the case of Alexander. Though Paul is not so concerned about himself, he is concerned for Timothy when he passes through Troas to pick up his belongings so he warns Timothy to 'guard himself' and not take any risks when Alexander is in the region. Just as Timothy and Paul are to guard the deposit entrusted to them (2 Tim. 1.12, 14) from false teaching, in the same way Timothy needs to protect himself from this false teacher who could do him harm and thereby frustrate their future ministry plans. Alexander has gone to great lengths (lit. 'exceedingly') to oppose the preached gospel message which Paul describes in a unique way as 'our words' which are the 'sound health producing words' of the gospel referred to earlier (1.13).

Trial at Rome (4.16-18a)

The sense of Paul's isolation continues (united through the use of the same verb, *egkataleipō*, in 4.9) as he explains his experience of the first trial through the lens of Psalm 22, the Lord's Prayer and the experience of Christ's last days. The uniqueness of Paul's reflection on this situation is his overwhelming sense of the Lord's presence, deliverance and purposefulness for this event that results in stirring up more confidence as he considers future ministry.

When Paul writes about his 'first defence', he could be referring to the initial hearing after his arrest in Troas that resulted in his transfer to Rome. Under Roman law a complaint (*postulatio*) is lodged with the local magistrate (*praetor*). If the complaint is deemed worthy of further investigation a summons (*citatio*) is issued and the accused is brought in for further questioning. During the investigation (*interrogatio*) the magistrate seeks more information to determine if there are grounds for a trial or to allow the accused an opportunity for a confession of guilt. At this point the case is dismissed or the judge draws up an inscription (*inscriptio*) stating the charges, which are signed by the accuser. This would have been the process in Troas where Alexander would have brought charges against Paul, which led to his arrest, interrogation, inscription and sudden departure to Troas. This explains why he did not have his cloak and books at hand.

Paul had already stood before Nero *circa* AD 62 (note that he was around 22 years old) and was acquitted. But clearly this situation seems more difficult and dire. Rome has changed. Nero has worsened since the death of Burrus (poisoned?), the prefect of the praetorian guards, and the retirement of Seneca, who were his two wise guardians. He became increasingly influenced by the anti-Semitic, anti-Christian despotism of Tigellinus, the new prefect of Rome. Paul would be very familiar with the stories of Nero lighting his parties with Christians and other forms of persecution. So when Paul arrived in Rome he was probably taken to the Mamertine prison since this Roman custody seems to afford him less freedom than his former Roman custody when he was under house arrest. This change of incarceration, since he is in chains (2 Tim. 1.16; 2.9), is probably a reflection of the gravity of his charges and the increased hostility of Rome toward Christians.

His 'first trial' in Rome would have been a repeat of the *interrogatio* he had in Troas. The Roman judge would determine if his case should go to trial. Paul says that 'no one appeared with [him] but all abandoned [him]'. It is possible that he means that no one was willing to be his defence counsel (*patronus*) and thereby he had to represent himself. It is also possible that none of the church members of Rome were willing to stand by him at his trial in much the same way the disciples did not come near at Jesus' trial and crucifixion for fear of being associated with a prominent leader of what was perceived by many as a subversive movement. Both scenarios are equally possible and he could have both in mind but most important for the reader is the feeling of isolation Paul is experiencing. In spite of this Paul, like Stephen (Acts 7.60) and Jesus (Lk. 23.34), is able to offer grace and mercy in the face of his friends' failure. The optative of *logizomai* is used, showing that there is not a hint of malice in Paul's heart; this clause could be translated in this way: 'I wish in no way that their cowardice and abandonment be counted against them'.

Paul was able to get through this situation because the Lord stood by him (*paristēmi*) and strengthened him. On another occasion the Lord stood by (*paristēmi*) Paul through an angel assuring him that he would not lose his life in the storm but would stand before (the same verb) Caesar (Acts 27.23-24). In Paul's mind knowing the Lord is beside him enables him to do what he is called to accomplish. In this instance the Lord empowered him so that through him the message of the gospel was fully proclaimed and all the Gentiles there heard it. Some commentators understand this clause to mean that Paul's ministry has been brought to completion or to its fulfillment, thereby pointing to his death, but this does not make sense of the

Greek text. It is the message that was fulfilled, not Paul's ministry (note that *message* is the subject of the sentence, 'ministry' is not even found in the verse). But even if one reads the text as 'Paul's preaching ministry has been fulfilled', it makes no sense either when compared with Rom. 15.19 (note that the same verb is used: *plērophoreō*). Certainly in this text Paul means 'I have fully proclaimed the gospel of Christ from Jerusalem all the way around to Illyricum', otherwise it means that Paul fulfilled his preaching ministry and never preached again. Obviously he preached again since he intends to preach in Rome when he arrives (Rom. 1.15) and unquestionably he preached many times again in the area between Jerusalem and Illyricum.

Undisputedly Paul did not preach the gospel to all Gentiles everywhere on this occasion. Rather Paul has in mind a variety of Gentiles who would have been in attendance at his trial, like the members of the judicial court, possibly Nero, civic leaders and their spouses, dignitaries, clerical help etc. Paul is pleased because this legal case gave him the opportunity to proclaim the gospel, much as he did before Felix and Agrippa (Acts 24; 26), in accordance with his calling to preach to the Gentiles (Gal. 2.8) and leaders (Acts 9.15) and in agreement with Ps. 22.27-28.

At this point Paul's hope is that the verdict from his *interrogatio* will be *non liquet*, meaning that there are no grounds for a trial and therefore he will be released. He is quite confident of this and describes this in metaphorical terms as 'I have been rescued from the mouth of the lion'. Some scholars associate 'lion' with Satan on the basis of similarity of language in the Lord's prayer (Mt. 6.13) and 1 Pet. 5.8. But if Paul were referring to Satan he probably would have included the article, 'the Lion', yet he does not. Others identify 'the mouth of the lion' with being thrown to real lions as in the case of Daniel or the reference in Heb. 11.33 (literally 'mouths of lions') or possibly the reference to Christians being covered with animals and torn by wild dogs (Tacitus, *Ann.* 15.44.2-8). The singular 'mouth of lion' and the fact that feeding people to the lions was not a first-century punishment, especially not for Roman citizens, suggest that another interpretation should be found. Josephus makes a statement in *Antiquities* 18.228, 'the lion is dead' in reference to the Roman Emperor Tiberius, which has led some to postulate that Paul is referring to Nero before whom he gave his defence. Since Paul had spoken before Nero years earlier (*circa* AD 62) and because Paul was a major leader of the Christian movement, there is a good chance that Paul did present his case before him. Nevertheless the most likely meaning for the phrase is 'death'. Funerary inscriptions with a lion clutching the head of a man are used to symbolize the power of death. David experienced deliverance from real lions (1 Sam. 17.37) and could therefore be seen as being comfortable, as the notional psalmist, in using the lion as a symbol to portray death (Pss. 7.3; 35.17). Again, the most likely background is Psalm 22. There the psalmist describes the threat of death in terms of 'roaring lions...opening their mouths wide against me', 'the sword' and 'powerful dogs seeking my life'. He cries out, 'deliver me from the mouth of lions' (Ps. 22.21). Therefore most likely Paul is avowing that he has been delivered from having his case go to a subsequent trial and a verdict of death. History would prove otherwise.

Verse 18 continues with the theme of deliverance from v. 17 connected through the use of the same verb in both verses: *hruomai*. There are echoes of the Lord's Prayer in this verse in which Paul is sure that God will deliver him from evil deeds (Mt. 6.13). Unquestionably Paul is not saying that God will deliver him from *every* evil deed anymore than he believes that he preached to *every* Gentile during his first trial (4.17). Similarly he is not saying that God will deliver him from the consequences of the evil deeds of others. Paul has had too much experience of suffering at the hands of others to think this. He is saying that so far in his life he has averted death through the help and grace of God.

So far Paul has declared what God has delivered him *from*. Now he will proclaim what God is saving him *to*. The other side of the story is that regardless of what happens or how many days he lives he knows that through all of this, God will save him into his heavenly kingdom. The overwhelming usage of *sōzō* in the Pauline corpus is in the future tense suggesting that salvation for the believer, though a present reality, is not fully realized until death. One must finish the whole race. His perspective is future-oriented, knowing that though he is regularly at risk of death, he is certain of the Lord's spiritual protection to hold him fast to the end (Phil. 1.6; Rom. 8.37-39).

Doxology (4.18b)

The use of the relative pronoun, *hō* ('to whom'), links this with the preceding vv. 9-17. Paul follows the typical structure of the *doxology form* as a declarative statement, stating *the one to whom praise is given* ('the Lord'), *the form of praise* ('glory'), *the extent of time of this praise* ('forever and ever') and *the response* confirming the appropriateness of this praise ('amen'). Although Paul's imprisonment has resulted in abandonment and desolation, as he reflects on the presence and help of God during this time he cannot help but break out in praise of God, realizing he alone is worthy of all glory. This doxology is identical to Gal. 1.5 and Heb. 13.21 and very close to other doxologies in terms of content and structure (Rom. 16.27; Phil. 4.20; 1 Pet. 4.11).

Final Greetings (4.19-22)

Typically in the *Greetings* literary form the author asks the recipient to pass on greetings to the author's friends. Similarly the author passes on greetings to the recipient from friends of the recipient that the author knows. This would be followed by a prayer or wish for health. Paul often builds on this minimal Hellenistic greeting by interspersing additional material (cf. 1 Thess. 5.26-28). The structure of this final greeting is as follows:

Personal Greeting to Author's Friends (4.19)
    Information about Mutual Friends (4.20)
        Request for Timothy to Come before Winter (4.21a)
Personal Greeting from Recipient's Friends (4.21b)
Prayer: for Timothy (4.22a)
    for Ephesians (4.22b)

Figure 15. *Greetings Form in 2 Tim. 4.19-22*

Personal Greeting to Paul's Friends (4.19)

Paul sends his personal greetings to Priscilla and Aquila, his fellow workers and tent-makers who risked their lives for Paul (Rom. 16.3), and the household of Onesiphorus. Typically the personal greetings in the Pauline corpus are given in the second person plural (20 of 22 times) but this greeting is given in the singular (note that the other exception is Tit. 3.15) thereby stressing that Timothy himself pass on the greeting to these people personally.

Paul first met the couple, Priscilla and Aquila, in Corinth after they had been expelled from Rome because of the edict of Claudius (Acts 18.2). They left their church (1 Cor. 16.19) and travelled with Paul to Ephesus where they ministered for more than 18 months, including instructing Apollos (Acts 18.26). From there they went to Rome where they led a church (Rom. 16.3). Now they are back in Ephesus probably as a support to Timothy. Aquila is a Jew from Pontus (along the south shore of the Black Sea) as likely is his wife, Priscilla. When the couple's names are mentioned together, Priscilla's name is mentioned first (five times) which is contrary to the culture, except in 1 Cor. 16.19 (cf. Acts 18.2). It is doubtful that this is a gesture of courtesy to a woman since when another couple is mentioned together, Andronicus and Junia in Rom. 16.7, it is the husband's name that is listed first which is just four verses after Paul refers to Priscilla and Aquila (Rom. 16.3). The reversal of order may because she held a higher social rank than Aquila or she held the primary ministry role of the couple.

Paul sends personal greetings to the household of Onesiphorus and not personally to Onesiphorus. Some suggest that he is alive but not around based on *Acts Paul and Thecla* 2.2, which says Onesiphorus was residing in Iconium. *Acts of Paul and Thecla* is probably not a reliable source so it is more likely that the omission of Onesiphorus is due to the fact that he is no longer alive.

Information about Erastus and Trophimus (4.20)

The identity of Erastus is not clear. He may be the city administrator mentioned in Rom. 16.23 based on an inscription found in Old Corinth though some suggest the Greek term Paul uses to describe Erastus (*oikonomos*) and the Latin Corinthian inscription (*aedile*) do not refer to the same position. He may be the 'servant' who left Ephesus to accompany Timothy to Macedonia during Paul's third missionary journey (Acts 19.22). It is possible that these are references to the same person and that Erastus went on to Corinth from Macedonia and later became a city administrator. If in fact Erastus were residing in Corinth then the scenario is probably that when Paul travelled from Nicopolis to Ephesus he passed through Corinth and there Paul tried to recruit Erastus but he chose to remain in Corinth.

Trophimus was from the province of Asia and was one of those who accompanied Paul to Macedonia after the riot in Ephesus (Acts 20.1, 4). Later, Trophimus, a Gentile, is seen together with Paul in Jerusalem. Some Jews make the false assumption that Paul took him into the temple area beyond the Court of the Gentiles. This led to Paul's arrest (Acts 21.28-29). The text, referring to the time after Paul's release from his first Roman imprisonment, says, 'I left Trophimus sick in Miletus'. This could mean that on his way to Ephesus from Corinth, Paul is arrested in Miletus where Trophimus falls sick as Paul is taken away to Rome. This is doubtful since surely Timothy would have been aware of Paul's arrest and Trophimus's sickness since Miletus is only 50 kilometres from Ephesus. As I said in the introduction, Paul was in all likelihood arrested in Troas (250 kilometres from Ephesus) after leaving his winter retreat in Nicopolis and passing through Corinth. So it is more probable that Trophimus is accompanying Paul to Rome after his arrest in Troas and falls sick on the journey and is left at port in Miletus. Paul is making Timothy aware of this.

Request for Timothy to Come before Winter (4.21a)

This request is a more specific form of 4.9 (cf. Tit. 3.12) asking Timothy to come 'before winter'. With winter approaching Paul will need his cloak and therefore Timothy will have to get on a boat before the shipping lanes on the Mediterranean and Adriatic seas close for travel between November and April. This detail helps us determine a date of writing around late spring or early to mid summer.

Personal Greeting from Recipient's Friends (4.21b)

This greeting given in the third person consists of four names and a general reference to 'all the brothers'. Of the three names listed, one is Greek (Claudia) and three of them are Latin and quite certainly belonged to the Roman church though it is difficult to know whether they were leaders of the Roman church. It is likely these people were Timothy's friends more than Paul's though there is no mention of them elsewhere in the NT. If Paul knew these people then they might constitute some of those who would not appear on his behalf at his first trial (4.16).

Eubulus is not mentioned elsewhere in the NT but the name is found in the Apocryphal *Acts of Paul* 7.1. Later tradition purports that Pudens, a Roman senator, converted to Christianity and was subsequently martyred under Nero. His home housed Peter and was also used as a meeting place for a church, called *Pudentiana*. Because of the proximity of the names on the list (but note they are not side by side; cf. Priscilla and Aquila in 2 Tim. 4.19), some have speculated that Pudens was the husband of Claudia and father of Linus. This hypothesis is mainly based on a tenuous reading of the Roman poet Martial's *Epigrams* (1.31; 4.13; around AD 40–102) and should probably be dismissed.

More is known about Linus. Irenaeus (*circa* AD 130–200) states that Peter and Paul handed over the leadership of the 'church' to Linus. It is not clear whether Irenaeus means the church in Rome or the whole known church. Subsequent writers confirm it to be the former since he is referred to as the Bishop of Rome (see Eusebius, *HE* 3.2, 4; Chrysostom, *Hom.* 10; Valentinius, *Chrono. 354* 13; *Lib. pont.* 6).

Claudia is the only woman in the list. Little is known about her though she is proclaimed to be the mother of Linus (*Apost. Const.* 7.46).

Prayer: for Timothy (4.22a)

It is quite common to overlook these final greetings but to do so is to miss something that would be very important to the recipients. The prayer of blessing for Timothy draws upon the background of the OT where God temporarily imparts his presence and power to individuals to perform a special function (Gen. 28.15; Judg. 6.16; Ps. 90.15). Surprisingly this formula is only found in a greeting twice in the OT (Judg. 6.12; Ruth 2.4; cf. *Jos. Asen.* 26.2). This concept of the blessing of God's presence and power is also found in the NT. Jesus experiences this on earth (Jn 8.29; 16.32), as does Mary (Lk. 1.28). Jesus is the 'anointed one', Immanuel or 'God with us' (Mt. 1.23), and therefore is the source and the one who imparts blessing on individuals or groups directly (disciples in Jn 14.16; Paul in Acts 18.9) or indirectly through a prayer of blessing made on behalf of others (Rom. 15.33; 2 Cor. 13.11; Phil. 4.9; 2 Thess. 3.16). 2 Tim. 4.22a should be understood in light of these NT texts. The *Prayer of Blessing* is a literary formula with the loosely stylized structure of *The One Blessing* (God or Jesus), *Verb of Blessing* (usually 'to be', sometimes omitted) and *Object of Blessing*. The *Verb of Blessing* is omitted in this text and therefore the emphasis could be *declarative*, 'God is with your spirit' as a word of assurance for Timothy, or it could be a *wish*, 'may God [continue] to be with your spirit'. Both elements are probably present as a means of blessing someone through the certainty of invoking God's presence through prayer. This prayer relates back to Timothy's calling and divine empowerment for his task in Ephesus (2 Tim. 1.6-7; cf. 1 Tim. 4.14), therefore assuring Timothy of God's sustaining power to enable him to persevere and to fulfill his calling.

Prayer: for Ephesians (4.22b)
Paul ends the letter with a *Grace Benediction* ('grace be with you') found in each of the letters of Paul. This literary formula has a set structure of *Wish of Grace, Divine Source* and *Recipient*. The prayer of grace for the Ephesians exemplifies Paul's concern for the Ephesian church, particularly their need to live in the grace by which they were called and saved (1.9) and to be strengthened in this grace (2.1). The *Divine Source* phrase, 'of our Lord Jesus Christ', is consistently added in the undisputed Pauline letters (Gal. 6.18; Phil. 4.23; 1 Thess. 5.28). Remarkably this phrase is missing in this benediction as it is in 1 Tim. 6.21b. 'Lord' is probably tacitly understood as the modifier from the preceding phrase, 'may the Lord be with your spirit'. Though Paul has made reference to a larger circle of readers in 2 Tim. 4.19, it is nevertheless surprising to have a plural *Recipient* in a letter addressed to an individual. The plural referent suggests that this letter was to be read publically for the benefit of the church. If one accepts the variant reading of 'amen' at the end of the book then it gives credence to a liturgical setting.

Bibliography

Commentaries
Barclay, William, *The Letters to Timothy, Titus and Philemon* (Edinburgh: Saint Andrew Press, 1956).
Barrett, C.K., *The Pastoral Epistles* (Oxford: Clarendon Press, 1963).
Bernard, J.H., *The Pastoral Epistles* (Cambridge: Cambridge University Press, 1906).
Brown, Ernest F., *The Pastoral Epistles* (London: Methuen, 1917).
Calvin, John, *Commentaries on the Epistles to Timothy, Titus, and Philemon* (trans. William Pringle; Edinburgh: T. Constable, 1856).
Collins, Raymond F., *1 & 2 Timothy and Titus: A Commentary* (NTL; Louisville, KY: Westminster/John Knox Press, 2002).
Davies, Margaret, *The Pastoral Epistles* (London: Epworth Press, 1996).
Dibelius, Martin, *Die Pastoralbriefe* (Tubingen: J.C.B. Mohr, 1966).
Dibelius, Martin, and Hans Conzelmann, *The Pastoral Epistles* (Philadelphia: Fortress Press, 1972).
Donelson, Lewis R., *Colossians, Ephesians, First and Second Timothy, and Titus* (Louisville, KY: Westminster/John Knox Press, 1996).
Ellicott, C.J., *A Critical and Grammatical Commentary on the Pastoral Epistles* (Boston: Draper, 1867).
Fee, Gordon D., *1 and 2 Timothy, Titus* (NIBC; Peabody, MA: Hendrickson, 1984).
Fiore, Benjamin, *The Pastoral Epistles* (Collegeville, MN: Liturgical Press, 2007).
Gorday, Peter, *Colossians, 1–2 Thessalonians, 1–2 Timothy, Titus, Philemon* (Chicago, IL: Fitzroy Dearborn Publishers, 2000).
Guthrie, Donald, *The Pastoral Epistles* (TNTC; London: Tyndale Press, 1957).
Hanson, A.T., *The Pastoral Epistles* (NCB; London: Marshall, Morgan and Scott, 1982).
Holtz, Gottfried, *Die Pastoralbriefe* (Berlin: Evangelische Verlagsanstalt, 1986).
Jeremias, Joachim, and Hermann Strathmann, *Die Briefe an Timotheus und Titus* (Göttingen: Vandenhoeck & Ruprecht, 1953).
Johnson, Luke Timothy, *The First and Second Letters to Timothy* (AB, 35a; New York: Doubleday, 2001).
Karris, Robert J., *The Pastoral Epistles* (Wilmington, DE: Michael Glazier, 1979).
Kelly, J.N.D., *A Commentary on the Pastoral Epistles: Timothy I and II, and Titus* (HNTC; Peabody, MA: Hendrickson, 1987).
Knight, George W., *The Pastoral Epistles* (NICNT; Grand Rapids: Eerdmans, 1992).
Laansma, Jon, *2 Timothy, Titus* (Cornerstone Biblical Commentary; Carol Stream, IL: Tyndale House Publishers, 2009).
Liefeld, Walter L., *1 and 2 Timothy/Titus* (The NIV Application Commentary from Biblical Text to Contemporary Life; Grand Rapids: Zondervan, 1999).
Lock, Walter, *A Critical and Exegetical Commentary on the Pastoral Epistles* (ICC; Edinburgh: T. & T. Clark, 1924).

Marshall, I. Howard, *A Critical and Exegetical Commentary on the Pastoral Epistles* (ICC; Edinburgh: T. & T. Clark, 1999).
Moellering, H. Armin, and Victor A. Bartling, *1 Timothy, 2 Timothy, Titus* (Concordia Commentary; Saint Louis, MO: Concordia Publishing House, 1970).
Montague, George T., *First and Second Timothy, Titus* (Grand Rapids: Baker Academic, 2008).
Moule, H.C.G., *The Second Epistle to Timothy* (London: The Religious Tract Society, 1905).
Mounce, William D., *Pastoral Epistles* (WBC, 46; Nashville: Thomas Nelson, 2000).
Ngewa, Samuel, *1 & 2 Timothy and Titus* (Grand Rapids, MI: Zondervan/HippoBooks, 2009).
Quinn, Jerome D., *The Letter to Titus* (New York: Doubleday, 1990).
Quinn, Jerome D., and William C. Wacker, *The First and Second Letters to Timothy* (Grand Rapids: Eerdmans, 2000).
Saarini, Risto, *The Pastoral Epistles with Philemon and Jude* (Brazos Theological Commentary on the Bible; Grand Rapids: Brazos Press, 2008).
Scott, E.F., *The Pastoral Epistles* (London: Hodder and Stoughton, 1936).
Simpson, E.K., *The Pastoral Epistles* (TNTC; London: Tyndale Press, 1954).
Spicq, C., *Saint Paul: Les Épîtres Pastorales* (Paris: Gabalda, 1969).
Stott, John, *The Message of 2 Timothy* (Leicester: Inter-Varsity Press, 1984).
Towner, Philip H., *1–2 Timothy & Titus* (IVPNTC; Leicester: Inter-Varsity Press, 1994).
Twomey, Jay, *The Pastoral Epistles through the Centuries* (Chichester: Wiley-Blackwell, 2009).
Wall, Robert W., and Richard B. Steele, *1 and 2 Timothy and Titus* (Grand Rapids, MI: Eerdmans, 2012).
Ward, Ronald A., *Commentary on 1 and 2 Timothy and Titus* (Waco, TX: Word Books, 1974).
Zehr, Paul M., *1 & 2 Timothy, Titus* (Scottdale, PA: Herald Press, 2010).

Primary Sources

Aelian, *Claudii Aeliani Varia Historia*, in Rudolph Hercher (ed.), *Claudii Aeliani Varia Historia* (Leipzig: B.G. Teubner, 1887).
Charlesworth, James H. (ed.), *The Old Testament Pseudepigrapha* (Garden City, NY: Doubleday, 1983).
Chronography of 354, http://www.tertullian.org/fathers/chronography_of_354_00_eintro.htm
Chrysostom, John, *The Homilies of St. John Chrysostom* (Oxford: James Parker and Co., 1854).
Clement, *The Writings of Clement of Alexandria*, in William Wilson (trans.), *Clement: The Writings of Clement of Alexandria* (ANCL; Edinburgh: T. & T. Clark, 1909).
Davis, Raymond (ed.), *The Book of Pontiffs* (Liverpool: University of Liverpool Press, 1989).
Dionysius of Halicarnassus, *De compositione*, in Stephen Usher (trans.), *Dionysius of Halicarnassus: Critical Essays*, II (LCL; London: Heinemann, 1985).
Dionysius of Halicarnassus, *Demosthenes*, in Stephen Usher (trans.), *Dionysius of Halicarnassus: The Critical Essays* (LCL; Cambridge: Harvard University Press, 1974).

Epictetus, *Discourses*, in P.E. Matheson, *The Discourses of Epictetus* (New York: Heritage Press, 1968).
Eusebius, *The Ecclesiastical History*, in J.E.L. Oulton (trans.), *Eusebius: The Ecclesiastical History* (LCL; London: Heinemann, 1926).
Galen, *On the Sects for Beginners; An Outline of Empiricism; On Medical Experience*, in R. Walzer and M. Frede (trans.), *Three Treatises on the Nature of Science* (Indianapolis, IN: Hackett Publishing, 1985).
Guthrie, Kenneth Sylvan (ed.), *The Pythagorean Sourcebook and Library* (Grand Rapids, MI: Phanes Press, 1978).
Herodotus, in A.D. Godley (trans.), *Herodotus* (LCL; Cambridge, MA: Harvard University Press, 1921).
Holmes, Michael W. (ed.), *The Apostolic Fathers: Greek Texts and English Translations* (Grand Rapids, MI: Baker Books, 1999).
Homer, *The Odyssey*, in A.T. Murray (trans.), *Homer: The Odyssey* (LCL; London: Heinemann, 1919).
Irenaeus, *Against the Heresies* (New York: Paulist Press, 1992).
James, M.R. (ed.), 'Acts of Peter', in M.R. James (trans.), *The Apocryphal New Testament* (Oxford: Clarendon Press, 1926).
Josephus, Flavius, *Antiquities of the Jews, Against Apion, Life of Josephus, Jewish War*, in H. St. J. Thackeray (trans.), *Josephus* (LCL; Cambridge, MA: Harvard University Press, 1966).
Longinus, *On the Sublime*, in Donald Russell (trans.), *On the Sublime* (LCL; Cambridge, MA: Harvard University Press, 1995).
Lucian, *The Works of Lucian of Samosata*, in H.W. Fowler and F.G. Fowler (trans.), *The Works of Lucian of Samosata* (Oxford: Clarendon Press, 1905).
Metzger, Bruce M. (ed.), 'Muratorian Canon', in Bruce M. Metzger (trans.), *Early Christian Writings*, http://www.earlychristianwritings.com/muratorian.html
Philo, *De aeternitate mundi*, in F.H. Colson (trans.), *Philo*, IX (LCL; London: Heinemann, 1941).
—*De agricultura*, in Albert C. Geljon and David T. Runia (trans.), *Philo of Alexandria, On cultivation* (Leiden: Brill, 2013).
—*De confusion linguarum*, in F.H. Colson and G.H. Whitaker (trans.), *De confusion linguarum* (LCL; London: Heinemann, 1932).
—*De congressu eruditionis gratia*, in F.H. Colson and G.H. Whitaker (trans.), *Philo*, IV (LCL; London: Heinemann, 1932).
—*De decalogo*, in F.H. Colson (trans.), *Philo*, VII (LCL; London: Heinemann, 1937).
—*De ebrietate*, in F.H. Colson and G.H. Whitaker (trans.), *Philo*, III (LCL; London: Heinemann, 1930).
—*De fuga et invention*, in F.H. Colson and G.H. Whitaker (trans.), *Philo*, V (LCL; London: Heinemann, 1937).
—*De migratione Abrahami*, in F.H. Colson and G.H. Whitaker (trans.), *Philo*, IV (LCL; London: Heinemann, 1932).
—*De specialibus legibus*, in F.H. Colson (trans.), *Philo*, VII (LCL; London: Heinemann, 1937).
—*De vita Mosis*, in F.H. Colson (trans.), *Philo*, VI (LCL; London: Heinemann, 1935).
—*In Flaccum*, in F.H. Colson (trans.), *Philo*, IX (LCL; London: Heinemann, 1941).
—*Legatio ad Gaium*, in F.H. Colson (trans.), *Philo*, X (LCL; Cambridge, MA: Harvard University Press, 1962).

—*Legum allegoriae*, in F.H. Colson and G.H. Whitaker (trans.), *Philo*, I (LCL; London: Heinemann, 1929).
—*Quis rerum divinarum heres sit*, in F.H. Colson and G.H. Whitaker (trans.), *Philo*, IV (LCL; London: Heinemann, 1932).
Plutarch, *The Complete Works of Plutarch: Essays and Miscellanies* (New York: Crowell, 1909).
—*Moralia*, in Bernadotte Perrin (trans.), *Plutarch's Lives* (LCL; London: Heinemann, 1914).
Polybius, *The Histories*, in W.R. Paton (trans.), *Polybius: The Histories* (LCL; London: Heinemann, 1922).
Roberts, Alexander, James Donaldson, A. Cleveland Coxe, Allan Menzies, Ernest Cushing Richardson and Bernhard Pick, *The Ante-Nicene Fathers: Translations of the Writings of the Fathers Down to A.D. 325* (Grand Rapids: Eerdmans, 1978).
Tacitus, *The Annals*, in John Jackson (trans.), *The Annals* (LCL; London: Heinemann, 1923).
Tertullian, *Prescription Against Heretics, Against Marcion, Ad Martyras*, in Peter Holmes (trans.), *Tertullian* (ANCL; Edinburgh: T. & T. Clark, 1867).
Thucydides, in Charles Forster Smith (trans.), *Thucydides* (LCL; London: Heinemann, 1919).
Virgil, *Aeneid*, in H. Rushton Fairclough (trans.), *Aeneid* (London: Heinemann, 1978).
Xenophon, *Cyropedia*, in Walter Miller (trans.), *Xenophon in Seven Volumes* (Cambridge, MA: Harvard University Press, 1914).

Secondary Sources

Aune, David E. (ed.), *Greco-Roman Literature and the New Testament: Selected Forms and Genres* (Atlanta, GA: Scholars Press, 1988).
—*Studies in New Testament and Early Christian Literature: Essays in Honor of Allen P. Wikgren* (Leiden: E.J. Brill, 1972).
Barton, J.M.T., '*Bonum Certamen Certavi... Fidem Servavi*: 2 Tim. 4:7', *Bib* 40 (1959), pp. 878-84.
Berger, K., 'Apostelbrief und apostolische Rede: Zum Formular frühchristlicher Briefe', *ZNW* 65 (1974), pp. 190-231.
—'Hellenistische Gattungen im Neuen Testament', in *ANRW* 25.2 (1984), pp. 1031-432.
Bernard, J.H., *The Pastoral Epistles* (Cambridge Greek Testament for Schools and Colleges; Cambridge: Cambridge University Press, 1906).
Best, E., *Paul and his Converts* (Edinburgh: T. & T. Clark, 1988).
Boobyer, G.H., *'Thanksgiving' and the 'Glory of God' in Paul* (Leipzig: Noske, 1929).
Braudel, F., *The Mediterranean and the Mediterranean World in the Age of Phillip II* (New York: Harper & Row, 1966).
Brown, C., 'Sacrifice', in *NIDNTT*, III, pp. 418-38.
Brown, E.F., *The Pastoral Epistles* (Westminster Commentaries; London: Methuen, 1917).
Bunn, L., '2 Timothy 2.23-26', *ExpTim* 41 (1929), 235-37.
Cadbury, Henry J., 'Erastus of Corinth', *JBL* 50 (1931), pp. 42-58.
Champion, L.G., 'Benedictions and Doxologies in the Epistles of Paul' (Inaugural Dissertation zur Erlangung der Doktorwürde, Ruprecht-Karls-Universität zu Heidelberg, 1934).

Classen, C.J., 'St Paul's Epistles and Ancient Greek and Roman Rhetoric', in Stanley E. Porter (ed.), *Rhetoric and the New Testament* (JSNTSup, 90; Sheffield: JSOT Press, 1993), pp. 265-91.
Clinton, R.J., *The Making of a Leader* (Colorado Springs: NavPress, 1988).
Clifford, J.W., *In the Presence of My Enemies* (New York: Norton, 1963).
Collins, J.J., 'Testaments', in M.E. Stone (ed.), *Jewish Writings of the Second Temple Period* (Philadelphia: Fortress Press, 1984), pp. 325-55.
Cook, D., '2 Timothy IV.6-8 and the Epistle to the Philippians', *JTS* 33 (1982), pp. 168-71.
Dahl, N.A., 'Letter', in K. Crim (ed.), *Interpreter's Dictionary of the Bible* (Nashville: Abingdon Press, 1976), pp. 538-40.
Dearman, J. Andrew, 'Seals', in Paul J. Achtemeier, Howard Clark Kee, Simon B. Parker and James D. Purvis (eds.), *Harper's Bible Dictionary* (San Francisco: Harper & Row, 1985), pp. 989-90.
Deissmann, A., *Licht vom Osten* (Tübingen: Mohr, 1908).
Delcor, M., 'Les Attaches Littéraires, L'origine Et La Signification De L'expression Biblique "Prendre À Temoin Le Ciel Et La Terre"', *VT* 16 (1966), pp. 8-25.
Denis, A., 'La Fonction apostolique et la liturgie nouvelle en Esprit. Étude thématique des métaphores pauliniennes du culte nouveau', *RSPT* 42 (1958), pp. 401-36, 617-56.
—'"Versé en libation (Phil 2,17) = Versé son sang?" A propos d'une réference de W. Bauer', *RSR* 45 (1957), pp. 567-70.
Dornier, P., 'Paul au soir de sa vie', *AsSeign* 60 (1975), pp. 62-66.
Doty, W., *Letters in Primitive Christianity* (GBS; Philadelphia: Fortress Press, 1973).
Douglas, J.D. (ed.), 'Jannes and Jambres'; 'Seals' (NBD; Wheaton, IL: Tyndale Press, 1982).
Duncan, G.S., 'Paul's Ministry in Asia—the Last Phase', *NTS* 3.3 (1957), pp. 211-18.
Ellis, E. Earle, 'Traditions in the Pastoral Epistles', in Craig A. Evans and William F. Stinespring (eds.), *Early Jewish and Christian Exegesis* (Atlanta, GA: Scholars Press, 1987), pp. 237-53.
Exler, F.X., *The Form of the Ancient Greek Letter: A Study in Greek Epistolography* (Washington, DC: Catholic University of America, 1923).
Fee, Gordon D., *God's Empowering Presence: The Holy Spirit in the Letters of Paul* (Peabody, MA: Hendrickson, 1994).
—*Pauline Christology: An Exegetical Theological Study* (Peabody, MA: Hendrickson, 2007).
—'Toward a Theology of 2 Timothy—from a Pauline Perspective', in *SBL 1997 Seminar Papers* (SBLSP, 36; Atlanta: Scholars Press, 1997), pp. 732-49.
Ferguson, E., *Backgrounds of Early Christianity* (Grand Rapids: Eerdmans, 1987).
Fiore, B., *The Function of Personal Example in the Socratic and Pastoral Epistles* (AnBib, 105; Rome: Biblical Institute Press, 1986).
Fitzgerald, John T. (ed.), *Greco-Roman Perspectives on Friendship* (Atlanta, GA: Scholars Press, 1997).
—'Last Wills and Testaments in Graeco-Roman Perspective', in J.T. Fitzgerald and T.H. Olbricht (eds.), *Early Christianity and Classical Culture: Comparative Studies in Honour of Abraham J. Malherbe* (Leiden: Brill, 2003), pp. 637-72.
Fitzmyer, J.A., 'Aramaic Epistolography', *Semeia* 22 (1981), pp. 25-58.

—'New Testament Epistles', in R.E. Brown (ed.), *New Jerome Biblical Commentary* (London: Geoffrey Chapman, 1990), pp. 769-71.
France, R.T., 'Pour', in *NIDNTT*, II, pp. 853-55.
Freeborn, J.C.K., '2 Tim. 4.11: "Only Luke Is with Me"', in E.A. Livingstone (ed.), *Studia Evangelica* VI (Texte und Untersuchungen zur Geschichte der altchristlichen Literatur, 112; Berlin: Akademie-Verlag, 1973), pp. 128-39.
Funk, R.W., 'The Apostolic Parousia: Form and Significance', in W.R. Farmer (ed.), *Christian History and Interpretation: Studies Presented to John Knox* (Cambridge: Cambridge University Press, 1967), pp. 249-68.
Gernet, L., 'La diamartyrie, procédure archaïque du droit athénien', in P.G.W. Glare (ed.), *The Oxford Latin Dictionary* (Oxford: Clarendon Press, 8th edn, 1990).
Goetzmann, J., '*Oikia*', in Colin Brown (ed.), *NIDNTT* (Exeter: Paternoster Press, 1976), pp. 247-51.
Hafemann, S.J., *Suffering and Ministry in the Spirit* (PBTM; Carlisle: Paternoster Press, 1990).
Harrelson, W., 'The Significance of Last Words for Intertestamental Ethics', in J.L. Crenshaw and J.T. Willis (eds.), *Essays in Old Testament Ethics* (New York: Ktav Publishing House, 1974), pp. 203-13.
Harrison, P.N., *The Problem of the Pastoral Epistles* (Oxford: Oxford University Press, 1921).
Hassett, M., 'Mamertine Prison', in *The Catholic Encyclopedia* (New York: Robert Appleton Company, 1910).
Hitchcock, F.R.M., 'The Latinity of the Pastorals', *ExpTim* 39 (1927/28), pp. 347-52.
Johnson, L.T., *Letters to Paul's Delegates* (The New Testament in Context; Valley Forge, PA: Trinity Press International, 1996).
Karris, R.J., 'The Background and Significance of the Polemic of the Pastoral Epistles', *JBL* 92 (1973), pp. 549-64.
—'The Function and Sitz im Leben of the Paraenetic Elements in the Pastoral Epistles' (PhD dissertation, Harvard University, 1971).
Käsemann, E., 'Das Formular einer neutestamentlichen Ordinationparänese', in W. Eltester (ed.), *Neutestamentliche Studien für R. Bultmann* (Berlin: Alfred Töpelmann, 1954), pp. 261-68.
Kolenkow, A.B., 'The Genre Testament and Forecasts of the Future in the Hellenistic Jewish Milieu', *JSJ* 6 (1975), pp. 57-71.
—'Testaments', in R.A. Kraft and G.W.E. Nickelsburg (eds.), *Early Judaism and its Modern Interpreters* (Philadelphia: Fortress Press, 1986), pp. 259-67.
Kostenberger, Andreas, and Terry L. Wilder (eds.), *Entrusted with the Gospel* (Nashville, TN: B & H Academic, 2010).
Kurz, W.S., *Farewell Addresses in the New Testament* (Zacchaeus Studies: New Testament; Collegeville, MN: Liturgical Press, 1990).
—'Luke 22:14-38 and Greco-Roman and Biblical Farewell Addresses', *JBL* 104 (1985), pp. 251-68.
Malherbe, A., 'Hellenistic Moralists and the New Testament', *ANRW* 26.1 (1992), pp. 267-333.
—'"In Season and out of Season": 2 Timothy 4:2', *JBL* 103 (1984), pp. 235-43.
—*Moral Exhortation: A Greco-Roman Sourcebook* (Philadelphia: Westminster Press, 1986).

Malkin, I., 'Libations', in S. Hornblower and A. Spawforth (eds.), *The Oxford Classical Dictionary* (Oxford: Oxford University Press, 1996), p. 854.
Marshall, I.H., 'Recent Study of the Pastoral Epistles', *Themelios* 23 (1997), pp. 3-37.
Martin, S.C., *Pauli testamentum: 2 Timothy and the Last Words of Moses* (Tesi gregoriana. Serie teologia, 18; Rome: Pontificia Università Gregoriana, 1997).
Martin, W.J., 'Poetry', in *NBD*, pp. 949-50.
McCown, C.C., 'Codex and Roll in the New Testament', *HTR* 34.4 (1941), pp. 219-50.
McRay, John, 'The Authorship of the Pastoral Epistles: A Consideration of Certain Adverse Arguments to Pauline Authorship', *ResQ* 7 (1963), pp. 2-18.
Medley, E., 'The Character of Timothy as Reflected in the Letters Addressed to Him by the Apostle Paul', *Exp* 2 (1895), pp. 223-34.
Michel, O., 'σπένδομαι', in *TDNT*, VII, pp. 528-36.
Miller, J.D., *The Pastoral Letters as Composite Documents* (New York: Cambridge University Press, 1997).
Mullins, T.Y., 'Disclosure: a Literary Form in the New Testament', *NovT* 7 (1964), pp. 44-50.
—'Formulas in New Testament Epistles', *JBL* 91 (1972), pp. 380-90.
—'Greeting as a New Testament Form', *JBL* 87 (1968), pp. 418-26.
Munck, J., 'Discourses d'adieu dans le Nouveau Testament et dans la littérature biblique', in J. von Allmen (ed.), *Aux Sources de la tradition chrétienne* (Paris: Delachaux & Niestlé, 1950), pp. 155-70.
Mundle, W., 'Command', in *NIDNTT*, I, pp. 340-41.
O'Brien, P.T., *Introductory Thanksgivings in the Letter of Paul* (NovTSup, 49; Leiden: E.J. Brill, 1977).
Peaston, M., 'Disengagement', *ExpTim* 93.6 (1982), pp. 180-82.
Perdue, L.G., 'The Death of the Sage and Moral Exhortation: From Ancient Near Eastern Instructions to Graeco-Roman Paraenesis', *Semeia* 50 (1990), pp. 81-109.
Pfitzner, V.C., *Paul and the Agon Motif* (NovTSup, 16; Leiden: E.J. Brill, 1976).
Porter, S.E., *Idioms of the Greek New Testament* (Sheffield: JSOT Press, 1992).
—'Paul as Epistolographer and Rhetorician?', in idem, *The Rhetorical Interpretation of Scripture* (JSNTSup, 180; Sheffield: Sheffield Academic Press, 1999), pp. 222-48.
—'The Theoretical Justification for Application of Rhetorical Categories to Pauline Epistolary Literature', in T.H. Olbricht and S.E. Porter (eds.), *Rhetoric and the New Testament* (JSNTSup, 90; Sheffield: JSOT Press, 1993), pp. 100-122.
Prior, M., *Paul the Letter-Writer* (JSNTSup, 23; Sheffield: JSOT Press, 1989).
Purdue, L.G., 'The Death of the Sage and Moral Exhortation: From Ancient Near Eastern Instructions to Graeco-Roman Paraenesis', *Semeia* 50 (1990), pp. 81-109.
Quinn, J.D., 'Paraenesis and the Pastoral Epistles', in M. Carrez (ed.), *De la Torah au Messie. Mélanges Henri Cazelles* (Paris: Editions du Cerf, 1981), pp. 495-501.
—'The Holy Spirit in the Pastoral Epistles'; in Daniel Durken (ed.), *Sin, Salvation and the Spirit* (Collegeville, MN: The Liturgical Press, 1979), pp. 345-68.
—'Paraenesis and the Pastoral Epistles: Lexical Observations Bearing on the Nature of the Sub-genre and Soundings on its Role in Socialization and Liturgies', *Semeia* 50 (1990), pp. 189-210.
—'The Pastoral Epistles', *BiTod* 23 (1985), pp. 228-38.
—'Paul's Last Captivity', in E.A. Livingstone (ed.), *Studia Biblica: Papers on Paul*

and Other New Testament Authors (JSNTSup, 3; Sheffield: JSOT Press, 1978), pp. 289-99.

Rapske, B., *Paul in Roman Custody* (The Book of Acts in its First Century Setting, 3; Grand Rapids: Eerdmans, 1994).

Reinhartz, A., 'On the Meaning of the Pauline Exhortation "μιμεταί μου γίνεσθε—become imitators of me"', *SR* 16 (1987), pp. 393-403.

Richards, W., *Difference and Distance in Post-Pauline Christianity: An Epistolary Analysis of the Pastorals* (Studies in Biblical Literature, 44; New York: Peter Lang, 2002).

Rigaux, B., *Saint Paul et ses lettres* (Paris: Desclée de Brouwer, 1962).

Robert, J.H., 'The Eschatological Transitions to the Pauline Letter Body', *Neot* 20 (1986), pp. 29-35.

Roberts, J.W., 'Note on the Adjective *pas* in 2 Timothy 3.16', *ExpTim* 76 (1965), p. 359.

Robertson, A.T., *A Grammar of the Greek New Testament in the Light of Historical Research* (New York: Hodder & Stoughton, 1919).

—*Word Pictures in the New Testament* (New York: Richard R. Smith, 1930).

Roller, O., *Das Formular der paulinischen Briefe: Ein Beitrag zur Lehre vom antike Briefe* (Stuttgart: W. Kohlhammer, 1933).

Rose, H.J., 'The Clausulae of the Pauline Corpus', *JTS* 25 (1924), pp. 17-43.

Saldarini, A.J., 'Last Words and Deathbed Scenes in Rabbinic Literature', *JQR* 68 (1977), pp. 28-45.

Sanders, J.T., 'The Transition from Opening Epistolary Thanksgiving to Body in the Letters of the Pauline Corpus', *JBL* 81 (1962), pp. 348-62.

Schubert, P., 'Form and Function of the Pauline Letters', *JR* 19 (1939), pp. 365-77.

—*Form and Function of the Pauline Thanksgivings* (BZNW, 20; Berlin: Alfred Töpelmann, 1939).

Smalley, S.S., 'The Testament of Jesus: Another Look', in E.A. Livingstone (ed.), *Studia Evangelica* VI (Texte und Untersuchungen zur Geschichte der altchristlichen Literatur, 112; Berlin: Akademie-Verlag, 1973), pp. 495-501.

Smith, C.A., 'The Consequences of the Increase in and the Changed Role of Letter-Writing for the Early Church', *IBS* 24 (2002), pp. 146-74.

—'Complaining', in Doug Magnum (ed.), *Lexham Lexical Dictionary* (Bellingham, WA: Logos, 2014).

—'Church Leadership', in Doug Magnum (ed.), *Lexham Lexical Dictionary* (Bellingham, WA: Logos, 2014).

Smith, R.E., and J. Beekman, 'A Literary-Semantic Analysis of Second Timothy', in M.F. Kopesec and J. Callow (eds.), *Semantic Structure of Written Communication* (Dallas, TX: Summer Institute of Linguistics, 1981).

Spence, R.M., '2 Timothy 3.15-16', *ExpTim* 8 (1896), pp. 563-65.

Stanley, D.M., '"Become imitators of me": The Pauline Conception of Apostolic Tradition', *Bib* 40 (1959), pp. 859-77.

Steen, H.A., 'Les clichés épistolaires dans les lettres sur papyrus grecques', *Classica et medievalia* 1 (1938), pp. 119-76.

Stowers, S.K., *Letter Writing in Greco-Roman Antiquity* (Philadelphia: Westminster Press, 1986).

Sundberg, A.C., 'Enabling Language in Paul', *HTR* 79 (1986), pp. 270-77.

Towner, P.H., 'The Portrait of Paul and the Theology of 2 Timothy: The Closing Chapter of the Pauline Story', *HBT* 21 (1999), pp. 151-70.

Trentham, C.A., *Studies in Timothy* (Nashville, TN: Convention Press, 1959).
Twomey, J., *The Pastoral Epistles through the Centuries* (Chichester: Wiley-Blackwell, 2009).
—'I Have Fought the Good Fight', *Scr* 10 (1958), pp. 110-15.
Van Leeuwen, C., 'δέ', in *THAT*, II, p. 1122.
Van Unnik, W.C., '*Dominus Vobiscum*: The Background of a Liturgical Formula', in *Sparsa Collecta III* (Leiden: E.J. Brill, 1983), pp. 362-91.
Verner, David C., *The Household Code: The Social World of the Pastoral Epistles* (SBLDS; Chico, CA: Scholars Press, 1983).
Von Nordheim, E., *Die Lehre der Alten. I. Das Testament als Literaturgattung im Judentum der hellenistisch-römischen Zeit* (Arbeiten zur Literatur und Geschichte des hellenistischen Judentums, 13; Leiden: E.J. Brill, 1980).
Warfield, B.B., *The Inspiration and Authority of the Bible* (Philadelphia: The Presbyterian and Reformed Publishers Company, 1948).
Ward, R.A., *Commentary on 1 and 2 Timothy and Titus* (Waco, TX: Word Books, 1974).
Watson, D.F., 'The Contributions and Limitations of Greco-Roman Rhetorical Theory for Constructing the Rhetorical and Historical Situations of a Pauline Epistle', in Stanley E. Porter (ed.), *The Rhetorical Interpretation of Scripture* (JSNTSup, 180; Sheffield: Sheffield Academic Press, 1999), pp. 125-51.
—'Paul's Speech to the Ephesian Elders (Acts 20.17-38): Epideictic Rhetoric of Farewell', in Duane F. Watson (ed.), *Persuasive Artistry: Studies in New Testament Rhetoric in Honor of George A. Kennedy* (JSNTSup, 50; Sheffield: JSOT Press, 1991), pp. 184-208.
Weima, J.A.D., *Neglected Endings: The Significance of the Pauline Letter Closings* (JSNTSup, 101; Sheffield: JSOT Press, 1994).
White, J.L., 'Ancient Greek Letters', in D.E. Aune (ed.), *Greco-Roman Literature and the New Testament* (Atlanta, GA: Scholars Press, 1988), pp. 85-106.
—*The Body of the Greek Letter* (SBLDS, 2; Missoula, MT: Scholars Press, 1975).
—'Introductory Formulae in the Body of the Pauline Letter', *JBL* 90 (1971), pp. 91-97.
—'Saint Paul and the Apostolic Letter Tradition', *CBQ* 45 (1983), pp. 433-44.
Wilson, J.P., 'The Translation of 2 Timothy 2.26', *ExpTim* 49 (1937), p. 45.
Winter, B.W., 'The Entries and Ethics of Orators and Paul (1 Thess 2:1-12)', *TynBul* 44 (1993), pp. 55-74.

Scripture Index

Old Testament

Genesis		1.9	154	Judges	
1.26	80	5.21	41	2.8	105
1.28	80	5.23	41	6.12	176
1.30	93	6.2	41	6.16	176
2.20-25	93	6.4	41	13.4-7	153
2.25	154	19.15	26		
4.1	41	24.16	96	*Ruth*	
6.12	122	26.36	32	2.4	176
24.3	142				
28.15	176	*Numbers*		*1 Samuel*	
35.14	114	4.37	155	1.11	153
39.12	101	4.41	155	1.14	154
39.21	54	6.1-23	153	2.11	155
50.15	170	6.27	95	2.18	155
50.17	170	15.1-10	153	2.27	140
		16.15	105	3.1	155
Exodus		16.26-35	96	17.37	172
2	100	16.3	100		
2.11-25	100	16.4	105	*2 Samuel*	
3.21	54	16.5	96, 105	3.39	170
7.1	121	24.2	137	7.12-16	71
7.11	105, 120, 129			23.1	137
		Deuteronomy		23.16	153
7.12	120	5.22	137		
7.22	105, 120	6.5	116	*1 Kings*	
7.8-12	121	6.7-9	56	17.24	140
8.7	120	11.1	116	21.8	95
9.11	120, 122	11.13	116		
11.3	54	11.22	116	*2 Kings*	
12.31-42	100	19.9	116	2.9-14	169
24.4	137	21.18	113	9.7	105
24.6	154	25.1	26	18.12	105
28.11	95, 96	25.2	26		
28.36	96	30.16	116	*1 Chronicles*	
29.40	153	30.19-20	142	28.19	135
32.16	135	30.20	116		
33.7	154	31.6	165	*Ezra*	
				7.24	155
Leviticus		*Joshua*			
1.13	154	24.29	105	*Nehemiah*	
1.17	154			9.38	95

Scripture Index

Job
36.10   97

Psalms
7.3   172
19.7   134
22   163-64
22.21   164, 173
22.22   164
22.27-28 172
23.6   97
25.1-3   34
34.14   96
34.19   127
35.17   172
36.1   105
42.4   97
44.2   54
44.22   127
55.17   26
62.12   170
90.15   176
105.43   74
105.6   74
106.32   127
119.21   113
134.1   105
135.1   105

Proverbs
1.7   116
2.6   68
3.7   90, 96
4.1-8   116
4.14-15 117
8.5   104
10.14   115, 149
11.5   90
13.3   115
14.8   123
15.1   109
15.14   104
21.17   116
22.15   123
24.12   170
25.22   118
27.20b   115
28.18   61

30.1   137
31.1   137

Ecclesiastes
7.4   116
9.11   158

Isaiah
26.13   96
28.16   95
3.9   121
42.1-9   105
42.2-3   105
49.1   105
49.1-7   105
49.6   105
50.4-9   105
50.6   105
52.1   96
52.13–53.12 105
53.7   105

Jeremiah
8.6   158
23.10   158
32.11-14 95

Ezekiel
22.9   114

Daniel
3.39   51
6.4   61
6.10   26
12.1   109

Hosea
9.7   137

Joel
2.28   110
2.32   103

Zephaniah
1.9   42

Haggai
2.23   95

Zechariah
14.6   42

APOCRYPHA
1 Esdras
4.34   139
8.52   158

Tobit
10.13   41

Judith
2.10   139
16.9   118

Sirach
3.21   110
9.18   115
17.26   96
51.23   104

Wisdom
2.19   106
2.23   37
3.19   110
6.18   38
8.7   88
12.4   114
16.29   114

1 Maccabees
2.49   139
14.34   139

2 Maccabees
2.21   8
3.15   41
3.24   8
4.4   110
5.4   8
7.34   114
8.32   114
12.12   88
12.39-45 51
12.45   160

Scripture Index

New Testament

Matthew
1.23	176
1.25	41
2.13	101
5.7	50
5.11-12	129
5.12	106
5.43-46	106
6.4-6	161
6.13	127, 172, 173
6.18	161
6.24	62
7.6	88, 109, 111
7.7	50
7.21	117
8.26	32, 146
8.28	110
9.13	131
9.37-38	89
10.11-15	145
10.14	109
10.21	79
10.22	79
10.22-23	128
10.33	81
10.38	100
12.29	98
13.24	56, 98
13.31	56
15.17	68
16.9	68
16.11	68
16.22	146
16.27	161
17.9	70
18.15	139
18.21-35	161
19.13	146
19.28	80
20.1	89
20.8	89
21.42	135
22.14	74
22.37	104
22.37-38	112
22.39	112
23.8-10	106
23.12	113
24.6ff.	75
24.6-31	75
24.10	79
24.10-13	112
24.13	74, 79, 112
24.32	131
25.36	50
26.56	134
26.69-75	81
27.3	82, 100
27.5	82
27.29	63
27.46	165
27.51-53	93
28.12	111
28.19-20	134
28.20	106

Mark
1.1	72
1.11	20
1.25	146
2.17	77
2.26	97
3.5	106
3.27	98
5.37	165
7.35	72
8.17	68
8.31	34, 41
8.33	146
8.34	61, 81, 128
8.38	33, 41, 89
9.9	70
9.24	83
6.21	145
10.18	140
10.30	126
10.45	70, 161
10.48	146
12.6	20
12.10	135
12.24	135
13.24-27	109
12.25	93
13.27	74
13.34	150
13.37	149
14.11	145
14.31	79
14.33	165
15.17	161
15.21	169
15.29-30	106
16.11	82, 83
16.16	82, 83

Luke
1.1	151
1.1-4	169
1.3	124
1.15	153
1.28	176
1.41	133
1.44	133
2.12	133
2.16	133
2.29	99
2.37	26
4.17	169
4.21	135
4.39	146
5.31	45
6.11	11, 123
6.16	11, 115
6.48-50	94
7.10	45
7.42	161
8.14	61
8.47	30
9.21	146
9.26	33
10.37	21
10.40	151
12.9	81
12.48	56
13.16	72
13.24	157
14.11	40
16.1	114
16.7	133
16.14	113
16.24	49
17.3	146

Scripture Index

Luke (cont.)		20.5	94	16–17	126
17.31	98	20.9	70	16.1-2	126
18.15	133	21.4	94	16.1-4	40
19.10	77			16.1	28, 34, 124
20.35	75	Acts		16.2-3	133
21.21	101	1.17	151	16.2	126, 133
21.24	118	1.25	151	16.8-11	167
21.34-35	108	2.27	165	16.18	142
22.30	80	2.31	165	16.20-21	73
23.16	107	3.12	128	16.26	72
23.32	75	4.17	92, 122	17.3	56
23.32-39	73	4.24	99	17.34	87
23.33	75	4.6	169	18.2	174
23.34	171	6	5	18.3	61
23.39	75	6.6	31	18.9	41
23.40	146	6.11	113	18.9	176
24.11	82, 83	7.22	107	18.10	41
24.32	135	7.52	11, 115	18.18	153
24.41	82, 83	7.60	171	18.19	58
24.43	83	8.1	42	18.26	58, 174
24.44-47	134	8.17-19	31	18.27-28	88
24.45	83	8.35	135	19	129
24.46	70	8.9	94, 120	19.6	31
		9.3-10	41	19.9	40, 59
John		9.12	31	19.19	134
1.9	77	9.15	98, 153,	19.19-20	120
2.19-22	95		155, 172	19.22	175
3.19	77	9.17	31	19.25	89
3.20	139	9.22	55	19.33	169, 170
4.27	94	9.36	100, 140	19.36	115
5.39	134	10.42	143, 161	20.1	175
5.46	134	11.23	125	20.4-5	168
6.14	77	13–14	126	20.4	175
6.45	131	13.1-12	121	20.23	72
7.13	94	13.2	150	20.24	74, 151,
7.15	133	13.8	120		153, 158,
7.42	135	13.10	90		159
8.29	176	13.13	167	20.24a	158
8.31	131	13.45	126	20.24b	158
10.12	101	13.47	105	20.28-30	5
12.40	68	13.50	127	20.29-30	13, 56, 58,
12.42	94	14.5-6	127		115
13.15	19	14.19	127	20.29-31	15
14.16	176	14.22	128	20.30	113, 138
15.1	65	14.23	56	21.13	153
15.20	128	15.2	104	21.28-29	175
16.28	77	15.7	104	21.29	4, 14
16.32	176	15.36-41	167	22.4	129
18.37	77	15.38	150	22.7	129

Scripture Index   191

22.24	30	3.25	8	9.23	98
23.1	8, 25	4.5	9	10.11	135
24	172	4.11	95	10.12-13	103
24.4	122	4.17	38	11.9	108
24.16	8, 26	4.20	54, 55	11.26	127
25	172	4.24	70	11.31	21
25.20	104	5.2	21, 89	12.1	88
26.29	72	5.3-4	40, 89, 126, 127	12.3	33
27.2	13			12.6	31
27.23-24	171	5.3	80	12.9	27
28	4	5.5	125	12.12	74
28.21	133	5.8	125	12.14	129
28.24	82, 83	5.12	36	12.20	118
28.30-31	40	5.15	121	14.13	38
		5.17	80	14.9-10	143
Romans		5.18	121	14.14	43
1.1	105, 154	5.19	121	14.15	36
1.2-4	72, 134	5.21	121	14.20	36
1.3-4	75	6.1-11	94	15.4	135
1.3	71	6.4	37	15.5	79, 126
1.4	33, 35	6.8	77, 78, 79	15.7	36
1.5	9	6.9	70	15.13	33, 35, 51
1.7	20	6.11-12	78	15.14	43
1.8-9	49	6.12	101	15.16-17	155
1.9	25	6.13	89, 100	15.16	25, 99, 155
1.11	27	6.16	88	15.19	33, 35, 166, 172
1.13	66	6.19	89		
1.15	172	6.23	31	15.20	95, 168
1.16	33, 41	7.6	133	15.28	95
1.18	128	7.15	128	15.31	127
1.21-28	117	7.23	118	15.32	49
1.24	101	7.24	127	15.33	176
1.25	25	8.14	119	16.1	5
1.28-31	111, 113	8.15-16	36	16.3	174
1.30	113	8.15	32	16.7	26, 174
1.31	114	8.18-25	160	16.11	26
2.4	107, 125	8.18	126, 153	16.12	65
2.5-8	161	8.28-29	40	16.21	26
2.6	170	8.28	125	16.22	2, 11
2.7	37, 100	8.29	74, 96	16.23	175
2.15	170	8.33	74	16.25	36
2.17-24	116	8.36	127	16.27	173
2.20	116	8.37-39	173		
2.27	133	8.38	43	*1 Corinthians*	
2.29	133	9.1	8	1.1	19, 22
3.2	83	9.11	125	1.2	99, 103
3.3	82, 83	9.21	98	1.4-9	24
3.21-27	75	9.22	125, 170	1.9	76
3.21	8	9.23	21	1.11	16

192 Scripture Index

1 Corinthians (cont.)		10.6	44	1.10	127
1.16	50, 63	10.13	76	1.18	76
1.18-25	29, 39	10.14	101	1.22	32
1.18-2.5	148	10.27	8	2.11	16, 152
1.21-25	141	11.1	7, 19, 44,	2.14-16	72
1.23	34		88, 106	2.14	33
2.12	32	11.7-10	80	2.16	58
2.4	33, 35	11.23	152	3.6	46, 133
2.6–5.13	7	11.32	107	3.7	133
3.10-12	95	12.4	31	3.13	38
3.10	38	12.12-24	98	3.18	89
3.11	38	12.18	39	4.7	97, 98
4.1	43	12.26	40	4.9a	165
4.2	89	12.28	18, 31, 39	4.9b	165
4.4	25	13.7	74	4.16–5.5	160
4.5	36	13.13	125	5.1-5	66
4.6	131	14.1	102, 131	5.2	27
4.8	80	14.15	63	5.9-10	144
4.12	65, 129	14.24	146	6.3-10	21
4.15	105	14.35	131	6.3-13	40, 75
4.16-17	124	15.1-3	45	6.3	151
4.16	19	15.9	58, 152	6.4-10	20
4.17	20, 58, 125	15.10	65	6.4	69, 126
4.21	107	15.12	93	6.6	27
5.3	16	15.17	93, 94	7.3	79
5.6	107	15.19	37, 93, 94	8.4	151
5.7	98	15.20	70	8.6	166
6.2	80	15.23	66	8.16-21	166
6.11	99	15.25	38	8.23	166
6.12	91	15.26	36	10.5	118
6.18	101	15.42	37	11.13	89
6.19	32	15.50	37	11.20	148
7.1	16	15.53	37	11.23-33	20, 40
7.7	31	15.54	37	11.24-28	59
7.26	110	15.55	36	12.1-10	41
8.1	117	15.58	41, 150	12.7-10	40
8.10	92	16.2	38	12.8-10	127
9	7	16.10	150	12.9	33, 55
9.1	18	16.15	151	12.10	126
9.2	95	16.19	174	12.12	18
9.7	60, 65, 66			13.11	176
9.13	62	2 Corinthians			
9.18	38	1.1	19, 22	Galatians	
9.24	60	1.3-7	35	1.4	19, 129
9.24-26	159	1.6	75	1.5	173
9.24-27	157	1.6a	40	1.10	105
9.25	64, 157	1.8	48	1.13-17	7, 134
9.27	64	1.8-9	40	1.14	91, 129
10.1-13	120	1.8-10	21	1.15	105

Scripture Index   193

1.23	9	3.20	35	1.30	63, 157	
2.8	172	4.2	125, 147	2.5-11	53	
2.1-3	166	4.3	88	2.6-11	105	
2.10	88	4.8	118	2.7	105	
2.11-14	105	4.11	18	2.9-11	144	
2.11	152	4.12	151	2.17	155	
2.14	90	4.14	119	2.19-24	20	
2.17-21	161	4.15	106	2.22	20	
3.10	169	4.22	101	2.24	13, 155	
3.8	135	5.11	139, 146	2.25-30	59	
3.9	137	5.13	139, 146	2.25	18, 49, 59	
3.22	135, 137	5.16	110	3.2	89	
4.4-7	36	5.18	129	3.3	25	
4.30	135	5.20	114	3.4-6	6	
5.16	101	6.1	113	3.6	102	
5.22	125, 147	6.4	139	3.7-11	161	
5.23	107	6.10ff.	59	3.8	34, 129	
5.24	101, 119	6.10-18	157	3.10	33, 126,	
6.1	107	6.10	54, 55		15.	
6.8	37	6.16	129	3.12-14	30, 160	
6.11	133	6.17	105	3.12	102	
6.18	177	6.20-21	72	3.14	102	
		6.21-22	168	3.16	131	
Ephesians		6.21	20, 58, 168	3.17	44	
1.1	19, 22	6.24	37	4.1	64	
1.4	74			4.9	176	
1.13	90	Philippians		4.11	152	
1.17	51	1.1	5, 105	4.13	55, 62	
1.18	33	1.3-5	24	4.14-19	49	
1.19-20	33	1.6	140, 173	4.20	173	
1.20	95	1.7	72	4.23	177	
1.21	97	1.8	27	5.2	9	
2.1	37	1.9	33	6.3	9	
2.3	119	1.12-13	34	9.2	9	
2.6	94	1.12-18	73			
2.8-9	38	1.12-20	155	Colossians		
2.8-10	50	1.12-21	130	1.1	19, 22	
2.8	55	1.13	12	1.5	160	
2.10	100	1.14	72	1.13	144	
2.11-13	70	1.15-18	35, 41, 58	1.15	90	
2.11-14	21	1.17	72	1.21	129	
2.19-22	97	1.20	89	1.24	34, 40, 72,	
3.1	34	1.22	67		75, 126,	
3.2	43	1.23	119		130, 153	
3.4	68	1.23	156	1.25	43	
3.5	68	1.25	9, 67	1.29	157	
3.9	36	1.27–3.13	47	2.1	63, 157	
3.11	125	1.27	9	2.1	157	
3.16	33	1.29	40, 55, 67	3.1-11	78	

194 Scripture Index

Colossians (cont.)		1.10	34		79, 125,
3.1	94	2.2	56, 58		147
3.4	37	2.5	16, 70	1.18	30, 62,
3.5	101	2.8	8, 161		106, 151
3.12	74, 107	2.9-12	117	1.19-20	14
4.7	58, 168	2.13	46	1.20	25, 81, 92,
4.10	13, 168	3.2	129		99, 107,
4.11	49, 165	3.3	76, 129		108, 114,
4.12	157	3.5	79		115, 126,
4.13	165	3.8	26		170
4.14	165, 167	3.9	19, 44	2.1	58
4.17	151	3.16	176	2.2	9, 106
4.18	72			2.4	58, 90,
		1 Timothy			107, 108,
1 Thessalonians		1.1	22		119
1.2-16	24	1.2	50, 166	2.5	58
1.3	63	1.3-4	53, 159	2.6	34
1.7	44	1.3-5	113	2.7	39, 103
1.9-10	36	1.3-7	90	2.8	114
2.2	63, 157	1.3-11	129	2.11-12	106
2.7	106	1.3	13, 15, 56,	2.11	131
2.9	26		58, 67, 85	2.13	103
2.17	88, 119	1.4	44, 87,	2.15	131
2.19	63		104, 107	3.1-7	58
3.4	128	1.5	25, 27, 102	3.1	57, 76, 77,
3.6	27	1.6	74, 87		150, 158
3.10	26	1.7	59, 68,	3.2	33, 67,
3.11-13	51		105, 113,		106, 115
4.1	67		125	3.6	114, 116
4.4	98	1.8-11	26, 64, 134	3.7	63, 67,
4.8	32	1.8	46, 64, 169		106, 108,
4.13	16	1.9-10	111		114
4.13-18	93	1.9	91, 111,	3.8	44
4.16-18	143		114, 128	3.9	26, 125
4.17	66	1.10	22, 45, 92,	3.10	89
5.6	150		125, 138,	3.11	58, 114
5.8	45, 59,		148	3.14-16	91, 116,
	150, 157	1.11	75, 113		122
5.9-10	36	1.12	39, 42,	3.15	67, 95, 97
5.9	39		151, 168	3.16–4.5	148
5.12	65	1.13-16	22	3.16	9, 77, 128
5.17	26	1.13	6, 21, 50,	4.1-2	107
5.19	31		113, 149	4.1-6	160
5.23	8, 51	1.14	45, 55,	4.1	125, 136,
5.24	76		103, 149		138, 148
5.26-28	174	1.15-16	73	4.2	8, 25, 97,
5.28	177	1.15	21, 57, 76,		118, 119,
			77, 116		122
2 Thessalonians		1.16	21, 37, 44,	4.3	93, 107,
1.5	40		50, 73, 77,		116

Scripture Index 195

4.3b	15	6.3	9, 22, 45, 125, 145, 148	1.10	7, 8, 36, 37, 161
4.6	15, 124, 138			1.11-12	19, 20
4.7-8	9	6.4	45, 87, 106, 116, 116	1.11	6, 39
4.7-9	119			1.12	12, 30, 41, 42, 43, 46, 57, 82, 170
4.7	91, 104, 149, 159	6.5	9, 111, 122		
4.8	19, 37, 64, 79, 100, 128, 138	6.5b	113	1.13	9, 19, 39, 44, 44, 44, 45, 58, 62, 103, 125
		6.6-8	168		
		6.6-10	89, 104		
4.9-10	76	6.6-10	104		
4.9	57, 76	6.6	9	1.14	10, 42, 43, 46, 170
4.10	57, 58, 77, 157, 169	6.9	101, 102, 108, 119, 130		
				1.15-18	167
4.11	124			1.15	81. 92
4.12	20, 44, 45, 102, 141	6.10	74, 113, 147	1.16-18	96
				1.16	171
4.13	31	6.11	9, 54, 79, 101, 102, 103, 126, 128	1.17	88
4.14	30, 31, 32, 177			1.18	50. 51
				1.18	51
4.15	92, 122			2	60
4.16	44, 124	6.12	63, 79, 157	2.1-6	60
5	103	6.12a	158	2.1	67, 68, 79
5, 6	64	6.13	34, 143	2.2	16, 44, 59, 85, 124
5.1ff.	114	6.14	8, 36, 144, 161		
5.2	15, 89, 102, 114, 150			2.3	19, 35, 46, 62, 150
		6.19	37, 79, 95		
		6.20	41, 42, 43, 46, 91, 107, 131, 145, 148	2.4	88
5.4	26, 131			2.5	10, 51, 64, 64, 159
5.5	26				
5.6	36			2.6	65
5.8	81, 113, 169	6.21	74, 84	2.8-10	75
		6.21b	177	2.8	26, 64, 96
				2.9	35, 171
5.11	104	*2 Timothy*		2.10-12a	64
5.13	15, 63, 131	1.1	22, 79	2.10	69, 74
5.16	57	1.2	50, 54, 96	2.11-13	76, 77, 94
5.17	65, 66, 85, 169	1.3-5	24	2.11	76
		1.3	8, 26, 104	2.12	9, 10, 74, 89, 107
5.18	89, 135	1.4	164		
5.20	92, 94, 131, 139, 146	1.5	9, 43, 102, 103, 133	2.13	57, 131
				2.13b	77
		1.6-7	177	2.14-23	159
5.21	56, 102, 143	1.6–2.7	123	2.14-26	86
		1.6	30, 31, 151	2.14	100, 106
5.24	63	1.7-8	10, 54	2.15-18	160
6.1	99, 140	1.7	31, 32, 102, 124	2.15	88, 89, 98, 106, 122, 130, 164
6.2	57, 99				
6.2b	57	1.8	19, 40, 89		
6.3-10	62, 67	1.9	55, 125	2.16-18	113, 115

2 Timothy (cont.)		3.15		9, 103, 119, 133, 159		4.19-22	174
2.16	90, 122, 128	3.16		10, 135, 136, 137, 138		4.19	90, 176, 177
2.17-18	74, 81					4.20	14
2.17	14, 98, 99, 140					4.21	88, 156
		3.17		100, 159		4.22a	176
2.18	15, 87, 90, 92, 96, 119, 159	4.1-8		xi, xiii, 17, 142, 143, 144		*Titus* 1.1	18, 74, 105, 119, 154
2.19-21	168	4.1		8, 36, 161			
2.19	26, 92, 99, 117, 122	4.2		125, 139		1.2	36, 37
		4.3-4		89, 120, 159		1.5	13, 166
2.20-24	160						
2.21	99, 104	4.3		34, 39, 45, 101, 148		1.7	43
2.22	8, 9, 33, 45, 97, 106	4.4		47, 74		1.8	115
						1.9	57
2.23	91, 103, 107	4.5		62, 123, 168		1.11	94
						1.13	30
2.24-25	88, 125	4.6		xii, 152, 156		1.14	44, 47, 149
2.24	67, 98, 106, 113	4.7		9, 59, 63, 105, 158, 158, 158, 159		1.16	81, 102, 113, 116, 122
2.25-26	102, 159					2.2	79
2.25	119, 150					2.3	114
2.26	84, 114					2.4	133
3.1-8	98	4.8		8, 10, 30, 36, 37, 42, 64, 130, 157, 161, 170		2.7	44
3.2-4	110, 111					2.9	99
3.2	58					2.11	54
3.3-5	112					2.12	101
3.4	11, 113					2.13	8, 144, 161
3.5	9, 81, 128	4.9-10		46		3.1	87
3.6-8	58	4.9-18		21, 163		3.3	101, 111, 113, 119
3.6	9, 101, 102	4.9-22		164			
3.7	119, 131	4.9		23, 32, 88			
3.8	9, 15, 26, 100, 103, 120, 121	4.10		9, 23, 47, 115, 156		3.8	57, 76, 77
						3.9	91, 102, 104
		4.11-13					
3.9	11, 120, 129	4.11		12, 14, 15, 158, 165		3.10	104
						3.12	13, 14, 88, 164, 167, 175
3.10	9, 19, 21, 79, 102, 130, 147	4.13		xii, 13, 48			
		4.14		14, 48, 81, 115, 140		3.15	174
3.11	35, 40	4.15		122			
3.12	20, 40, 53, 100, 103, 126, 141	4.16-18		13		*Hebrews*	
		4.16		14, 40, 46, 47, 72,		1.1-3	26
						1.2	110
3.13	91, 118, 122, 140			115, 165, 167		2.7	63
						2.9	63
3.14-17	26	4.17		13, 158, 159, 165		2.11	30
3.14	131, 169					2.14	49
3.15-16	122	4.18		140		3.1-6	97

3.6	105	10	72, 105	1.16	134
3.12	146	11	100	1.21	134, 137
4.2	134	13	72	2.1	99
4.16	50, 145	22	13	2.5	39
5.8	44	23	13, 167	2.6	88
5.12	95	24	165	2.11	113
5.14	95			3.1	27
6.1	95	*James*		3.3	110
8.2	155	1.12	79, 161		
8.5	25	1.21	107	*1 John*	
9.9	25	4.16	113	2.16	113
9.21	97, 98	5.3	110	2.22-23	81
9.27	160	5.13	34, 72	3.8	107
10.23	76				
10.32	63, 79	*1 Peter*		*3 John*	
10.36-39	129	1.1	18	2	148
10.38	32	1.7	89		
10.39	32	1.13	150	*Jude*	
11.3	68	2.2	133	4	82, 99, 118
11.33	172	2.4	95	9	146
11.35	75	2.7	83	21	50
12.1-3	160	2.18	99		
12.1	63, 159	2.20	69, 79	*Revelation*	
12.2	70, 79	2.21-23	70	2.10	161
12.3	79, 157	2.21	79	3.19	139
12.5	139	3.7	82	4.4	63
12.7	139	3.15-16	107	4.10	63
12.8	139	4.5	143	5.10	80
12.11	139	4.7	150	6.2	63
12.14	103	4.11	173	6.10	99
12.23	161	5.4	64, 161	9.4	95
12.25	47	5.8	149, 150, 172	14.14	161
13.5	47			21.5	76
13.21	173	5.9	95	21.8	32
13.23	53			21.14	94, 95
		2 Peter		21.19	94
Philemon		1.1	18	22.6	76
2	5, 59	1.13	27		

Apocrypha and Pseudepigrapha

2 (Slavonic) Enoch		*4 Maccabees*		*Apocalypse of Elijah*	
50.3-4	150	1.26	113	1.13	149
		3.21	102		
3 Maccabees		6.28–7.9	154	*Letter of Aristeas*	
2.2	114	9.22	37	281	161
4.8	102	14.13-14	114	289	115
		17.12	37		
		17.21-24	154		

Joseph and Asenath
26.2   176

Odes of Solomon
8.15-16   96

Pseudo-Phocylides
129   137

Sibylline Oracles
308   137
406   137

Testament of Judah
2.1   54
21.8   91

Testament of Levi
8.2   161
13.2   134

Testament of Reuben
5.3   118

Testament of Solomon
19.3   129

Qumran
Damascus Document
4.5.17-19   121

Targums
Palestinian Targums
Exod. 7.11   121
Num. 22.21, 22   121

Targum Pseudo-Jonathan
Ps. 40.6   121

Mishnah
Nazir   153

Pirke Aboth
5.21   130

Philo
De aeternitate mundi
94.4   155

De agricultura
83   111
88   116

De decalogo
35   137

De ebrietate
152   154

In Flaccum
115   156
187   156

De fuga et inventione
81   111

Legum allegoriae
3.48   158

Legato ad Gaium
195   133

De migratione Abrahami
35   137

De plantatione
70   116

Quaestiones in Genesin
2.29.4   156

Quis rerum divinarum heres sit
106   133
159   133
182-84   154

De specialibus legibus
1.65   137
2.65   61
4.49   137

De vita Mosis
2.291   158

Josephus
Antiquities of the Jews
1.13   133
10.210   133
11.24   62
16.10   127
16.399   102
19.239   155

The Jewish War
2.135   91

Other Christian Authors

1 Clement
1.3   114
2.1   113
5.6-7   13, 39
6.2   114
15.4   132
16.2   113
20.2   158
40.5   151
42.1-4   59
42.3   132

44.2   59
44.5   156
45.2   10, 137
47.6   125
48.1   125
54.1–57.3   61

2 Clement
7.1-4   10
10.1   102
19.3   34

20.1-4   10

Acts of Paul
7.1   176

Acts of Paul and Thecla
2.2   174
2.4, 12-16   166
7–11   119
14   94
28   51

Scripture Index 199

Acts of Peter		Epistle to Diognetus		Irenaeus	
1–3	13	8.4	129	*Against All Heresies*	
				1.23.5	94
Apostolic Constitutions		Eusebius of Caesarea		3.3-4	59
2.54	96	*Historia ecclesiastica*			
7.46	176	2.22.2, 3	31	*Liber pontificalis*	
		3.2, 4	194	6	176
Barnabas		3.4	71		
4.6	148	3.4, 9	184	*Martyrdom of Polycarp*	
4.10	118			11.1	110
7.2	143	Fragments of Papias			
		10.1	136	Polycarp	
Chrysostom				*Philippians*	
Homilies		Hermas		2.1	161
4	56-57, 75	*Mandate*		4.1	128
10	169, 176	6.2.10	110	5.2	27, 98
		10.1.4	61	6.3	27
Clement of Alexandria				9.2	27
Stromata		Hermas			
1.2.21.2–		*Similitudes*		Pseudo-Clement of Rome	
3.24.4	87, 148	6.4	115	*Homiliae*	
4.7	10	19.1	115	3.28.3	156
		62.7	61		
Dio Chrysostom				Tertullian	
Orations		Hermas		*On the Proscribing*	
6.21	134	*Vision*		*of Heretics*	
12.51	133	1.5	146	25	10
28.3	94	16.9	27		
32.11	147			Tertullian	
77.26-28	120	Ignatius		*Ad Martyras*	
		Letter to Polycarp		3.24	59
Epistula Apostolorum		1.2	142, 158		
16	143				

Other Ancient Authors

Aelian		Aristotle		Dionysius of Halicarnassus	
Varia historia		*Rhetoric*		*Antiquitates romanae*	
4.22	117	2.17.6	116	11.24	62, 76
Antigonus of Carystus		Demosthenes		Epictetus	
Historiae mirabiles		*Zenothemis*		*Dissertationes*	
172	118	32.18	129	1.9	124
				1.9.19-21	116
Archelaus		Diodorus Siculus		3.1.5	61
Disputation with Manes		12.67.5	62	3.2.1-10	102
25	122	14.54.6	73	3.10.8	159
36	122			4.8.35-40	65

Epistle of Socrates
30.6   73

Galen
De Materia Medica
9   92

Herodotus
History
8.74.1   158

Homer
Odyssey
4.235-36   54

Horatius Flaccus
Epodes
8   120

Julius Victor
Ars rhetorica
27   18

Juvenal
Satires
6.434-56   120

Longinus
On the Sublime
22.2   129

Lucian
Alexander
6   119

Lucian
Piscator
42   121

Methodius
Symposium
5.1   133

Pausanias
Description of Greece
5.24.9a   65
5.24.9b   64

Pliny the Elder
Naturalis historia
30.1.11   121

Plutarch
Doctrine of the Philosophers
5.2   137

Plutarch
Moralia
6b   116
24   92
338F   57

Polybius
Histories
1.48.5   92
3.81.1   116

Quintus Curtius Rufus
Historiae Alexandri Magni
9.2.28   142

Secundus of Athens
Sententiae
20.1   156

Sophocles
Electra   156

Tacitus
Annals
15.44.2-8   172

Thucydides
History of the Peloponnesian War
2.100.2   90

Valentinius
Chronography of 354
13   176

Virgil
Aeneid
2.141-44   142

Xenophon
Cyropaedia
2.2.6   120

www.ingramcontent.com/pod-product-compliance
Lightning Source LLC
Chambersburg PA
CBHW050146170426
43197CB00011B/1982